STRUCTURED PROGRAMMING

A.P.I.C. Studies in Data Processing
General Editor: C. A. R. Hoare

A.P.I.C. Studies in Data Processing
No. 8

STRUCTURED PROGRAMMING , 1972.

O.-J. DAHL
Universitet i Oslo,
Matematisk Institut,
Blindern, Oslo, Norway

E. W. DIJKSTRA
Department of Mathematics,
Technological University,
Eindhoven, The Netherlands

C. A. R. HOARE
Department of Computer Science,
The Queen's University of Belfast,
Belfast, Northern Ireland

1972
ACADEMIC PRESS
LONDON AND NEW YORK

ACADEMIC PRESS INC. (LONDON) LTD.
24/28 Oval Road,
London NW1

United States Edition published by
ACADEMIC PRESS INC.
111 Fifth Avenue
New York, New York 10003

Second printing 1973
Third printing 1973
Fourth printing 1973
Fifth printing 1974
Sixth printing 1974

Library of Congress Catalog Card Number: 72–84452
ISBN Casebound edition 0–12–200550–3
ISBN Paperback edition 0–12–200556–2

MADE AND PRINTED IN GREAT BRITAIN BY
THE GARDEN CITY PRESS LIMITED
LETCHWORTH, HERTFORDSHIRE
SG6 1JS

PREFACE

In recent years there has been an increasing interest in the art of computer programming, the conceptual tools available for the design of programs, and the prevention of programming oversights and error. The initial outstanding contribution to our understanding of this subject was made by E. W. Dijkstra, whose Notes on Structured Programming form the first and major section of this book. They clearly expound the reflections of a brilliant programmer on the methods which he has hitherto unconsciously applied; there can be no programmer of the present day who could not increase his skills by a study and conscious application of these principles.

In the second monograph I have tried to describe how similar principles can be applied in the design of data structures. I have suggested that in analysing a problem and groping towards a solution, a programmer should take advantage of abstract concepts such as sets, sequences, and mappings; and judiciously postpone decisions on representation until he is constructing the more detailed code of the program. The monograph also describes a range of useful ideas for data representation, and suggests the criteria relevant for their selection.

The third monograph provides a synthesis of the previous two, and expounds the close theoretical and practical connections between the design of data and the design of programs. It introduces useful additional methods for program and data structuring which may be unfamiliar to many programmers. The examples show that structured programming principles can be equally applied in "bottom-up" as in "top-down" program design. The original inspiration, insight, and all the examples were contributed by O.-J. Dahl; I have only assembled the material, and added some additional explanations where I found it difficult to understand.

June 1972

C. A. R. HOARE

CONTENTS

I. Notes on Structured Programming

EDSGER W. DIJKSTRA

1. TO MY READER

These notes have the status of "Letters written to myself": I wrote them down because, without doing so, I found myself repeating the same arguments over and over again. When reading what I had written, I was not always too satisfied.

For one thing, I felt that they suffered from a marked verbosity. Yet I do not try to condense them (now), firstly because that would introduce another delay and I would like to "think on", secondly because earlier experiences have made me afraid of being misunderstood: many a programmer tends to see his (sometimes rather specific) difficulties as the core of the subject and as a result there are widely divergent opinions as to what programming is really about.

I hope that, despite its defects, you will enjoy at least parts of it. If these notes prove to be a source of inspiration or to give you a new appreciation of the programmer's trade, some of my goals will have been reached.

Prior to their publication in book form, the "Notes on Structured Programming" have been distributed privately. The interest then shown in them, for which I would like to express my gratitude here, has been one of the main incentives to supplement them with some additional material and to make them available to a wider public. In particular I would like to thank Bob Floyd, Ralph London and Mike Woodger for their encouraging comments and Peter Naur for the criticism he expressed. Finally I would like to express my gratitude to Mrs. E. L. Dijkstra-Tucker for her kind assistance in my struggles with the English language.

2. ON OUR INABILITY TO DO MUCH

I am faced with a basic problem of presentation. What I am really concerned about is the composition of large programs, the text of which may be, say, of the same size as the whole text of this chapter. Also I have to include

1

examples to illustrate the various techniques. For practical reasons, the demonstration programs must be small, many times smaller than the "life-size programs" I have in mind. My basic problem is that precisely this difference in scale is one of the major sources of our difficulties in programming!

It would be very nice if I could illustrate the various techniques with small demonstration programs and could conclude with "...and when faced with a program a thousand times as large, you compose it in the same way." This common educational device, however, would be self-defeating as one of my central themes will be that any two things that differ in some respect by a factor of already a hundred or more, are utterly incomparable.

History has shown that this truth is very hard to believe. Apparently we are too much trained to disregard differences in scale, to treat them as "gradual differences that are not essential". We tell ourselves that what we can do once, we can also do twice and by induction we fool ourselves into believing that we can do it as many times as needed, but this is just not true! A factor of a thousand is already far beyond our powers of imagination!

Let me give you two examples to rub this in. A one-year old child will crawl on all fours with a speed of, say, one mile per hour. But a speed of a thousand miles per hour is that of a supersonic jet. Considered as objects with moving ability the child and the jet are incomparable, for whatever one can do the other cannot and vice versa. Also: one can close one's eyes and imagine how it feels to be standing in an open place, a prairie or a sea shore, while far away a big, reinless horse is approaching at a gallop, one can "see" it approaching and passing. To do the same with a phalanx of a thousand of these big beasts is mentally impossible: your heart would miss a number of beats by pure panic, if you could!

To complicate matters still further, problems of size do not only cause me problems of presentation, but they lie at the heart of the subject: widespread underestimation of the specific difficulties of size seems one of the major underlying causes of the current software failure. To all this I can see only one answer, viz. to treat problems of size as explicitly as possible. Hence the title of this section.

To start with, we have the "size" of the computation, i.e. the amount of information and the number of operations involved in it. It is essential that this size is large, for if it were really small, it would be easier not to use the computer at all and to do it by hand. The automatic computer owes its right to exist, its usefulness, precisely to its ability to perform large computations where we humans cannot. We want the computer to do what we could never do ourselves and the power of present-day machinery is such that even small computations are by their very size already far beyond the powers of our unaided imagination.

Yet we must organise the computations in such a way that our limited powers are sufficient to guarantee that the computation will establish the desired effect. This organising includes the composition of the program and here we are faced with the next problem of size, viz. the length of the program text, and we should give this problem also explicit recognition. We should remain aware of the fact that the extent to which we can read or write a text is very much dependent on its size. In my country the entries in the telephone directory are grouped by town or village and within each such group the subscribers are listed by name in alphabetical order. I myself live in a small village and given a telephone number I have only to scan a few columns to find out to whom the telephone number belongs, but to do the same in a large city would be a major data processing task!

It is in the same mood that I should like to draw the reader's attention to the fact that "clarity" has pronounced quantitative aspects, a fact many mathematicians, curiously enough, seem to be unaware of. A theorem stating the validity of a conclusion when ten pages full of conditions are satisfied is hardly a convenient tool, as all conditions have to be verified whenever the theorem is appealed to. In Euclidean geometry, Pythagoras' Theorem holds for any three points A, B and C such that through A and C a straight line can be drawn orthogonal to a straight line through B and C. How many mathematicians appreciate that the theorem remains applicable when some or all of the points A, B and C coincide? Yet this seems largely responsible for the convenience with which Pythagoras' Theorem can be used.

Summarizing: as a slow-witted human being I have a very small head and I had better learn to live with it and to respect my limitations and give them full credit, rather than to try to ignore them, for the latter vain effort will be punished by failure.

3. On The Reliability Of Mechanisms

Being a programmer by trade, programs are what I am talking about and the true subject of this section really is the reliability of programs. That, nevertheless, I have mentioned "mechanisms" in its title is because I regard programs as specific instances of mechanisms, and that I wanted to express, at least once, my strong feeling that many of my considerations concerning software are, mutatis mutandis, just as relevant for hardware design.

Present-day computers are amazing pieces of equipment, but most amazing of all are the uncertain grounds on account of which we attach any validity to their output. It starts already with our belief that the hardware functions properly.

Let us restrict, for a moment, our attention to the hardware and let us wonder to what extent one can convince oneself of its being properly constructed. Some years ago a machine was installed on the premises of my University; in its documentation it was stated that it contained, among many other things, circuitry for the fixed-point multiplication of two 27-bit integers. A legitimate question seems to be: "Is this multiplier correct, is it performing according to the specifications?".

The naïve answer to this is: "Well, the number of different multiplications this multiplier is claimed to perform correctly is finite, viz. 2^{54}, so let us try them all." But, reasonable as this answer may seem, it is not, for although a single multiplication took only some tens of microseconds, the total time needed for this finite set of multiplications would add up to more than 10,000 years! We must conclude that exhaustive testing, even of a single component such as a multiplier, is entirely out of the question. (Testing a complete computer on the same basis would imply the established correct processing of all possible programs!)

A first consequence of the 10,000 years is that during its life-time the multiplier will be asked to perform only a negligible fraction of the vast number of all possible multiplications it could do: practically none of them! Funnily enough, we still require that it should do any multiplication correctly when ordered to do so. The reason underlying this fantastic quality requirement is that we do not know in advance, which are the negligibly few multiplications it will be asked to perform. In our reasoning about our programs we talk about "the product" and have abstracted from the specific values of the factors: we do not know them, we do not wish to know them, it is not our business to know them, it is our business not to know them! Our wish to think in terms of the concept "the product", abstracted from the specific instances occurring in a computation is granted, but the price paid for this is precisely the reliability requirement that *any* multiplication of the vast set will be performed correctly. So much for the justification of our desire for a correct multiplier.

But how is the correctness established in a convincing manner? As long as the multiplier is considered as a black box, the only thing we can do is "testing by sampling", i.e. offering to the multiplier a feasible amount of factor pairs and checking the result. But in view of the 10,000 years, it is clear that we can only test a negligible fraction of the possible multiplications. Whole classes of in some sense "critical" multiplications may remain untested and in view of the reliability justly desired, our quality control is still most unsatisfactory. Therefore it is not done that way.

The straightforward conclusion is the following: a convincing demonstration of correctness being impossible as long as the mechanism is regarded as a black box, our only hope lies in not regarding the mechanism as a black box. I shall call this "taking the structure of the mechanism into account".

From now onwards the type of mechanisms we are going to deal with are programs. (In many respects, programs are mechanisms much easier to deal with than circuitry, which is really an analogue device and subject to wear and tear.) And also with programs it is fairly hopeless to establish the correctness beyond even the mildest doubt by testing, without taking their structure into account. In other words, we remark that the extent to which the program correctness can be established is not purely a function of the program's external specifications and behaviour but depends critically upon its internal structure.

Recalling that our true concern is with really large programs, we observe as an aside that the size itself requires a high confidence level for the individual program components. If the chance of correctness of an individual component equals p, the chance of correctness of a whole program, composed of N such components, is something like

$$P = p^N.$$

As N will be very large, p should be very, very close to 1 if we desire P to differ significantly from zero!

When we now take the position that it is not only the programmer's task to produce a correct program but also to demonstrate its correctness in a convincing manner, then the above remarks have a profound influence on the programmer's activity: the object he has to produce must be usefully structured.

The remaining part of this monograph will mainly be an exploration of what program structure can be used to good advantage. In what follows it will become apparent that program correctness is not my only concern, program adaptability or manageability will be another. This stress on program manageability is my deliberate choice, a choice that, therefore, I should like to justify.

While in the past the growth in power of the generally available equipment has mitigated the urgency of the efficiency requirements, this very same growth has created its new difficulties. Once one has a powerful machine at one's disposal one tries to use it and the size of the problems one tackles adjusts itself to the scope of the equipment: no one thinks about programming an algorithm that would take twenty years to execute. With processing power increased by a factor of a thousand over the last ten to fifteen years, Man has become considerably more ambitious in selecting problems that now should be "technically feasible". Size, complexity and sophistication of programs one should like to make have exploded and over the past years it has become patently clear that on the whole our programming ability has not kept pace with these exploding demands made on it.

The power of available equipment will continue to grow: we can expect manufacturers to develop still faster machines and even without that development we shall witness that the type of machine that is presently considered as exceptionally fast will become more and more common. The things we should like to do with these machines will grow in proportion and it is on this extrapolation that I have formed my picture of the programmer's task.

My conclusion is that it is becoming most urgent to stop to consider programming primarily as the minimization of a cost/performance ratio. We should recognise that already now programming is much more an intellectual challenge: the art of programming is the art of organising complexity, of mastering multitude and avoiding its bastard chaos as effectively as possible.

My refusal to regard efficiency considerations as the programmer's prime concern is not meant to imply that I disregard them. On the contrary, efficiency considerations are recognised as one of the main incentives to modifying a logically correct program. My point, however, is that we can only afford to optimise (whatever that may be) provided that the program remains sufficiently manageable.

Let me end this section with a final aside on the significance of computers. Computers are extremely flexible and powerful tools and many feel that their application is changing the face of the earth. I would venture the opinion that as long as we regard them primarily as tools, we might grossly underestimate their significance. Their influence as tools might turn out to be but a ripple on the surface of our culture, whereas I expect them to have a much more profound influence in their capacity of intellectual challenge!

Corollary of the first part of this section:
Program testing can be used to show the presence of bugs, but never to show their absence!

4. ON OUR MENTAL AIDS

In the previous section we have stated that the programmer's duty is to make his product "usefully structured" and we mentioned the program structure in connection with a convincing demonstration of the correctness of the program.

But how do we convince? And how do we convince ourselves? What are the typical patterns of thought enabling ourselves to understand? It is to a broad survey of such questions that the current section is devoted. It is written with my sincerest apologies to the professional psychologist, because it will be amateurishly superficial. Yet I hope (and trust) that it will be sufficient to give us a yardstick by which to measure the usefulness of a proposed structuring.

Among the mental aids available to understand a program (or a proof of its correctness) there are three that I should like to mention explicitly:

(1) Enumeration

(2) Mathematical induction

(3) Abstraction.

4.1. ON ENUMERATION

I regard as an appeal to enumeration the effort to verify a property of the computations that can be evoked by an enumerated set of statements performed in sequence, including conditional clauses distinguishing between two or more cases. Let me give a simple example of what I call "enumerative reasoning".

It is asked to establish that the successive execution of the following two statements

$$\text{"}dd := dd/2;$$

$$\textbf{if } dd \leqslant r \textbf{ do } r := r - dd\text{"}$$

operating on the variables "r" and "dd" leaves the relations

$$0 \leqslant r < dd \tag{1}$$

invariant. One just "follows" the little piece of program assuming that (1) is satisfied to start with. After the execution of the first statement, which halves the value of dd, but leaves r unchanged, the relations

$$0 \leqslant r < 2*dd \tag{2}$$

will hold. Now we distinguish two mutually exclusive cases.

(1) $dd \leqslant r$. Together with (2) this leads to the relations

$$dd \leqslant r < 2*dd; \tag{3}$$

In this case the statement following **do** will be executed, ordering a decrease of r by dd, so that from (3) it follows that eventually

$$0 \leqslant r < dd,$$

i.e. (1) will be satisfied.

(2) **non** $dd \leqslant r$ (i.e. $dd > r$). In this case the statement following **do** will be skipped and therefore also r has its final value. In this case "$dd > r$" together with (2), which is valid after the execution of the first statement leads immediately to

$$0 \leqslant r < dd$$

so that also in the second case (1) will be satisfied.

Thus we have completed our proof of the invariance of relations (1), we have also completed our example of enumerative reasoning, conditional clauses included.

4.2. ·ON MATHEMATICAL INDUCTION

I have mentioned mathematical induction explicitly because it is the only pattern of reasoning that I am aware of that eventually enables us to cope with loops (such as can be expressed by repetition clauses) and recursive procedures. I should like to give an example.

Let us consider the sequence of values

$$d_0, d_1, d_2, d_3, \ldots \ldots \tag{1}$$

given by

for $i = 0$ $d_i = D$ (2a)

for $i > 0$ $d_i = f(d_{i-1})$ (2b)

where D is a given value and f a given (computable) function. It is asked to make the value of the variable "d" equal to the first value d_k in the sequence that satisfies a given (computable) condition "prop '. It is given that such a value exists for finite k. A more formal definition of the requirement is to establish the relation

$$d = d_k \tag{3}$$

where k is given by the (truth of the) expressions

prop (d_k) (4)

and   **non** prop (d_i) for all i satisfying $0 \leqslant i < k$ (5).

We now consider the following program part:

"$d: = D$;

     while non prop (d) **do** $d: = f(d)$"   (6)

in which the first line represents the initialisation and the second one the loop, controlled by the (hopefully self-explanatory) repetition clause **while...do.** (In terms of the conditional clause **if...do,** used in our previous example, a more formal definition of the semantics of the repetition clause is by stating that

"**while** B **do** S"

is semantically equivalent with

"**if** B **do**

         begin S; **while** B **do** S **end**"

expressing that "**non** B" is the necessary and sufficient condition for the repetition to terminate.)

Calling in the construction "**while** B **do** S" the statement S "the repeated statement" we shall prove that in program (6):

after the nth execution of the repeated statement will hold (for $n \geqslant 0$)

$$d = d_n \tag{7a}$$

and $\qquad$ **non** prop (d_i) for all i satisfying $0 \leqslant i < n$. $\qquad$ (7b)

The above statement holds for $n = 0$ (by enumerative reasoning); we have to prove (by enumerative reasoning) that when it holds for $n = N(N \geqslant 0)$, it will also hold for $n = N + 1$.

After the Nth execution of the repeated statement relations (7a) and (7b) are satisfied for $n = N$. For the $N + 1$st execution to take place, the necessary and sufficient condition is the truth of

non prop (d)

which, thanks to (7a) for $n = N$ (i.e. $d = d_N$) means

non prop (d_N)

leading to condition (7b) being satisfied for $n = N + 1$. Furthermore, $d = d_N$ and (2b) leads to

$$f(d) = d_{N+1}$$

so that the net effect of the $N + 1$st execution of the repeated statement

"$d := f(d)$"

established the relation

$$d = d_{N+1}$$

i.e. relation (7a) for $N = N + 1$ and thus the induction step (7) has been proved.

Now we shall show that the repetition terminates after the kth execution of the repeated statement. The nth execution cannot take place for $n > k$ for (on account of 7b) this would imply

non prop (d_k)

thereby violating (4). When the repetition terminates after the nth execution of the repeated statement, the necessary and sufficient condition for termination, viz.

non (**non** prop (d))

becomes, thanks to (7a)

prop (d_n). $\qquad$ (8)

This excludes termination for $n < k$, as this would violate (5). As a result the repetition will terminate with $n = k$, so that (3) follows from (7a), (4) follows from (8) and (5) follows from (7b). Which terminates our proof.

Before turning our attention away from this example illustrating the use of mathematical induction as a pattern of reasoning, I should like to add some remarks, because I have the uneasy feeling that by now some of my readers (in particular experienced and competent programmers) will be terribly irritated, viz. those readers for whom program (6) is so obviously correct that they wonder what all the fuss is about: "Why his pompous restatement of the problem, as in (3), (4) and (5), because anyone knows what is meant by the first value in the sequence, satisfying a condition? Certainly he does not expect us, who have work to do, to supply such lengthy proofs, with all the mathematical dressing, whenever we use such a simple loop as that?" Etc.

To tell the honest truth: the pomp and length of the above proof infuriate me as well! But at present I cannot do much better if I really try to prove the correctness of this program. But it sometimes fills me with the same kind of anger as years ago the crazy proofs of the first simple theorems in plane geometry did, proving things of the same degree of "obviousness" as Euclid's axioms themselves.

Of course I would not dare to suggest (at least at present!) that it is the programmer's duty to supply such a proof whenever he writes a simple loop in his program. If so, he could never write a program of any size at all! It would be as impractical as reducing each proof in plane geometry explicitly and in extenso to Euclid's axioms. (Cf. Section "On our inability to do much.")

My moral is threefold. Firstly, when a programmer considers a construction like (6) as obviously correct, he can do so because he is familiar with the construction. I prefer to regard his behaviour as an unconscious appeal to a theorem he *knows*, although perhaps he has never bothered to formulate it; and once in his life he has convinced himself of its truth, although he has probably forgotten in which way he did it and although the way was (probably) unfit for print. But we could call our assertions about program (6), say, "The Linear Search Theorem" and knowing such a name it is much easier (and more natural) to appeal to it consciously.

Secondly, to the best of my knowledge, there is no set of theorems of the type illustrated above, whose usefulness has been generally accepted. But we should not be amazed about that, for the absence of such a set of theorems is a direct consequence of the fact that the type of object—i.e. programs—has not settled down. The kind of object the programmer is dealing with, viz. programs, is much less well-established than the kind of object that is dealt with in plane geometry. In the meantime the intuitively competent programmer is probably the one who confines himself, whenever acceptable, to program structures with which he is very familiar, while becoming very alert and careful whenever he constructs something unusual (for him). For an established style of programming, however, it might be a useful activity to look for a body of theorems pertinent to such programs.

Thirdly, the length of the proof we needed in our last example is a warning that should not be ignored. There is of course the possibility that a better mathematician will do a much shorter and more elegant job than I have done. Personally I am inclined to conclude from this length that programming is more difficult than is commonly assumed: let us be honestly humble and interpret the length of the proof as an urgent advice to restrict ourselves to simple structures whenever possible and to avoid in all intellectual modesty "clever constructions" like the plague.

4.3. ON ABSTRACTION

At this stage I find it hard to be very explicit about the role of abstraction, partly because it permeates the whole subject. Consider an algorithm and all possible computations it can evoke: starting from the computations the algorithm is what remains when one abstracts from the specific values manipulated this time. The concept of "a variable" represents an abstraction from its current value. It has been remarked to me (to my great regret I cannot remember by whom and so I am unable to give credit where it seems due) that once a person has understood the way in which variables are used in programming, he has understood the quintessence of programming. We can find a confirmation for this remark when we return to our use of mathematical induction with regard to the repetition: on the one hand it is by abstraction that the concepts are introduced in terms of which the induction step can be formulated; on the other hand it is the repetition that really calls for the concept of "a variable". (Without repetition one can restrict oneself to "quantities" the value of which has to be defined as most once but never has to be redefined as in the case of a variable.)

There is also an abstraction involved in naming an operation and using it on account of "what it does" while completely disregarding "how it works". (In the same way one should state that a programming manual describes an abstract machine: the specific piece of hardware delivered by the manufacturer is nothing but a—usually imperfect!—mechanical model of this abstract machine.) There is a strong analogy between using a named operation in a program regardless of "how it works" and using a theorem regardless of how it has been proved. Even if its proof is highly intricate, it may be a very convenient theorem to use!

Here, again, I refer to our inability to do much. Enumerative reasoning is all right as far as it goes, but as we are rather slow-witted it does not go very far. Enumerative reasoning is only an adequate mental tool under the severe boundary condition that we use it only very moderately. We should appreciate abstraction as our main mental technique to reduce the demands made upon enumerative reasoning.

(Here Mike Woodger, National Physical Laboratory, Teddington, England, made the following remark, which I insert in gratitude: "There is a parallel analogy between the unanalysed terms in which an axiom or theorem is expressed and the unanalysed operands upon which a named operation is expected to act.")

5. An Example Of A Correctness Proof

Let us consider the following program section, where the integer constants a and d satisfy the relations

$$a \geqslant 0 \text{ and } d > 0.$$

> "**integer** r, dd;
>
> $r := a$; $dd := d$;
>
> **while** $dd \leqslant r$ **do** $dd := 2*dd$;
>
> **while** $dd \neq d$ **do**
>
>   **begin** $dd := dd/2$;
>
>   **if** $dd \leqslant r$ **do** $r := r - dd$
>
> **end**".

To apply the Linear Search Theorem (see Section "On our mental aids", subsection "On mathematical induction") we consider the sequence of values given by

for $i = 0$ $dd_i = d$

for $i > 0$ $dd_i = 2*dd_{i-1}$

from which $dd_n = d*2^n$ (1)

can be derived by normal mathematical techniques, which also tell us that (because $d > 0$) for finite r

$$dd_k > r$$

will hold for some finite k, thus ensuring that the first repetition terminates with

$$dd = d*2^k$$

Solving the relation

$$d_i = 2*d_{i-1}$$

for d_{i-1} gives

$$d_{i-1} = d_i/2$$

and the Linear Search Theorem then tells us, that the second repetition will also terminate. (As a matter of fact the second repeated statement will be executed exactly the same number of times as the first one.)

At the termination of the first repetition,

$$dd = dd_k$$

and therefore,

$$0 \leqslant r < dd \qquad\qquad\qquad\qquad (2)$$

holds. As shown earlier (Section "On our mental aids.", subsection "On enumeration") the repeated statement of the second clause leaves this relation invariant. After termination (on account of "**while** $dd \neq d$ **do**") we can conclude

$$dd = d$$

which together with (2) gives

$$0 \leqslant r < d \tag{3}$$

Furthermore we prove that after the initialisation

$$dd \equiv 0 \bmod (d) \tag{4}$$

holds; this follows, for instance, from the fact that the possible values of dd are (see (1))

$$d*2^i \text{ for } 0 \leqslant i \leqslant k.$$

Our next step is to verify, that after the initial assignment to r the relation

$$a \equiv r \bmod (d) \tag{5}$$

holds.

(1) It holds after the initial assignments.

(2) The repeated statement of the first clause ("$dd := 2*dd$") maintains the invariance of (5) and therefore the whole first repetition maintains the validity of (5).

(3) The second repeated statement consists of two statements. The first ("$dd := dd/2$") leaves (5) invariant, the second one also leaves (5) invariant for either it leaves r untouched or it decreases r by the current value of dd, an operation which on account of (4) also maintains the validity of (5). Therefore the whole second repeated statement leaves (5) invariant and therefore the whole repetition leaves (5) invariant. Combining (3) and (5), the final value therefore satisfies

$$0 \leqslant r < d \text{ and } a \equiv r \bmod (d)$$

i.e. r is the smallest non-negative remainder of the division of a by d.

Remark 1. The program

```
"integer r, dd, q;
r: = a; dd: = d; q: = 0;
while dd ⩽ r do dd: = 2 * dd;
while dd ≠ d do
    begin dd: = dd/2; q: = 2 * q;
        if dd ⩽ r do begin r: = r − dd; q: = q + 1 end
end
```

assigns to q the value of the corresponding quotient. The proof can be established by observing the invariance of the relation

$$a = q * dd + r.$$

(I owe this example to my colleague N. G. de Bruijn.)

Remark 2. In the subsection "On mathematical induction." we have proved the Linear Search Theorem. In the previous proof we have used another theorem about repetitions (a theorem that, obviously, can only be proved by mathematical induction, but the proof is so simple that we leave it as an exercise to the reader), viz. that if prior to entry of a repetition a certain relation P holds, whose truth is not destroyed by a single execution of the repeated statement, then relation P will still hold after termination of the repetition. This is a very useful theorem, often allowing us to bypass an explicit appeal to mathematical induction. (We can state the theorem a little more sharply; in the repetition

"while *B* do *S*"

one has to show that S is such that the truth of

P and B

prior to the execution of S implies the truth of

P

after its execution.)

Remark 3. As an exercise for the reader (for which acknowledgement is due to James King, CMU, Pittsburgh, USA), prove that with integer A, B, x, y and z and

$$A > 0 \text{ and } B \geqslant 0$$

after the execution of the program section

> "$x := A$; $y := B$; $z := 1$;
>
> **while** $y \neq 0$ **do**
>
>   **begin if** odd (y) **do begin** $y := y - 1$; $z := z * x$ **end**;
>
> $y := y/2$; $x := x * x$
>
>   **end**"

finally $z = A^B$ will hold.

The proof has to show that (in spite of "$y := y/2$") all variables keep integer values; the method shows the invariance of

$$x > 0 \text{ and } y \geqslant 0 \text{ and } A^B = z * x^y$$

6. ON THE VALIDITY OF PROOFS VERSUS THE VALIDITY OF IMPLEMENTATIONS

In the previous section I have assumed "perfect arithmetic" and in my experience the validity of such proofs often gets questioned by people who argue that in practice one never has perfect arithmetic at ones disposal: admissible integer values usually have an absolute upper bound, real numbers are only represented to a finite accuracy etc. So what is the validity of such proofs?

The answer to this question seems to be the following. If one proves the correctness of a program assuming an idealised, perfect world, one should not be amazed if something goes wrong when this ideal program gets executed by an "imperfect" implementation. Obviously! Therefore, if we wish to prove program correctness in a more realistic world, the thing to do is to acknowledge right at the start that all operations appealed to in the program (in particular all arithmetic operations) need not be perfect, provided we state—rather axiomatically—the properties they have to satisfy for the proper execution of the program, i.e. the properties on which the correctness proof relies. (In the example of the previous section this requirement is simply exact integer arithmetic in the range [0, 2a].)

When writing a program operating on real numbers with rounded operations, one must be aware of the assumptions one makes, such as

$$b > 0 \text{ implies } a + b \geqslant a$$

$$a * b = b * a$$

$$-(a * b) = (-a) * b$$

$$0 * x = 0$$

$$0 + x = x$$

$$1 * x = x \text{ etc. etc.}$$

Very often the validity of such relations is essential to the logic of the program. For the sake of compatibility, the programmer would be wise to be as undemanding as possible, whereas a good implementation should satisfy as many reasonable requirements as possible.

This is the place to confess one of my blunders. In implementing ALGOL 60 we decided that "$x = y$" would deliver the value **true** not only in the case of exact equality, but also when the two values differed only in the least significant digit represented, because otherwise it was so very improbable that the value *true* would ever be computed. We were thinking of converging iterations that could oscillate within rounding accuracy. While we had been generous (with the best of intentions!) in regarding real numbers as equal, it quickly turned out that the chosen operation was so weak as to be hardly of any use at all. What it boiled down to was that the established truth of $a = b$ **and** $b = c$ did not allow the programmer to conclude the truth of $a = c$. The decision was quickly changed. It is because of that experience that I know that the programmer can only use his tool by virtue of (a number of) its properties; conversely, the programmer must be able to state which properties he requires. (Usually programmers don't do so because, for lack of tradition as to what properties can be taken for granted, this would require more explicitness than is otherwise desirable. The proliferation of machines with lousy floating-point hardware—together with the misapprehension that the automatic computer is primarily the tool of the numerical analyst—has done much harm to the profession!)

7. On Understanding Programs

In my life I have seen many programming courses that were essentially like the usual kind of driving lessons, in which one is taught how to handle a car instead of how to use a car to reach one's destination.

My point is that a program is never a goal in itself; the purpose of a program is to evoke computations and the purpose of the computations is to establish a desired effect. Although the program is the final product made by the programmer, the possible computations evoked by it—the "making" of which is left to the machine!—are the true subject matter of his trade. For instance, whenever a programmer states that his program is correct, he really makes an assertion about the computations it may evoke.

The fact that the last stage of the total activity, viz. the transition from the (static) program text to the (dynamic) computation, is essentially left to the machine is an added complication. In a sense the making of a program is therefore more difficult than the making of a mathematical theory: both program and theory are structured, timeless objects. But while the mathematical theory makes sense as it stands, the program only makes sense via its execution.

In the remaining part of this section I shall restrict myself to programs written for a sequential machine, and I shall explore some of the consequences of our duty to use our understanding of a program to make assertions about the ensuing computations. It is my (unproven) claim that the ease and reliability with which we can do this depends critically upon the simplicity of the relation between the two, in particular upon the nature of sequencing control. In vague terms we may state the desirability that the structure of the program text reflects the structure of the computation. Or, in other terms, "What can we do to shorten the conceptual gap between the static program text (spread out in "text space") and the corresponding computations (evolving in time)?"

It is the purpose of the computation to establish a certain desired effect. When it starts at a discrete moment t_0 it will be completed at a later discrete moment t_1 and we assume that its effect can be described by comparing "the state at t_0" with "the state at t_1". If no intermediate states are taken into consideration the effect is regarded as being established by a primitive action.

When we do take a number of intermediate states into consideration this means that we have parsed the happening in time. We regard it as a sequential computation, i.e. the time-succession of a number of subactions and we have to convince ourselves that the cumulative effect of this time-succession of subactions indeed equals the desired net effect of the total computation.

The simplest case is a parsing, a decomposition, into a fixed number of subactions that can be enumerated. In flowchart form this can be represented as follows.

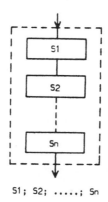

S1; S2; ......; Sn

The validity of this decomposition has to be established by enumerative reasoning. In this case, shortening of the conceptual gap between program and computation can be achieved by requiring that a linear piece of program text contains names or descriptions of the subactions in the order in which they have to take place. In our earlier example (invariance of $0 \leqslant r < dd$)

"$dd: = dd/2$;

if $dd \leqslant r$ do $r: = r - dd$"

this condition is satisfied. The primary decomposition of the computation is into a time-succession of two actions; in the program text we recognise this structure

"halve dd;

reduce r modulo dd".

We are considering all initial states satisfying $0 \leqslant r < dd$ and in all computations then considered, the given parsing into two subactions is applicable. So far, so good.

The program, however, is written under the assumption that "reduce r modulo dd" is not a primitive action, while "decrease r by dd" is. Viewing all possible happenings during "reduce r modulo dd" it then becomes relevant to distinguish that in some cases "decrease r by dd" takes place, while in the other cases r remains unchanged. By writing

"if $dd \leqslant r$ do decrease r by dd"

we have represented that at the given level of detail the action "reduce *r* modulo *dd*" can take one of two mutually exclusive forms and we have also given the criterion on account of which the choice between them is made. If we regard "**if** $dd \leqslant r$ **do**" as a conditional clause attached to "decrease *r* by *dd*" it is natural that the conditional clause is placed in front of the conditioned statement. (In this sense the alternative clause

"**if** condition **then** statement 1 **else** statement 2"

is "over-ordered" with respect to "statement 1" and "statement 2": they are just two alternatives that cannot be expressed simultaneously on a linear medium.)

The alternative clause has been generalised by C. A. R. Hoare whose "case-of" construction provides a choice between more than two possibilities. In flowchart form they can be represented as follows.

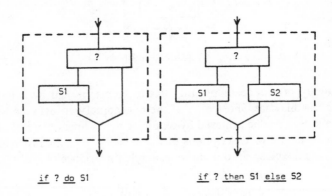

if ? do S1   if ? then S1 else S2

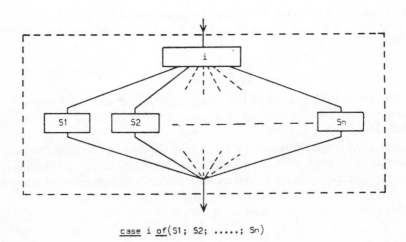

case i of(S1; S2; ......; Sn)

These flowcharts share the property that they have a single entry at the top and a single exit at the bottom: as indicated by the dotted block they can again be interpreted (by disregarding what is inside the dotted lines) as a single action in a sequential computation. To be a little bit more precise: we are dealing with a great number of possible computations, primarily decomposed into the same time-succession of subactions and it is only on closer inspection—i.e. by looking inside the dotted block—that it is revealed that over the collection of possible computations such a subaction may take one of an enumerated set of distinguished forms.

The above is sufficient to consider a class of computations that are primarily decomposed into the same set of enumerated subactions; they are insufficient to consider a class of computations that are primarily decomposed into a varying number of subactions (i.e. varying over the class of computations considered). It is here that the usefulness of the repetition clauses becomes apparent. We mention "**while** condition **do** statement" and "**repeat** statement **until** condition" that may be represented in flowchart form as follows.

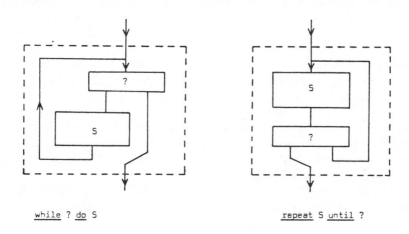

while ? do S   repeat S until ?

These flowcharts also share the property of a single entry at the top and a single exit at the bottom. They enable us to express that the action represented by the dotted block is on closer inspection a time-succession of "a sufficient number" of subactions of a certain type.

We have now seen three types of decomposition; we could call them "concatenation", "selection" and "repetition" respectively. The first two are understood by enumerative reasoning, the last one by mathematical induction.

The programs that can be written using the selection clauses and the repetition clauses as only the means for sequencing control, permit straightforward translation into a programming language that is identical but for the fact that sequencing control has to be expressed by jumps to labelled points. The converse is not true. Alternatively: restricting ourselves to the three mentioned types of decomposition leads to flowcharts of a restricted topology compared with the flowcharts one can make when arrows can be drawn from any block leading into any other. Compared with that greater freedom, to restrict oneself to the clauses presents itself as a sequencing discipline.

Why do I propose to adhere to this sequencing discipline? The justification for this decision can be presented in many ways and let me try a number of them in the hope that at least one of them will appeal to my readers.

Eventually, one of our aims is to make such well-structured programs that the intellectual effort (measured in some loose sense) needed to understand them is proportional to program length (measured in some equally loose sense). In particular we have to guard against an exploding appeal to enumerative reasoning, a task that forces upon us some application of the old adage "Divide and Rule", and that is the reason why we propose the step-wise decompositions of the computations.

We can understand a decomposition by concatenation via enumerative reasoning. (We can do so, provided that the number of subactions into which the computation is primarily parsed, is sufficiently small and that the specification of their net effect is sufficiently concise. I shall return to these requirements at a later stage, at present we assume the conditions met.) It is then feasible to make assertions about the computations on account of the program text, thanks to the triviality of the relation between the progress through the computations and the progress through the program text. In particular: if on closer inspection one of the subactions transpires to be controlled by a selective clause or a repetition clause, this fact does not impose any burden on the understandability of the primary decomposition, because there only the subaction's net effect plays a role.

As a corollary: if on closer inspection a subaction is controlled by a selective clause the specific path taken is always irrelevant at the primary level (the only thing that matters is that the correct path has been taken). And also: if on closer inspection a subaction is controlled by a repetitive clause, the number of times the repeated statement has been executed is, as such, irrelevant (the only thing that matters is that it has been repeated the correct number of times).

We can also understand the selective clauses as such, viz. by enumerative reasoning; we can also understand the repetition clause, viz. by mathematical induction. For all three types of decomposition—and this seems to me a great help—we know the appropriate pattern of reasoning.

There is a further benefit to be derived from the proposed sequencing discipline. In understanding programs we establish relations. In our example on enumerative reasoning we established that the program part

$$\text{``}dd := dd/2;$$
$$\textbf{if } dd \leqslant r \textbf{ do } r := r - dd\text{''}$$

leaves the relation

$$0 \leqslant r < dd$$

invariant. Yet, even if we can ensure that these relations hold before execution of the quoted program part, we cannot conclude that they always hold, viz. not necessarily between the execution of the two quoted statements. In other words: the validity of such relations is dependent on the progress of the computation, and this seems typical for a sequential process.

Similarly, we attach meanings to variables: a variable may count the number of times an event of a given type has occurred, say the number of lines that has been printed on the current page. Transition to the next page will be followed immediately by a reset to zero, printing a line will be followed immediately by an increase by 1. Again, just before resetting or increasing this count, the interpretation "number of lines printed on the current page" is non-valid. To assign such a meaning to a variable, again, can only be done relative to the progress of the computation. This observation raises the following question: "How do we characterise the progress of a computation?"

In short, we are looking for a co-ordinate system in terms of which the discrete points of computation progress can be identified, and we want this co-ordinate system to be independent of the variables operated upon under program control: if we need values of such variables to describe progress of the computation we are begging the question, for it is precisely in relation to this progress that we want to interpret the meaning of these variables.

(A still more stringent reason not to rely upon the values of variables is presented by a program containing a non-ending loop, cycling through a finite number of different states. Eternal cycling follows from the fact that a different points of progress the *same* state prevails. But then the state is clearly incapable of distinguishing between these two *different* points of progress!)

We can state our problem in another way. Given a program in action and suppose that before completion of the computation the latter is stopped at one of the discrete points of progress. How can we identify the point of interruption, for instance if we want to redo the computation up to the very same point? Or also: if stopping was due to some kind of dynamic error, how can we identify the point of progress short of a complete memory dump?

For the sake of simplicity we assume our program text spread out in (linear) text space and assume an identifying mechanism for the program points corresponding to the discrete points of computation progress; let us call this identifying mechanism "the textual index". (If the discrete points of computation progress are situated in between successive statement executions, the textual index identifies, say, semicolons.) The textual index is a kind of generalised order counter, its value points to a place in the text.

If we restrict ourselves to decomposition by concatenation and selection, a single textual index is sufficient to identify the progress of the computation. With the inclusion of repetition clauses textual indices are no longer sufficient to describe the progress of the computation. With each entry into a repetition clause, however, the system could introduce a so-called "dynamic index", inexorably counting the ordinal number of the corresponding current repetition; at termination of the repetition the system should again remove the corresponding dynamic index. As repetition clauses may occur nested inside each other, the appropriate mechanism is a stack (i.e. a last-in-first-out-memory). Initially the stack is empty; at entry of a repetition clause a new dynamic index(set to zero or one) is added on the top of the stack; whenever it is decided that the repetition is not terminated the top element of this stack is increased by 1; whenever it is decided that a repetition is terminated, the top element of the stack is removed. (This arrangement reflects very clearly that after termination of a repetition the number of times, even the fact that it was a repetition, is no longer relevant.)

As soon as the programming language admits procedures, then a single textual index is no longer sufficient. In the case that a textual index points to the interior of a procedure body, the dynamic progress of the computation is only characterised when we also describe to which call of the procedure we refer, but this can be done by giving the textual index pointing to the place of the call. With the inclusion of the procedure the textual index must be generalised to a stack of textual indices, increased by one element at procedure call and decreased by one element at procedure return.

The main point is that the values of these indices are outside the programmer's control; they are defined (either by the write-up of his program or by the dynamic evolution of the current computation) whether he likes it or not. They provide independent co-ordinates in which to describe the progress of the computation, a "variable-independent" frame of reference in which meanings to variables can be assigned.

There is, of course, even with the free use of jumps, a programmer independent co-ordinate system in terms of which the progress of a sequential computation can be described uniquely, viz. a kind of normalised clock that counts the number of "discrete points of computation progress" passed since program start. It is unique, but utterly unhelpful, because the textual index is no longer a constituent component of such a co-ordinate system.

The moral of the story is that when we acknowledge our duty to control the computations (intellectually!) via the program text evoking them, that then we should restrict ourselves in all humility to the most systematic sequencing mechanisms, ensuring that "progress through the computation" is mapped on "progress through the text" in the most straightforward manner.

8. On Comparing Programs

It is a programmer's everyday experience that for a given problem to be solved by a given algorithm, the program for a given machine is far from uniquely determined. In the course of the design process he has to select between alternatives; once he has a correct program, he will often be called to modify it, for instance because it is felt that an alternative program would be more attractive as far as the demands that the computations make upon the available equipment resources are concerned.

These circumstances have raised the question of the equivalence of programs: given two programs, do they evoke computations establishing the same net effect? After suitable formalisation (of the way in which the programs are given, of the machine that performs the computations evoked by them and of the "net effect" of the computations) this can presumably be made into a well-posed problem appealing to certain mathematical minds. But I do not intend to tackle it in this general form. On the contrary: instead of starting with two arbitrarily given programs (say: independently conceived by two different authors) I am concerned with alternative programs that can be considered as products of the same mind and then the question becomes: how can we conceive (and structure) those two alternative programs so as to ease the job of comparing the two?

I have done many experiments and my basic experience gained by them can be summed up as follows. Two programs evoking computations that establish the same net effect are equivalent *in that sense* and *a priori* not in any other. When we wish to compare programs in order to compare their corresponding computations, the basic experience is that it is impossible (or fruitless, unattractive, or terribly hard or what you wish) to do so when on the level of comparison the sequencing through the two programs differs. To be a little more explicit: it is only attractive to compare two programs and the computations they may possibly evoke, when paired computations can be parsed into a time-succession of actions that can be mapped on each other and the corresponding program texts can be equally parsed into instructions, each corresponding to such an action.

This is a very strong condition. Let me give a first example.

Excluding side-effects of the boolean inspections and assuming the value "$B2$" constant (i.e. unaffected by the execution of either "$S1$" or "$S2$"), *we* can establish the equivalence of the following two programs:

"**if** $B2$ **then**

begin while $B1$ **do** $S1$ **end**

else

begin while $B1$ **do** $S2$ **end**"   (1)

and

"**while** $B1$ **do**

begin if $B2$ **then** $S1$ **else** $S2$ **end**"   (2)

The first construction is primarily one in which sequencing is controlled by a selective clause, the second construction is primarily one in which sequencing is controlled by a repetitive clause. I can establish the equivalence of the output of the computations, but I cannot regard them as equivalent in any other useful sense. I had to force myself to the conclusion that (1) and (2) are "hard to compare". Originally this conclusion annoyed me very much. In the meantime I have grown to regard this incomparability as one of the facts of life and, therefore, as one of the major reasons why I regard the choice between (1) and (2) as a relevant design decision, that should not be taken without careful consideration. It is precisely its apparent triviality that has made me sensitive to the considerations that should influence such a choice. They fall outside the scope of the present section but I hope to return to them later.

Let me give a second example of incomparability that is slightly more subtle.

Given two arrays $X[1:N]$ and $Y[1:N]$ and a boolean variable "equal", make a program that assigns to the boolean variable "equal" the value: "the two arrays are equal element-wise". Empty arrays (i.e. $N = 0$) are regarded as being equal.

Introducing a variable j and giving to "equal" the meaning "among the first j pairs no difference has been detected", we can write the following two programs.

"$j: = 0$; equal: = **true**;

while $j \neq N$ **do**

begin $j: = j + 1$; equal: = equal **and** $(X[j] = Y[j])$ **end**"   (3)

and

"$j: = 0$; equal: = **true**;

while $j \neq N$ **and** equal **do**

begin $j: = j + 1$; equal: = $(X[j] = Y[j])$ **end**".   (4)

Program (4) differs from program (3) in that repetition is terminated as soon as a pair-wise difference has been detected. For the same input the number of repetitions may differ in the two programs and therefore the programs are only comparable in our sense as long as the last two lines of the programs are regarded as describing a single action, not subdivided into subactions. But what is their relation when we do wish to take into account that they both end with a repetition? To find this out, we shall prove the correctness of the programs.

On the arrays X and Y we can define of $0 \leqslant j \leqslant N$ the $N + 1$ functions $EQUAL_j$ as follows:

for $j = 0$ $EQUAL_j = $ **true**,

for $j > 0$ $EQUAL_j = EQUAL_{j-1}$ **and** $(X[j] = Y[j])$.   (5)

In terms of these functions it is required to establish the net effect

$$equal = EQUAL_N.$$

Both programs maintain the relation

$$equal = EQUAL_j \qquad (6)$$

for increasing values of j, starting with $j = 0$.

It is tempting to regard programs (3) and (4) as alternative refinements of the same (abstract) program (7):

    "$j: = 0$; equal: $= EQUAL_0$;

    while "perhaps still: equal $\neq EQUAL_N$" **do**

        begin $j: = j + 1$; "equal: $= EQUAL_j$" **end**"   (7)

in which "perhaps still: equal $\neq EQUAL_N$" stands for some sort of still open primitive. When this is evaluated

$$equal = EQUAL_j$$

will hold and the programs (3) and (4) differ in that they guarantee on different criteria that "equal" will have its final value $EQUAL_N$.

In program (3) the criterion is very naïve, viz.

$$j = N.$$

At the beginning of the repeated statement

$$equal = EQUAL_j$$

still holds. After the execution of "$j: = j + 1$" therefore

$$equal = EQUAL_{j-1}$$

holds and the assignment statement

    "equal: $=$ equal **and** $(X[j] = Y[j])$"

is now a straightforward transcription of the recurrence relation (5).

To come to program (4) some analysis has to be applied to the recurrence relation (5), from which can be derived (by mathematical induction again) that

$EQUAL_j$ = **false** implies $EQUAL_N$ = **false**, and therefore $EQUAL_j$ = **false** implies $EQUAL_j$ = $EQUAL_N$. If this situation arises, the equality "equal = $EQUAL_N$" can also be guaranteed and this leads to program (4). The set of (sub)computations the repeated statement has to cope with in program (4) is restricted to those with the initial state "equal = **true**" and therefore in program (4) the assignment "equal: = $EQUAL_j$," can be abbreviated to

$$\text{"equal:} = (X[j] = Y[j])\text{"}$$

And now it is clear why the introduction of (7) as an abstraction of (3) and (4) was misleading. With "perhaps still: equal $\neq EQUAL_N$" we have stated the meaning of truth and falsity of a boolean expression without stating the expression itself and that was very tricky. We have tried to interpret (7) as a program in which part of the sequencing at its own level was undefined and varying over its refinements. As a result we have tried to view the last lines of (7) as a model for the last lines of both (3) and (4), but this was misleading because the computations to be evoked by them cannot be brought into a one-to-one correspondence.

So much for programs that we consider as incomparable. Examples of comparable programs will be encountered in the following sections. A final remark: we have stated that "paired computations can be parsed into a time-succession of actions that can be mapped on each other". We have not required that actions so paired should have the same net effect! We may compare alternative programs for the same job but also different programs for similar jobs.

9. A First Example Of Step-Wise Program Composition

In the section "On understanding programs." I have stressed the need for systematic sequencing so that the structure of the computations could be reflected in the structure of our program: in this way we can speak of the joint structuring of program and computations. In the current section I shall now try to give a little more content to the still rather vague notion of structuring computations. It will be a first effort to exploit our powers of abstraction to reduce the appeal made to enumerative reasoning; it will be a consequent application of the decompositions mentioned in the section "On understanding programs.".

Instead of presenting (as a ready-made product) what I would call a well-structured program I am going to describe in very great detail the composition process of such a program. I do this because programs are not there: on the contrary, they have to be made, and the kind of programs I am particularly interested in are those which I feel to be reasonably well suited to our powers of construction and conception.

The task is to instruct a computer to print a table of the first thousand prime numbers, 2 being considered as the first prime number.

Note 1. This example has been chosen because on the one hand it is sufficiently difficult to serve as a model for some of the problems encountered in programming, and on the other hand its mathematical background is so simple and familiar that our attention is not usurped by the problem.

Note 2. I do not claim that my final program will be "the best one", measured by whatever yardstick any of my readers might care to choose. At least two readers of a previous version of this presentation—in which remainders were computed via a divide operation—reacted quite vehemently to it: "But everyone knows that the most efficient way to generate prime numbers is by using the Sieve of Eratosthenes." thereby blocking their ability to read any further!

The basic pattern of my approach will be to compose the program in minute steps, deciding each time as little as possible. As the problem analysis proceeds, so does the further refinement of my program.

When an algorithm has to be made, the desired computation has to be composed from actions corresponding to a well-understood instruction repertoire.

The simplest form of the program is

description 0:

begin "print first thousand prime numbers" **end**

and when "print first thousand prime numbers" refers to an instruction from the well-understood repertoire, the description 0 solves the problem. For the sake of argument we assume that this instruction does *not* occur in the well-understood repertoire. Therefore we have to conceive a computation composed from "more primitive" actions that establishes the desired net effect. Our first proposal is to separate the generation of the prime numbers and their printing, and we propose description 1:

begin variable "table p";

    "fill table p with first thousand prime numbers";

    "print table p"

end,

describing that our computation consists of a time-succession of two actions and takes place in a state space containing a single variable, called "table p". The first action assigns a value to this variable, the second action is controlled by the (then current) value of this variable.

Again, when "fill table p with first thousand prime numbers" and "print table p" occur in the well-understood repertoire (and "table p" occurs among the implicitly available resources) then our problem is solved. Again, for the sake of argument, we assume this not to be the case. This means that in our next refinement we have to express how the effect of these two actions can be established by two further (sub)computations. Apart from that we have to decide, how the information to be contained in the intermediate value of the still rather undefined object "table p" is to be represented.

Before going on, I would like to stress how little we have decided upon when writing down description 1, and how little of our original problem statement has been taken into account. We have assumed that the availability of a resource "table p" (in some form or other) would permit us to compute the first thousand prime numbers before printing starts, and on this assumption we have exploited the fact that the computation of the primes can be conceived independently of the printing. Of our original problem statement we have not taken into account very much more than that at least a thousand different prime numbers do exist (we had to assume this for the problem statement to make sense). At this stage it is still fairly immaterial what the concept "prime number" really means. Also, we have not committed ourselves in the least as regards the specific layout requirements of the print-out to be produced. Apparently it is the strength of our approach that the consequences of these two rather independent aspects of our original problem statement seem to have been allocated in the respective refinements of our two constituent actions. It suggests that we have been more or less successful in our effort to apply the golden principle "divide and rule".

Resuming our discussion, however, we have to ask ourselves, to what extent the two subcomputations can now be conceived independently of each other. To be more precise "Have we now reached the stage that the design of the two subalgorithms (that have to evoke the two subcomputations) can be conceived by two programmers, working independently of each other?".

When the two actions can no longer be regarded as invoked by instructions from the well-understood repertoire, neither can the variable "table p" any longer be regarded as an implicitly available resource. And in a way similar to the one in which we have to decompose the actions into subactions, we have to choose how the variable "table p" will be composed, viz. what data structure we select to represent the information to be handed over via "table p" from the first action to the second. At some point this has to be decided and the questions are "when?" and "how?".

In principle, there seem to be two ways out of this. The first one is to try to postpone the decision on how to structure "table p" into (more neutral, less problem-bound) components. If we postpone the decision on how to structure "table p", the next thing to do is to refine one of the actions or both. We can do so, assuming a proper set of operations on the still mysterious object "table p"; finally we collect these operations and in view of their demands we design the most attractive structure of "table p".

Alternatively, we can try to decide, here and now, upon the structure of "table p". Once it has been decided how the table of the first thousand primes will be represented, the refinements of both actions can be done fairly independently of each other.

Both ways are equally tricky, for what will be an attractive algorithm for, say, the first subcomputation will greatly depend on the ease and elegance with which the assumed operations on "table p" can be realised, and if one or more turn out to be prohibitively clumsy, the whole edifice falls to pieces. Alternatively, if we decide prematurely upon a structure for "table p" we may well discover that the subcomputations then turn out to be awkward. There is no way around it: in an elegant program the structure of "table p" and the computations referring to it must be well-matched. I think that the behaviour of the efficient programmer can be described as trying to take the easiest decision first, that is the decision that requires the minimum amount of investigation (trial and error, iterative mutual adjustment etc.) for the maximum justification of the hope that he will not regret it.

In order not to make this treatment unduly lengthy we assume that the programmer finds the courage to decide that now the structure of "table p" is the first thing to be decided upon. Once this position has been taken, two alternatives immediately present themselves. On the one hand we can try to exploit that "a table of the first 1000 primes" is not just a table of a thousand numbers—as would be a table of the monthly wages of 1000 employees in a factory—but that all these numbers are different from each other. Using this we can arrange the information with a linear boolean array (with consecutive elements associated with consecutive natural numbers) indicating whether the natural number in question is a prime number or not. Number theory gives us an estimation of the order of magnitude of the thousandth prime number and thereby a boundary of the length of the array that will suffice. If we arrange our material in that way we have prepared an easy mechanism to answer the question "is n (less than the maximum) prime or not?". Alternatively, we can choose an integer array in which the successive prime numbers will be listed. (Here the same estimate, obtained by means of number theory, will be used, viz. when a maximum value of the integer array elements needs to be given *a priori*.) In the latter form we create a mechanism suited to answer the question "what is the value of the kth prime number, for $k \leqslant 1000$?".

We grant the programmer the courage to choose the latter representation. It seems attractive in the printing operation in which it is requested to print the prime numbers and not to print natural numbers with an indication whether they are prime or not. It also seems attractive for the computing stage, if we grant the programmer the clairvoyance that the analysis of whether a given natural number is a prime number or not, will have something to do with the question of whether prime factors of the number to be investigated can be found.

The next stage of our program refinement then becomes the careful statement of a convention regarding the representation of the still mysterious object "table p" and a redefinition of the two operations in terms of this convention.

The convention is that the information to be contained in "table p" will be represented by the values of the elements of the "**integer array** $p[1:1000]$", such that for $1 \leqslant k \leqslant 1000$ $p[k]$ will be equal to the kth prime number, when the prime numbers are arranged in order of increasing magnitude. (If a maximum value of the integers is implicitly understood, we assume that number theory allows us to state that this is large enough.)

When we now want to describe this new refinement we are faced with a new difficulty. Our description 1 had the form of a single program, thanks to the fact that it was a refinement of the single action named "print the first thousand prime numbers", referred to in description 0. (In more conventional terms: description 1 could have the form of a procedure body.) This no longer holds for our next level, in which we have to refine (simultaneously, in a sense) three named entities, viz. "table p" and the two actions, and we should invent some sort of identifying terminology indicating what refines what.

For the continuation of our discussion we make a very tentative proposal. We say: description 0 is a valid text expressed in terms of a single named action "print first thousand prime numbers"; let this be identified by the code 0a.

Description 1 is called "1" because it is the next refinement of description 0; it contains a refinement of 0a—the only term in which description 0 is expressed—and is itself expressed in terms of three named entities to which we attach the codes:

"table p"   1a

"fill table p with first thousand prime numbers"   1b

"print table p"   1c

code numbers, starting with 1, because description 1 is expressed in terms of them, and "a", "b" and "c" being attached for the purpose of distinction.

Now we have to describe our convention chosen for the representation of the information to be contained in "table p", but this convention pertains to all three elements 1a, 1b and 1c. Therefore we call this description 2; it should contain the descriptions of the three separate elements (I use the equality sign as separator) description 2:

1a = "**integer array** $p[1:1000]$"

1b = "make for k from 1 through 1000 $p[k]$ equal to the kth prime number"

1c = "print $p[k]$ for k from 1 through 1000".

Description 2 is expressed in terms of three named entities to which we give (in the obvious order) the codes 2a, 2b and 2c. (In code numbers, description 2 is very meagre: it just states that for 1a, 1b and 1c, we have chosen the refinements 2a, 2b and 2c respectively.)

Remark. In the representation of the information to be contained in "table p", we have chosen not to exploit the fact that each of the values to be printed occurs only once, nor that they occur in the order of increasing magnitude. Conversely, this implies that the action that has to take place under the name of 2c is regarded as a specific instance of printing any set of thousand integer values (it could be a table of monthly wages of thousand numbered employees!). The net effect of the printing action in this example is an uniquely defined as the first thousand prime numbers are: we conceive it, however, as a specific instance of a larger class of occurrences. In the further refinement of 2c we deal with this whole class, the specific instance in this class being defined by the values of the elements of the array p. When people talk about "defining an interface" I often get the feeling that they overlook the pre-supposed generalisation, the conception of the class of "possible" actions.

When 2b and 2c occur among the well-understood repertoire of instructions (and therefore 2a among the resources implicitly available) our whole problem is solved. For the sake of argument we again assume this not to be the case, and so we find ourselves faced with the task of conceiving subcomputations for the actions 2b and 2c. But now, thanks to the introduction of level 2, the respective refinements of 2b and 2c can be designed independently.

The refinement of 2b: "*make for k from 1 through 1000 $p[k]$ equal to the kth prime number*".

We are looking for description 2b1, i.e. the first refinement of 2b. We introduce a fresh numbering after 2b (rather than calling our next description "3 something") in order to indicate the mutual independence of the refinements of 2b and 2c respectively.

In description 2b1 we have to give an algorithm describing how the elements of the array p will get their values. This implies that we have to describe, for instance, in what order this will happen. In our first refinement we shall describe just that and preferably nothing more. An obvious, but ridiculous version starts as follows (with "version number" enclosed within parentheses):

2b1(1):

begin $p[1]:=2; p[2]:=3; p[3]:=5; p[4]:=7; p[5]:=11; \ldots\ldots\ldots$ **end**

implying that the programmer's knowledge includes that of a table of the first thousand primes. We shall not pursue this version as it would imply that the programmer hardly needed the machine at all.

The first prime number being given ($=2$), the thousandst being assumed unknown to the programmer, the most natural order in which to fill the elements of the array p seems to be in the order of increasing subscript value, and if we express just that we arrive (for instance) at

2b1(2):

begin integer $k, j; k: = 0; j: = 1;$

    while $k < 1000$ **do begin** "increase j until next prime number";

$$k: = k + 1; p[k]: = j \textbf{ end}$$

end

By identifying k as the number of primes found and by verifying that our first prime number ($=2$) is indeed the smallest prime number larger than 1 ($=$ the initial value of j), the correctness of 2b1(2) is easily proved by mathematical induction (assuming the existence of a sufficient number of primes).

Description 2b1(2) is a perfect program when the operation described by "increase j until next prime number"—call it 2b1(2)a—occurs among the repertoire, but let us suppose that it does not. In that case we have to express in a next refinement how j is increased (and, again, preferably nothing more). We arrive at a description of level 2b2(2)

2b1(2)a $=$

begin boolean $j$prime;

    repeat $j: = j + 1;$

        "give to $j$prime the meaning: j is a prime number"

    until $j$prime

end

Remark. Here we use the repeat-until clause in order to indicate that j has always to be increased at least once.

Again its correctness can hardly be subject to doubt. If, however, we assume that the programmer knows that, apart from 2, all further prime numbers are odd, then we may expect him to be dissatisfied with the above version because of its inefficiency. The price to be paid for this "lack of clairvoyance" is a revision of version 2b1(2). The prime number 2 will be dealt with separately, after which the cycle can deal with odd primes only. Instead of 2b1(2) we come to

2b1(3):

begin integer k, j; $p[1] := 2$; $k := 1$; $j := 1$;

    while $k < 1000$ *do*

        begin "increase odd j until next odd prime number";

            $k := k + 1$; $p[k] := j$

        end

end

where the analogous refinement of the operation between quotes—"2b1(3)a" say—leads to the description on level 2b2(3):

2b1(3)a =

begin boolean $j$prime;

    repeat $j := j + 2$;

        "give for odd j to $j$prime the meaning: j is a prime number";

    until $j$prime

end

The above oscillation between two levels of description is in fact nothing else but adjusting to our convenience the interface between the overall structure and the primitive operation that has to fit into this structure. This oscillation, this form of trial and error, is definitely not attractive, but with a sufficient lack of clairvoyance and being forced to take our decisions in sequence, I see no other way: we can regard our efforts as experiments to explore (at a rather low cost!) where the interface can probably be most conveniently chosen.

Remark. Both 2b1(2) and 2b1(3) can be loosely described as

begin "set table p and j at initial value";

    while "table p not full" **do**

    begin "increase j until next prime number to be added";

        "add j to table p"

    end

end

but we shall not do this as the sequencing in the two versions differs (see "On comparing programs") and we regard them as "incomparable". By choosing 2b1(3) we decide that our trial 2b1(2)—as 2b1(1)—is no longer applicable and therefore rejected.

The change from 2b1(2) to 2b1(3) is justified by the efficiency gain at the levels of higher refinement. This efficiency gain is earned at level 2b2, because now j can be increased by 2 at a time. It will also manifest itself in the still open primitive at level 2b2(3) where the algorithm for "give for odd j to $j$prime the meaning: j is a prime number" has only to cater for the analysis of odd values of j.

Again: in 2b2(3) we have refined 2b1(3) with an algorithm which solves our problem when "give for odd j to $j$prime the meaning: j is a prime number"— call it "2b2(3)a"—occurs among the well-understood repertoire. We now assume that it does not, in other words we have to evoke a computation deciding whether a given odd value of j has a factor. It is only at this stage that the algebra really enters the picture. Here we make use of our knowledge that we only need to try prime factors: furthermore we shall use the fact that the prime numbers to be tried can already be found in the filled portion of the array p.

We use the facts that

(1) j being an odd value, the smallest potential factor to be tried is $p[2]$, i.e. the smallest prime number larger than 2

(2) the largest prime number to be tried is $p[\text{ord} - 1]$ when $p[\text{ord}]$ is the smallest prime number whose square exceeds j.

(Here I have also used the fact that the smallest prime number whose square exceeds j can already be found in the table p. In all humility I quote Don Knuth's comment on an earlier version of this program, where I took this fact for granted:

"Here you are guilty of a serious omission! Your program makes use of a deep result of number theory, namely that if p_n denotes the nth prime number we *always* have

$$p_{n+1} < p_n{}^2."$$

Peccavi.)

If this set is not empty, we have a chance of finding a factor, and as soon as a factor has been found, the investigation of this particular j value can be stopped. We have to decide in which order the prime numbers from the set will be tried, and we shall do so in order of increasing magnitude, because the smaller a prime number the larger the probability of its being a factor of j.

When the value of ord is known we can give for "give for odd j to $j$prime the meaning: j is a prime number" the following description on level 2b3(3):

2b2(3)a =

begin integer n; $n := 2$; $j$prime: = **true**;

　　while $n <$ ord **and** $j$prime **do**

　　begin "give to $j$prime the meaning: $p[n]$ is not a factor of j"; $n := n + 1$

　　end

end

But the above version is written on the assumption that the value of ord, a function of j, is known. We could have started this refinement with

begin integer n, ord;

  ord: = 1; **while** p[ord] $\uparrow$ 2 $\leqslant$ j **do** ord: = ord + 1;

 . . . .

i.e. recomputing the value of "ord" afresh, whenever it is needed. Here some trading of storage space for computation time seems indicated: instead of recomputing this function whenever we need it, we introduce an additional variable ord for its current value: it has to be set when j is set, it has to be adjusted when j is changed.

This, alas, forces upon us some reprogramming. One approach would be to introduce, together with j, an integer variable ord and to scan the programs in order to insert the proper operations on ord, whenever j is operated upon. I do not like this because at the level at which j is introduced and has a meaning, the function "ord" is immaterial. We shall therefore try to introduce ord only at its appropriate level and we shall be very careful.

For 2b: "make for k from 1 through 1000 $p[k]$ equal to the kth prime number" we write (analogous to level 2b1(3))

level 2b1(4):·

begin integer k, j; $p[1]$: = 2; k: = 1;

  "set j to one";

  while $k < 1000$ **do**

  begin "increase odd j until next odd prime number";

    k: = $k + 1$; $p[k]$: = j

  end

end

expressed in terms of

2b1(4)a "increase odd j until next odd prime number"

2b1(4)b "set j to one".

In our next level we only introduce the subcomputation for 2b1(4)a; the other is handed down.

level 2b2(4):

2b1(4)a =

begin boolean $j$prime;

  repeat "increase j with two";

    "give for odd j to $j$prime the meaning: j is a prime number"

  until $j$prime

end;

2b1(4)b = 2b2(4)b

expressed in terms of

2b2(4)b   still meaning "set j to one"

2b2(4)c   "increase j with two"

2b2(4)d   "give for odd j to $j$prime the meaning: j is a prime number".

It is only at the next level that we need to talk about ord. Therefore we now write

level 2b3(4): **integer** ord;

2b2(4)b =

begin j: = 1; "set ord initial" **end**;

2b2(4)c =

begin j: = j + 2; "adjust ord" **end**;

2b2(4)d =

begin integer n; n: = 2; $j$prime: = **true**;

     while n < ord **and** $j$prime **do**

     begin "give to $j$prime the meaning: $p[n]$ is not a factor of j";

         n: = n + 1

     end

end

expressed in terms of

2b3(4)a   "set ord initial"

2b3(4)b   "adjust ord"

2b3(4)c   "give to $j$prime the meaning: $p[n]$ is not a factor of j".

In our next level we give two independent refinements. (Note. We could have given them in successive levels, but then we should have to introduce an arbitrary ordering to these two levels. We could also try to treat the refinements separately—i.e. as separately as 2b and 2c—but we feel that it is a little premature for this drastic decision.) We are going to express

(1) that, ord being a non-decreasing function of j and j only increasing in value, adjustment of ord implies a conditional increase;

(2) that, whether $p[n]$ is a factor of j is given by the question whether the remainder equals zero.

This leads to

level 2b4(4):

2b3(4)a = 2b4(4)a

2b3(4)b =

begin while "ord too small" **do** "increase ord by one" **end**;

2b3(4)c =

begin integer r;

    "make r equal to remainder of j over $p[n]$";

    $j$prime: $= (r \neq 0)$

end

expressed in terms of

2b4(4)a   still meaning "set ord initial"

2b4(4)b   "ord too small"

2b4(4)c   "increase ord by one"

2b4(4)d   "make r equal to remainder of j over $p[n]$"

If we have a built-in division, the implementation of "make r equal to the remainder of j over $p[n]$" can be assumed to be an easy matter. The case that the refinement of 2b4(4)d can be treated independently is now left to the interested reader. To give the algorithm an unexpected turn we shall assume the absence of a convenient remainder computation. In that case the algorithm

$$\text{"}r: = j;\ \textbf{while}\ r > 0\ \textbf{do}\ r: = r - p[n]\text{"}$$

would lead to the (non-positive) remainder but it would be most unattractive from the point of view of computation time. Again this asks for the introduction of some additional tabulated material (similar to the way in which "ord" has been introduced).

We want to know whether a given value of j is a multiple of $p[n]$ for $n < $ ord. In order to assist us in this analysis we introduce a second array in the elements of which we can store multiples of the successive prime numbers, as close to j as is convenient. In order to be able to give the size of the array we should like to know an upper bound for the value of ord; of course, 1000 would be safe, but number theory gives us 30 as a safe upper bound. We therefore introduce

integer array mult [1:30]

and introduce the convention that for $n < $ ord, mult $[n]$ will be a multiple of $p[n]$ and will satisfy the relation

$$\text{mult } [n] < j + p[n]$$

a relation that remains invariantly true under increase of j. Whenever we wish to investigate, whether $p[n]$ is a factor of j, we increase mult $[n]$ by $p[n]$ as long as

$$\text{mult } [n] < j.$$

After this increase mult $[n] = j$ is the necessary and sufficient condition for j to be a multiple of $p[n]$.

The low maximum value of ord has another consequence: the inspection "ord too small" can be expressed by

$$\text{``}p[\text{ord}] \uparrow 2 \leqslant j\text{''}$$

but this inspection has to be performed many times for the same value of ord. We may assume that we can speed up matters by introducing a variable (called "square") whose value equals $p[\text{ord}] \uparrow 2$.

So we come to our final

level 2b5(4):

integer square; **integer array** mult $[1:30]$;

2b4(4)a =

begin ord: $= 1$; square: $= 4$ **end**;

2b4(4)b =

(square $\leqslant j$);

2b4(4)c =

begin mult [ord]: $=$ square; ord: $=$ ord $+ 1$; square: $= p[\text{ord}] \uparrow 2$ **end**;

2b4(4)d =

begin while mult $[n] < j$ **do** mult $[n]$: $=$ mult $[n] + p[n]$; r: $= j -$ mult $[n]$ **end**

which has made our computation close to an implementation of the Sieve of Eratosthenes!

Note. In the refinement of 2b4(4)d, when mult$[n]$ is compared with the current value of j, mult$[n]$ is increased as much as possible; this could have been done in steps of $2 * p[n]$, because we only submit odd values of j and therefore are only interested in odd multiples of $p[n]$. (The value of mult$[1]$ remains, once set, equal to 4.)

The refinement of 2c "print $p[k]$ for k from 1 through 1000" is left to the reader. I suggest that the table should be printed on five pages, each page containing four columns with fifty consecutive prime numbers.

$$* \qquad *$$
$$*$$

Here I have completed what I announced at the beginning of this section, viz. "to describe in very great detail the composition process of such a [well-structured] program". I would like to end this section with some comments.

The most striking observation is that our treatment of a very simple program has become very long, too long indeed for my taste and wishes, even if I take into account that essentially we did two things: we made a program and we discussed extensively the kind of considerations leading to it. It is not so much the length of the latter part that bothers me (writers fill whole novels with the description of human behaviour); what bothers me is the length of the texts at the various levels. Therefore we may expect that notational technique will be one of our main concerns.

But we have also had encouraging experiences. Giving full recognition to the fact that the poor programmer cannot decide all at once, we succeeded to a large extent in building up this program one decision at a time, and in our example quite a lot of programming was already done in its definite form while major decisions were still left open: irrespective of whether the final decisions are taken this way or that way, the coding of the earlier levels remains valid. In view of the requirement of program manageability, this is very encouraging.

10. On Program Families

In our previous section we have considered the design of a program for a given task, but in doing so, we have considered our final program as an isolated object, a structure standing all by itself and to be judged on its private merits. Its structure was the result of successive decompositions; the purpose of this structure was to make a program in such a way that its correctness could be proved without undue intellectual labour.

In this section I am going to explain why I prefer to regard a program not so much as an isolated object, but rather as a member of a family of "related programs". In traditional terminology we can think about related programs either as alternative programs for the same task or as similar programs for similar tasks.

Why cannot the programmer confine his attention to the program he has to make and why has he to take into account such a whole family as well? For one thing, it is hard to claim that you know what you are doing unless you can present your act as a deliberate choice out of a possible set of things you could have done as well. But if we want to give due recognition to the difficulties that are specific to the construction of large complicated programs, there is a very practical justification. (And we *have* to recognise these specific difficulties: experience has shown that someone's proven ability to do an excellent job on a given scale is by no means a guarantee that, when faced with a much larger job, he will not make a mess of it.)

Certainly, one of the properties of large programs is that they have to be modified in the course of their life-time. A very common reason is that the program, although logically correct, turns out to evoke unsatisfactory computations (for instance unsatisfactory in one or more quantitative aspects). A second reason is that, although the program is logically correct and even satisfactorily meeting the original demands, it turns out to be a perfect solution for not quite the right problem; one is faced with a re-statement of the problem and adaptation of the program.

The naïve approach to this situation is that we must be able to modify an existing program (and for this the curious term "program maintenance" has established itself). The task is then viewed as one of text manipulation; as an aside we may recall that the need to do so has been used as an argument in favour of punched cards as against paper tape as an input medium for program texts. The actual modification of a program text, however, is a clerical matter, which can be dealt with in many different ways; my point is that if we have our grip on the program text primarily as on a linear sequence of symbols, the task to establish and to describe what has to be modified tends to become prohibitively difficult when the texts get longer and longer.

If a program has to exist in two different versions, I would rather not regard (the text of) the one program as a modification of (the text of) the other. It would be much more attractive if the two different programs could, in some sense or another, be viewed as, say, different children from a common ancestor, where the ancestor represents a more or less abstract program, embodying what the two versions have in common. Hopefully, this common ancestor can be readily recognised in the (prae-)documentation. The intentions are

(1) that the two versions share their respective correctness proofs as far as possible;

(2) that the two versions share (mechanically) as far as possible the common (or "equal") coding;

(3) that the regions affected by the modification are already well-isolated, a condition which is not met when the transition requires "brain-made" modifications scattered all over the text.

Well, this is a lofty goal. It has been inspired by the potential similarity between the task of program modification and program composition: when a program has been built up to an intermediate stage of refinement, what has then been written down is in fact a suitable "common ancestor" for all possible programs produced by further refinements. It is the similarity between "the decision to be changed" and "the decision still left open": in both cases we are left with what remains when we abstract from such a decision.

There is a second source of inspiration to be found in our experience. In the process of step-wise program composition, proceeding from outside inwards, going towards progressive refinements, we have in the earlier stages not only postponed deciding how certain things would be done, but we have also postponed committing ourselves as to exactly what had to be done: with progressing refinement, more detail about the actual problem statement has been brought into the picture. (Later examples will show this even more clearly than the problem of the prime table.) As a result, our first levels of refinement are equally applicable for the members of a whole class of problem statements.

In other words, in the step-wise approach it is suggested that even in the case of a well-defined task, certain aspects of the given problem statement are ignored at the beginning. That means that the programmer does not regard the given task as an isolated thing to be done, but is invited to view the task as a member of a whole family; he is invited to make the suitable generalisations of the given problem statement. By successively adding more detail he eventually pins his algorithm down to a solution for the given problem.

All this is well-known, each competent programmer does so all the time. Yet I stress it for a variety of reasons. If the given problem statement is an elaborate affair, i.e. too much to be grasped in a single glance, he *must* approach (and dissect) the problem statement in this way (see the section "On our inability to do much"). Secondly, if the given problem is perfectly defined, it is a wise precaution to anticipate as many future changes in the problem statement as one can foresee and accommodate. This remark is not an invitation to make one's program so "general" that it becomes, say, unacceptably inefficient, as might easily happen, when the generalisations of the problem statement are ill-considered (which might easily happen when they have been dictated by the Sales Department!) But in my experience, even in traditional programming, it is a very worth-while exercise to look for feasible generalisations of conceivable utility, because such considerations may give clear guidance as to how the final program should be structured. But such considerations boil down to ..... conceiving (more or less explicitly) a whole program family!

In an earlier section ("On the reliability of mechanisms.") the need for careful program structuring has been put forward as a consequence of the requirement that program correctness can be proved. In this section we are faced with another reason: program structure should be such as to anticipate its adaptations and modifications. Our program should not only reflect (by structure) our understanding of it, but it should also be clear from its structure what sort of adaptations can be catered for smoothly. Thank goodness, the two requirements go hand in hand.

11. ON TRADING STORAGE SPACE FOR COMPUTATION SPEED

In present-day sequential computers (spring 1969) we can distinguish two main components, an active one (the processor) and a passive one (the store). The active component has the specific function to be fast, the passive one has the specific function to be large. The following is written on the assumption that this functional division is here to stay for a sufficient period of time to make a study of its consequences relevant.

From the point of view of the programmer, storage space and computation time are then two distinct resources and I regard it as one of the responsibilities of the programmer—rather than of the system—to allocate them, i.e. to divide the load between them. It is to the consequences of this responsibility that the present section is devoted. This section is not devoted to techniques of estimating the various loads, i.e. to give quantitative criteria by which to influence the programmer's choice: it is devoted to the logical relation between the alternatives between which the programmer may choose.

Note. It is not inconceivable that some of the choices can be left to the system. In all but the most trivial cases, however, design and establishment of the equivalence seem to require mathematical invention from the side of the programmer. All efforts to automate this problem-solving activity fall outside the scope of this monograph.

In its most simple form we are faced with a computation that regularly needs the value of "FUN(arg)", where "FUN" is a given, computable function defined on the current value of one or more stored variables, collectively called "arg". In version *A* of the program, only the value of arg is stored and the value of FUN(arg) is computed whenever needed. In version *B*, an additional variable, "fun" say, is introduced, whose sole purpose is to record the value of "FUN(arg)" corresponding to the current value of arg.

Where version *A* has

"arg:= ...." (i.e. assignment to arg)

version *B* will have

"arg:= .....; fun:= FUN(arg)"

thereby maintaining the relation

fun = FUN(arg)   .

As a result of the validity of this relation, wherever version *A* calls for the evaluation of FUN(arg), version *B* will call for the current value of the variable fun.

There are two possible reasons to prefer version *B* to version *A*. When the value of FUN(arg) is more frequently requested than assignments to arg take place, version *B* could require less computation time. If necessary the technique can be refined by the introduction of a further (boolean) variable "fun up to date", indicating whether the relation "fun = FUN(arg)" is assumed to hold. Assignment to arg is then associated with

"fun up to date:= **false**" ;

whenever the value of FUN(arg) is needed, inspection of this boolean variable will tell, whether FUN(arg) has to be computed afresh; if so, the computed value will be assigned to fun and in accordance with its meaning "fun up to date" will be set to **true**. Let us call the last program version C. It is clear that these three programs, only differing where version A assigns to arg or uses the value of FUN(arg), are equivalent as far as their output is concerned; it is certainly not inconceivable that version B or C is derived from version A by mechanical means.

But quite often the situation is not as simple as that and now we come to the second reason for introducing such a variable "fun". Often it is very unattractive to compute FUN(arg) from scratch for arbitrary values of arg, while it is much easier to compute how the value of FUN(arg) changes when the value of arg is changed. In that case, the adjustment of the value of "fun" is more intimately linked with the nature of the functional dependence than is suggested by

"arg:= . . . . ; fun:= FUN(arg)".

Often this possibility is not only intimately linked to the nature of the functional dependence, but also to the "history of the variable arg" as the computation proceeds! We have seen a very striking example in the program for the prime table (see Section "A first example of step-wise program composition") with the introduction of "ord", which is functionally dependent on "j", viz. "ord" is the minimum value satisfying

$$p[\text{ord}] \uparrow 2 > j$$

where the adjustment of "ord" was a very attractive operation thanks to the fact that "j" was monotonically increasing in time.

In my understanding of programs I want such additional variables that store redundant information, to be clearly recognised as such, even if it is a somewhat undefined functional relationship as in the case of the table "mult" from the same example. I am strongly inclined to view such programs as, say, optimising refinements of a more abstract program, even when the optimisation effected by the additional variables is essential when we want to make a program with a realistic performance. From the point of view of efficiency such an additional variable may be so vital that it may strike one as irresponsible daydreaming to conceive a level in which its presence has been abstracted from. The way in which such an additional variable is manipulated is often experienced as the body of the algorithm: it is often there that we harvest the fruits of our mathematical ingenuity. The point is that, although the possibility of at least one such optimising refinement is essential for making something with a realistic performance, on closer inspection one often discovers that such an optimising refinement is far from unique, even on its coarsest level.

Note. I remember one program in which the additional information was so redundant that not only the value of "fun" could be derived from that of "arg" but also the other way round. Suddenly the relation between "fun" and "arg" became symmetric, and I have been seriously bothered by the question: what entitled me to treat them so asymmetrically? The program in question generated all the solutions of a combinatorial puzzle. On closer inspection it turned out that there was a second combinatorial puzzle, where it could be proved that there existed a one-to-one correspondence between the solutions of the two problems. If I had solved the second combinatorial problem I would have found the role of "fun" and "arg" interchanged! In traditional programming, where such functional dependencies are not explicitly shown, the two puzzles would probably be solved by identical programs, whereas I made two differently structured programs. And I think rightly so, because the single program for the two puzzles needed a different proof for its correctness, depending on which puzzle it was supposed to solve, and this seems somewhat unfair when we also wish that our understanding of the computations be reflected in the structure of our programs!

12. On A Program Model

Before we have a program we must have composed it; after we have a program —if there was any sense in making it—we shall have it executed. In this section I shall not stress the activities of program composition and of program execution too much, and I shall try to view the program as a static object. We want to view it as a highly structured object and our main question is: what kind of structures do we envisage and why? Our hope is that eventually we shall arrive at a program structure that is both nice to compose and nice to execute. Mentally, of course, I am unable to ignore these processes, but at present I do not want to discuss them; in particular: I do not want to discuss a design methodology (whether to work "from outside inwards" or the other way round), nor do I want to discuss implementation consequences now. Again, in order not to complicate matters too much, I shall restrict myself to sequential programs.

If I judge a program by itself, my central theme, I think, is that I want the program written down as I can understand it, I want it written down as I would like to explain it to someone. However, without further qualification these are just motherhood statements, so let me try and see whether I can be more specific.

Let us consider a very simple computation, in which three distinct actions can be distinguished to take place in succession, say: input of data, manipulation (i.e. the computation proper) and the output of the results. One way of representing the program is as a long string of statements:

begin

       . . . .

       . . . .

       . . . .

       . . . .

       . . . .

       . . . .

end

The next form adds some labels for explanatory purposes:

             begin

begin of input: . . . .

                         . . . .

begin of manipulation: . . . .

                         . . . .

begin of output: . . . .

                         . . . .

             end

suggesting to us, when we read the text, what is going to happen next.

Still better, we write:

             begin

input: **begin** . . . .

                         . . . . **end**;

manipulation: **begin** . . . .

                         . . . . **end**;

output: **begin** . . . .

                         . . . . **end**

          end

where the labels are considered less as markers of points in the program text than as names of regions—as indicated by the bracket pairs "**begin – end**"—that follow the label, or as names of the three actions in which the computation has been decomposed. However, if we take this point of view, the three "labels" are still comments, i.e. explanatory noise for the benefit of the interested (human) reader, whereas I would like to consider them as an integral part of the program. I want my program text to reflect somewhere the fact that the computation has been decomposed into a time-succession of the three actions, whatever form these might take upon closer inspection. A way of doing this is to write somewhere the (textual) succession of the three (abstract) statements

"input; manipulation; output"

on the understanding that the time-succession of these three actions will indeed be controlled from the above textual succession, whereas the further refinements of these three actions will be given "somewhere else", perhaps separately, but certainly without relative ordering.

Well, if closed subroutines had not been invented more than twenty years ago, this would have been the time to do it! In other words: we are returning to familiar grounds, to such an extent that many of my readers will even feel cheated! I don't, because one should never be ashamed of sticking to a proven method as long as it is satisfactory. But we should get a clear picture of the benefits we should like to derive from it, if necessary we should adjust it, and finally we should create a discipline for using it. Let me therefore review the subroutine concept, because my appreciation for it has changed in the course of the last year.

I was introduced to the concept of the closed subroutine in connection with the EDSAC†, where the subroutine concept served as the basis for a library of standard routines. Those were the days when the construction of hardware was a great adventure and many of the standard routines were means by which (scarce!) memory and computation time could be traded for circuitry: as the order code did not comprise a divide instruction, they had subroutines for division. Yet I do not remember having appreciated subroutines as a means for "rebuilding" a given machine into a more suitable one, curiously enough. Nor do I remember from those days subroutines as objects to be conceived and constructed by the user to reflect his analysis: they were more the standard routines to be used by the user. Eventually I saw them mainly as a device for the reduction of program length. But the whole program as such remained conceived as acting in a single homogeneous store, in an unstructured state space; the whole computation remained conceived as a single sequential process performed by a single processor. In the following years, in the many programming courses I gave, I preached the gospel faithfully and I have often explained how the

† "The Preparation of Programs for an Electronic Digital Computer; with Special Reference to the EDSAC and the use of a Library of Subroutines", M. V. Wilkes, D. J. Wheeler and S. Gill, Addison-Wesley Press, 1951.

calling sequence handed over the return address and how the subroutine would then begin by setting "the link"—i.e. the return jump—at its own end. At present I would rather view the main program as having its own instruction counter that just continues "counting" upon the completion of the subroutine execution and would certainly not regard the "sleeping value" as a parameter handed over to the subroutine. (Still the old view has found its way into the hardware of many machines. We have seen machines in which a subroutine jump stored the link at "address zero" of the subroutine and ordered instruction fetch to be resumed at "address one", an arrangement which makes re-entrant code and recursive subroutines somewhat hard to implement. And even in this decade we find machines which store at program interrupt the "program status" of the interrupted program at a location associated with the interrupt rather than with the interrupted program!)

Ten years later, when ALGOL 60 emerged, the scene changed and we did not talk any more about closed subroutines: we called them "procedures" instead. They remained to be appreciated by the programmer as a very handy means for shortening the program text, and more and more programmers started to use them for the purpose of structuring, so that program adaptation to foreseen changes in problem specification could be confined to the replacement of one or more procedure bodies, or to a procedure call with some actual parameters changed. But the main novelty was the concept of the local variables.

This was reflected in two important aspects. The first one was the concept of "scope", i.e. the idea that not all variables are homogeneously accessible all through the program: local variables of a procedure are inaccessible from outside the procedure body, because outside it they are irrelevant. What local variables a procedure needs to do its private task is its private concern; it is no concern of the calling main program and the fact that the main program can (and must!) be conceived independently of these local variables is judiciously reflected. We may have some misgivings about the specific scope rules, as embodied in ALGOL 60, but we should appreciate them as a very significant step in the right direction.

The second aspect of the novelty was given by the fact that procedures could be used recursively, more precisely, that a procedure was allowed to call itself, either directly or indirectly. The virtue of this facility has been the subject of many hot debates; as far as I can see the discussion has died down. The argument against recursive procedures was always an efficiency argument: non-re-entrant code could be executed so much more efficiently. But with the advent of multiprogramming another need for flexible storage allocation has emerged. And if there are still machines in which non-re-entrant code can be executed much more efficiently, i.e. in which the use of recursive routines is punished by too heavy a penalty, then I would venture the opinion that the structure of such a machine should now be called somewhat old-fashioned. The recursive procedure, however, forced upon us the recognition of the difference between its (static) text and its (dynamic) activation—its "incarnation" as it has been called. The procedure text is one thing; the set of local variables it operates upon this time is quite another matter.

So far, so good, but now some of its shortcomings (and I don't care, whether you call them linguistic or conceptual). Local variables are "created" upon procedure entry, and are "annihilated" upon procedure exit. It is precisely this automatic control over the life-time of variables pertaining to a procedure incarnation that allows us to implement the (recursive) procedures by means of a stack (i.e. a last-in-first-out storage arrangement). The fact that local variables pertaining to an incarnation only exist during the incarnation make it impossible for the procedure to transmit information behind the scenes from one incarnation to the next. To overcome this the concept "own" has been introduced, but this is no solution to the problem: what own variables are really good for becomes very unclear in the case of recursion and, secondly, it is impossible to write a set of procedures sharing a number of own variables. (We can simulate this by declaring them in an outer block, embracing the procedure declarations, but then the scope rules make them too generally accessible: they can then no longer be regarded as "behind the scenes".) Our conclusion—by no means new and by no means only mine!—is that the concept "own" as introduced in ALGOL 60 must be regarded as ill-considered, and that we must look for new ways to control and describe life-time, accessibility and identity of local variables.

But I have still another complaint about the procedure concept, and that is that it is still primarily regarded as a means for shortening the program text (although it may be a text of unknown length as in the case of recursion). The semantics of the procedure call are described in terms of the famous "copy rule": the procedure call is to be understood as a short-hand, because, semantically speaking, we should replace it with a copy of the text of the procedure body (with suitable adjustments of identifiers and substitutions for parameters) whereupon the thus modified text will be executed by the same machine as the one executing the main program. It remains (a representation for) a single program text to be executed by a single sequential machine. And it is precisely this picture of a single machine that does not satisfy me any longer.

I want to view the main program as executed by its own, dedicated machine, equipped with the adequate instruction repertoire operating on the adequate variables and sequenced under control of its own instruction counter, in order that my main program would solve my problem if I had such a machine. I want to view it that way, because it stresses the fact that the correctness of the main program can be discussed and established regardless of the availability of this (probably still virtual) machine: I don't need to have it, I only need to have its specifications as far as relevant for the proper execution of the main program under consideration.

For me, the conception of this virtual machine is an embodiment of my powers of abstraction, not unlike the way in which I can understand a program written in a so-called higher level language, without knowing how all kinds of operations (such as multiplication and subscription) are implemented and without knowing such irrelevant details as the number system used in the hardware that is eventually responsible for the program execution.

In actual practice, of course, this ideal machine will turn out not to exist, so our next task—structurally similar to the original one—is to program the simulation of the "upper" machine. In programming this simulation we have to decide upon data structures to provide for the state space of the upper machine; furthermore we have to make a bunch of algorithms, each of them providing an implementation of an instruction assumed for the order code of the upper machine. Finally, the "lower" machine may have a set of private variables, introduced for its own benefit and completely outside the realm and scope of the upper machine. But this bunch of programs is written for a machine that in all probability will not exist, so our next job will be to simulate it in terms of programs for a next-lower machine, etc. until finally we have a program that can be executed by our hardware.

If we succeed in building up our program along the lines just given, we have arranged our program in layers. Each program layer is to be understood all by itself, under the assumption of a suitable machine to execute it, while the function of each layer is to simulate the machine that is assumed to be available on the level immediately above it.

Why this model? What are the benefits we hope to derive from it? Let me try to list them.

(1) Our experience as recorded in "A first example of step-wise program composition" strongly suggests that the arrangement of various layers, corresponding to different levels of abstraction, is an attractive vehicle for program composition.

(2) It is not vain to hope that many a program modification can now be presented as replacement of one (virtual) machine by a compatible one.

(3) We may hope that the model will give us a better grip on the problems that arise when a program has to be modified while it is in action. If a machine at a given level is stopped between two of its instructions, all lower machines are completely passive and can be replaced, while all higher machines must be regarded as engaged in the middle of an instruction: their state must be considered as being in transition. In a sequential machine the

state can only be interpreted in between instruction executions and the picture of this hierarchy of machines, each having its own instruction counter —"counting its instructions"—seems more profitable if we wish to decide at any given moment, what interpretations are valid. In the usual programming language in which computational progress is measured in a homogeneous measure—say "the grain" of one statement—I feel somewhat helpless when faced with the question of which interpretations are valid when.

(4) We may hope that the model will even assist us in recovery problems —total or partial—when some malfunctioning has been detected. (Recently I have been involved in the design and construction of a multiprogramming system, but one of the most annoying things was our total inability to estimate (mechanically) the scope of the disaster when a memory cell gave a parity alarm. The only safe reaction we could implement was instantaneous machine stop, hardly a solution to be proud of!)

(5) The picture of a layered hierarchy of machines provides a counter poison to one of the dangers evoked by ruthless application of the principle "Divide and Rule", viz. that different components are programmed so independently of each other that duplication of work (or worse) takes place. The fact that a layer contains "a bunch of programs" to be executed by some conceptual machine stresses the fact that the programs of this bunch are invited to share the same primitives. Separation of tasks is a good thing, on the other hand we have to tie the loose ends together again!

13. A SECOND EXAMPLE OF STEP-WISE PROGRAM COMPOSITION

With a picture of program structure as a layered hierarchy of machines emerging, my fingers are itching to play with it, i.e. to make another program. The notational techniques employed should not be regarded as a well-considered proposal: they have been chosen to suit my fancy and should be regarded as part of the experiment.

The problem is the following one. There is given a line printer which is controlled by two commands "NLCR" (New Line Carriage Return) which defines the utmost left position of the next line as the "currently printable position", and the command "PRSYM(n)" which prints a character identified by the value of the integer parameter n on the currently printable position and defines the position immediately to the right of the printed position as the new currently printable position. (For our discussion we can regard lines of infinite length as permissible.) We shall only make use of two specific values of n, called "space" and "mark" respectively. "PRSYM (space)" causes the currently printable position to remain blank, "PRSYM (mark)" will print a given, visible character, some sort of asterisk say.

Furthermore two integer function of an integer argument are given, satisfying

for $0 \leqslant i < 1000 : 0 \leqslant fx(i) < 100$ and $0 \leqslant fy(i) < 50$.

Now we have to make a program printing 50 lines, numbered from top to bottom by a y-coordinate running from 49 through 0, the positions on a line being numbered from left to right by an x-coordinate running from 0 through 99. On the thousand positions (or less in the case of coincidence) given by

$x = fx(i)$ **and** $y = fy(i)$ for some i satisfying $0 \leqslant i < 1000$

a mark has to be printed; all other positions on the paper have to remain blank. In other words: a curve is given in a discrete parameter representation and we wish to use the line printer as a digital plotter.

I have used this problem extensively in viva voce examinations and the majority of the students quickly discover that, due to the absence of OLCR (Old Line Carriage Return) and of a "backspace", the order in which the printable positions have to be served is dictated by the printing commands and, secondly, that this order has nothing to do with the order of the marks if we number them, say, in the order of increasing i. As a result they quickly conclude that the use of storage seems indicated: first the thousand i-values should be scanned, i.e. the page image should be stored in a convenient manner, while afterwards, under control of the stored image, the page should be printed. (To be more precise: we assume that the computer has sufficient store for this purpose and that the computation of the function values "fx (i)" and "$fy(i)$" may be so time-consuming that we wish to have them computed only once for each i-value.)

We now document this design decision, and I propose the following piece of text:

COMPFIRST

begin

draw: {build; print};

var image;

instr build(image), print(image)

end

The above piece of documentation, which is considered as an integral part of the final program, should be interpreted as follows.

It refers to a machine called "COMPFIRST" (we use capitals for machine names and try to express the type of decision reflected in the program made for them).

The next line gives a named algorithm: its name is "draw" (this being assumed to be the name of the total program to be made, that has to "draw" a curve), the algorithm expresses the desired time-succession of two actions, building the image in store, followed by printing paper under control of the stored value.

In the last two lines we give the declarations (or declaration headings), naming the components of the machine for which the above algorithm is intended. The first line describes that the name "image" will be used for the data structure that has to accommodate the page image; the variable "image" is the only component of the state space of this machine. Its instruction code comprises two instructions, named "build" and "print" respectively.

Before proceeding, it should be noted that we have used abbreviations, some of which I do not yet know whether they are very wise or very foolish. They have both to do with the fact that the variable "image" is a unique variable of this type.

If the state space should have contained two images, I would have written

"**type** image;

image **var** image1, image2"

expressing that the state space comprises two variables (called "image1" and "image2" respectively), with the same set of possible values, this set being characterised by their **type**, called "image". In a later step the **type** image would enjoy further detailing and this would apply to both variables. As the set of variables of this type contains only one element, I have ventured not to distinguish between the set (called "image") and its only element (also called "image"). When descriptions in COMPFIRST (such as "build(image)") refer to "image", they refer to the variable; when later structuring detail is given, it refers to the type image.

The last line contains the code of instructions which are like the procedure heading. In general they contain the type of the parameters, where the call contains the variables as actual parameters. Again this seems foolish if the parameter is uniquely given by its type and for this reason we have mentioned the actual parameter in the declaration, and have omitted the mentioning of "image" in the code describing the algorithm "draw". Thus we can reserve the explicitly mentioned actual parameters for the case where this combinatorial freedom is actually used.

Before proceeding, I would like to stress that our little algorithm named "draw" can and should be regarded as a program written for a machine. We should write the manual for this machine; in it we have to state

(1) that the operation "build" assigns a value to the variable "image" specifying the image to be printed on paper as given by the functions fx and fy.

(2) that the operation "print" prints the picture on paper as specified by the current value of the variable "image".

The fact that it can really be regarded as an algorithm for a machine is perhaps most easily seen when we consider alternative algorithms for "draw" e.g.

draw: {print; build}

is wrong, because now the action "print" is undefined;

draw: {build; build; print}

is correct but unnecessarily time-consuming, because the second action "build" assigns to "image" the value it already has;

draw: {build; print; print}

would make sense: it would print the picture twice.

We now resume our programming task. If we had machine "COMPFIRST" at our disposal, the little program named "draw" to be executed by it would do the job. For the sake of argument and in order to be realistic we now assume that we do not have at our disposal such a machine tailored to our needs, and therefore our next task (similar to the previous one!) is to make such a machine.

There are three named entities assumed, viz. "build", "print" and "image", where the first two refer to the latter one. As a consequence, a further detailing of the latter one will affect the two first ones; also, it is very hard to give any further detailing of the action "print" without any further commitments as to the structure of "image". The action "build", however, admits a further detailing all by itself. And it is for that reason that we take "build" as our first candidate for further refinement.

We have to describe how the variable "image" will get its value corresponding to the proper positioning of the thousand marks. As a total operation, it assigns a value to a variable, whose earlier value was undefined: anticipating that the marks will be added "one at a time", we see, that addition of a next mark will turn out to be an action operating on an already defined value of the variable "image". It therefore seems attractive to view the whole setting of the marks as operating on an already defined value, viz. the one corresponding to the blank page. This decision leads to

CLEARFIRST

begin

build: {clear; setmarks};

instr clear(image), setmarks(image)

end

where the action "clear" assigns to image the value corresponding to a picture of fifty blank lines, where the action "setmarks" adjusts the initial value of image to the one in which the thousand (or less) marks of the curve have been added.

Again, CLEARFIRST is a machine for which alternative programs could have been written, e.g.

build: {clear}

would make sense, but would produce fifty blank lines as output;

build: {setmarks; clear}

would contain an undefined operation;

build: {clear; clear; setmarks}

would contain a superfluous operation, just as

build: {clear; setmarks; setmarks}

would, because the second action "setmarks" would only add marks to the picture that would already be there and therefore would not change the value of "image".

(Note on notation used. The algorithm explaining "build" in terms of "clear" and "setmarks" does so without explicitly mentioning "image", because we do not wish to use the actual parameter notation in algorithms unless its actual combinatorial freedom is in fact used in this machine.

Furthermore, "build" being a one-parameter operation no separate identifier for its formal parameter has been introduced. Also this abbreviation on my part could turn out to be very unwise.)

The next step in the design of the computation—because it can be made without any further commitments—is to describe how the thousand marks of the curve will be dealt with in turn. For the time being I propose the following write-up:

ISCANNER

begin integer i;

setmarks: {$i:= 0$; **while** $i < 1000$ **do** {add mark; i **plus** 1}};

instr add mark(i, image)

end

This algorithm is to be understood in a machine whose instruction repertoire comprises "add mark(i, image)" which will change the value of "image" in accordance with the addition of the ith mark. It describes the order in which the marks are dealt with; it shows all marks will be dealt with exactly once.

But this is not all: a new variable (viz. "i") has been introduced, the algorithm appeals to a set of actions referring to this variable ("$i:= 0$", "$i < 1000$" and "i **plus** 1") and if I were completely consistent, it seems that I should list them at the bottom, as possibly requiring further clarification at a later stage, just as "add mark". I have not done so (I have treated them along the same lines as the **while-do** clause). From the point of view of language semantics this separate treatment of an implicitly understood type **integer** does not seem attractive, and it seems hard to justify, why the type **integer** is treated differently from the type "image": both are implicitly understood in this machine.

Yet I have done it. All the time I design programs for non-existing machines and add: "if we now had a machine comprising the primitives here assumed, then the job is done". This is, logically speaking, correct; in practice it is a joke, because we know very well that we cannot assume a general purpose machine to be available whose instruction code is so very well tailored to our needs. We should not close our eyes—nor feign to do so!—to our responsibility to provide such primitives in a later stage of the design. When I now appeal to a well-understood type "integer" and the operations defined on variables of such a type in this exceptional manner, I do so with the intention of expressing that—although these facilities have to be provided in some form or another—providing these facilities fall outside the scope of the programmer's responsibility and also that the programmer will accept any reasonable implementation of them.

Again we are left with a primitive that admits further refinement without commitments regarding the other primitives. We have to describe how dealing with mark no. i can be expressed in terms of dealing with a position on the page: we create the machine dealing with the computation of this position.

COMPPOS

begin integer x,y;

add mark: $\{x := fx(i); y := fy(i); \text{mark pos}\}$;

instr mark pos (x, y, image)

end

where "mark pos" will change the current value of the variable "image" in accordance with the addition of a mark with the co-ordinates "x" and "y" on the picture to be printed.

(Note. In the last refinement it is explicitly assumed that the functions $fx(i)$ and $fy(i)$ can be evaluated in any order of their argument values. If these two thousand function values were to be read from an input stream, pair wise in a prescribed order of i-values, then the last two machines would have to be merged into a single one.)

By now I see no possibility of further refinement without committing myself to the structure of the still rather vague type "image". How do we propose that this value will be stored? We have to structure the variables of type "image", or, what amounts to exactly the same thing, we have to choose a representation for its possible values.

While lecturing at various places I have described versions of this program to different audiences, and it may be worth-while to point out that at least twice part of my audience was deeply troubled by the time I had reached this stage. They felt for instance, that I could not claim that my program, as far as developed, was correct; they objected to my remark that

draw: {build; print; print}

would produce the same picture twice, for how did I know, that "print" did not (by means of some side-effect) change the value of "image" before I had *made* the primitive "print"? The answer to this, of course, is that "print" has to do what has been stated and should not do what has not been stated. But then more objections came: I had failed to show that the representation was unique, perhaps it was such, that "print" was only a partial function, undefined for some possible values of "image", etc. The answer to this seems to be the following: legitimate as such concerns are, they should be dealt with at the right moment, i.e. not before we commit ourselves to a representation. It is apparently the strength of our approach that so much of the program could be written down independently of the representation to be chosen for the values of the type "image". What we have done so far seems indeed a judicious exploitation of our power of abstraction (here abstraction of the particular representation to be chosen for the data structure "image").

But even if we now come to the conclusion that the time has come to decide upon the data structure for the type "image" we still do not need to commit ourselves completely. Faced with the question how to structure our variable now, we can take our decisions step-wise, just as we have done with the algorithmic refinements encountered so far.

We recall that the origin of the problem was to be found in the circumstance that the printing primitives "PRSYM" and "NLCR" forced the computation to produce the picture line after line going from top to bottom. Let us try to give recognition to that fact by regarding the image as composed of an array of lines. I then come to the following next level.

LINER
begin integer j;
image: {**array** line[0 : 49]};
print: {j:= 49; **while** $j \geqslant 0$ **do** {lineprint(line[j]); j **minus** 1}};
clear: {j:= 49; **while** $j \geqslant 0$ **do** {lineclear(line[j]); j **minus** 1}};
mark pos: {linemark(line[y])};
type line;
instr lineprint(line), lineclear(line), linemark(x, line)
end

In the last line but one we have introduced a type called "line"; a type, I recall, is regarded as a collection of distinguishable values and a variable of such a type can, at any moment, have one of this collection as its value. The first line of code expresses that the type "image" is composed of an array of 50 elements of type "line", numbered from 0 through 49, and, being the only type composed from this type, again we abstain from introducing a new identifier (wisely or not).

Then, "print", "clear", and "mark pos", being operations that were understood as operating on an "image" are translated in algorithms expressed in terms of operations on a line. In the code of these algorithms, the (true) actual parameter specifies which line; at the end of the description we give the instruction list, indicating that the actions operate on "a line"; we have given the type, but not the parameter.

This level introduces some new features. To start with (as in explaining "image") we treat the structural refinement of a data type on a footing very similar to the algorithmic refinements (as applied to "print", "clear" and "mark pos"). Before this level, our approach could have been regarded as an effort to establish a discipline for "subroutinisation"—if the reader will excuse this horrible term!—now we observe that that characterisation of our effort covers only half of what we are trying to do, as we are trying to apply a similar technique to data structures as well. Secondly, our previous machine explained just one entity (instruction or data type) in contrast to "LINER", which explains a whole bunch of them. The point is that we try to associate with each level a separate design decision; the decision taken here is to understand the image from now onwards in terms of lines, and therefore all operations dealing with an image as such have to be translated in terms of operations dealing with its lines. The image has been "explained away", the only unusual type we still have to deal with is the type "line" and that is what we are going to do now. I draw your attention to the fact that in the level to come, we have to deal with lines: that lines are used to compose images from is no longer relevant!

To represent a line we have many different possibilities, e.g. a list of the the x-coordinates of the positions where a mark should be printed (possibly sorted in order of increasing x-value), a boolean array of 100 elements, each element indicating whether the corresponding position on the line of the picture should be marked, or an integer array of 100 elements, each element having the value "mark" or "space" of the PRSYM-parameter for the corresponding printable position. The last representation caters for extension when different curves (with different marks) have to be printed in the same picture; therefore we select the last one.
This leads to

LONGREP

begin integer k;

line: {**integer array** sym[0 : 99]};

lineprint: {$k := 0$; **while** $k < 100$ **do** {PRSYM(sym[k]); k **plus** 1}; NLCR};

lineclear: {$k := 0$; **while** $k < 100$ **do** {sym[k] := space; k **plus** 1}};

linemark: {sym[x] := mark}

end

This however leads to an implementation filling out the line with spaces at the righthand side of the rightmost mark: it is like banging the space bar until the bell rings when we want to effect the transition to a new paragraph while writing a letter!

The next version suppresses superfluous PRSYM-commands and even leaves those elements of the variable of type "line" undefined that do not need to be defined. With each line a counter "f" is associated, giving the number of PRSYM-commands to be given for that line. Clearing a line now shrinks into setting "f" to zero!

SHORTREP

begin integer k;

line: {**integer** f; **integer array** sym[0 : 99]};

lineprint: {$k := 0$; **while** $k < f$ **do** {PRSYM(sym[k]); k **plus** 1}; NLCR};

lineclear: {$f := 0$};

linemark: {sym[x] := mark;

    if $f \leqslant x$ **do** {$k := f$; **while** k $< x$ **do** {sym[k] := space; k **plus** 1};

        $f := x + 1$}}

end

Note added later.

The above program is essentially the program as I have shown it to at least five different audiences. Now, two months later, while thinking at leisure about correctness proofs, I suddenly realise that the given algorithm for "linemark" betrays my past, for it is a piece of lousy coding, compared with the following alternative:

linemark: {**while** $f \leqslant x$ **do** {sym[f] := space; f **plus** 1};

    sym[x] := mark}

a version which guarantees that whenever "sym[x] := mark" is executed, the relation "$x < f$" will always be satisfied: it is precisely the function of the first line to see to this. The reader is invited to try to understand both versions of linemark and to compare both reasonings. He will then agree with my judgement that the original version is lousy.

The second version jumped into my mind on account of the following observation. The conditional clause

"if *B* do *S*"

is used in programs in two different ways. On the one hand we have the applications, in which the execution of the statement *S* does not invalidate the truth of *B*, on the other hand we have the situations in which the execution of the statement *S* is guaranteed to invalidate the truth of *B*. In the latter case, it is the function of the conditional statement to ensure that after its execution *B* will not hold. It is then, essentially, a shortcut for

"while *B* do *S*",

which has the property of invalidating the truth of *B* (provided that it stops), but the justification of the shortcut requires a separate proof that the repeated statement will be executed at most once. (In "A first example of step-wise program composition" we did not bother to introduce this shortcut on level 2b4(4) where he wrote

"while "ord too small" **do** "increase ord by one"";

here a conditional clause would have done the job!)

14. ON WHAT WE HAVE ACHIEVED

One of the metaphors in which I find myself thinking about the program structure envisaged regards the program as a necklace, strung from individual pearls.

We have described the program in terms of levels and each level contained "refinements" of entities that were assumed available in higher levels. These refinements were either dynamic refinements (algorithms) or static refinements (data structures) to be understood by an appropriate machine. I use the term "pearl" for such a machine, refinements included.

Our previous program consists of a necklace of six pearls, in order either

COMPFIRST

CLEARFIRST

ISCANNER

COMPPOS

LINER

LONGREP

or

COMPFIRST

CLEARFIRST

ISCANNER

COMPPOS

LINER

SHORTREP.

LONGREP and SHORTREP are two different pearls, they explain the same concepts (from the "upper face") into the same concept (of the "lower face"); only the particular refinements differ: they are as alternative programs for the same job and the same machine.

Changing a program will be treated as replacing one or more pearls of the original necklace by one or more other pearls. The pearl is the individual unit from which programs are composed. Making a program (as a member of a class of related programs) is now regarded as a two-stage process: making pearls (more than strictly necessary) and then stringing a fitting necklace out of (a selection of) them.

The reasons for this two-stage approach are many. In designing a program we have to consider many, many alternative programs and once our program is finished, we will have to change it (into one of the alternative ones). As long as programs are regarded as linear strings of basic symbols of a programming language and, accordingly, program modification is treated as text manipulation on that level, then each program modification must be understood in the universe of all programs (right or wrong!) that can be written in that programming language. No wonder that program modification is then a most risky operation! The basic symbol is too small and meaningless a unit in terms of which to describe this. The pearl, embodying the independent design decision or, as the case may be, an isolated aspect of the original problem statement, is meant to be the natural unit for such modifications.

To rephrase the same argument: with the birth of ALGOL 60, syntax was discovered as a powerful means for expressing structure in a program text. (Syntax became so glorified that many workers in the field identified Computing Science with Syntactic Analysis!) It was slightly overlooked, however, that by expressing structure via syntax, this structure is only given very indirectly, i.e. to be derived by means of a parsing algorithm to be applied to a linear sequence of basic symbols. This hurts if we realise that many a program modification leaves large portions of the structure unaffected, so that after painful re-parsing of the modified text the same structure re-emerges! I have a strong feeling that the adequacy of context-free methods for the representation of structure has been grossly overestimated. (In my immediate environment the following program bug in an ALGOL 60 program was brought to my attention. A program produced erroneous output with a completely checking implementation which in addition to the program text requires a final "**progend**" after the last "**end**"; this additional character is refused everywhere else so that a correct "**begin – end**" bracketing can be established. It turned out that

(1) somewhere in the program a closing string quote was omitted;

(2) somewhere further down in the program text an opening string quote was omitted;

(3) the "**begin – end**" structure of the resulting program was syntactically correct;

(4) the identifiers declared between the two omissions were only used between the two omissions, so that even context-dependent checks were unable to give alarm.

Having already my doubts as to the adequacy of context-free methods for expressing macroscopic structure, I was delighted when this bug was shown to me!)

The more I think about pearls, the more I feel that something like them is the only way out of it, if we recognise our responsibility to take (for a large program) say a thousand (possible) versions into consideration. You cannot expect the programmer to make all these thousand versions from scratch, independent of each other. The only way I see to produce such a potential variety is by a combinatorial technique, i.e. by making more pearls (say 250) than needed for a single necklace (say 200) and stringing a necklace from a particular selection. I see no other feasible way. The other mechanism to achieve great variety by combinatorial means is permutation, but this is denied to us because the final necklace must be a fitting necklace and, given the pearls, the order in which they have to be strung on the thread to produce a fitting necklace is pretty well defined. And also: if it is not, the permissible change of order is pretty irrelevant!

Also, the pearl gives a clear status to an "incomplete" program, consisting of the top half of a necklace: it can be regarded as a complete program to be executed by a suitable machine (of which the bottom half of the necklace gives a feasible implementation). As such, the correctness of the upper half of the necklace can be established regardless the choice of the bottom half. Between two successive pearls we can make a "cut" which is a manual for a machine, provided by the part of the necklace below the cut and used by the program represented by the part of the necklace above the cut. This manual serves as an interface between the two parts of the necklace. We feel this form of interface more helpful than regarding data-representation as an interface between operations, in particular more helpful towards ensuring the combinatorial freedom required when a program has to be adapted.

Another remark concerns the range of validity of concepts along the necklace. For instance, the concept "image" is introduced in our top pearl "COMPFIRST" and is explained away in our bottom pearl but one, viz. "LINER". If we now come to the conclusion that the program as envisaged is too demanding on storage space so that we cannot afford to introduce the variable "image", we are faced with a major program revision and we have to replace the top five pearls by other ones, because that is the range of validity of the concept "image"! The bottom pearl (either "LONGREP" or "SHORTREP"), however, can be retained. (I mention this as an example of the fact that pearl exchange is by no means restricted to exchange of the bottom pearl.)

With respect to the validity range of concepts along the necklace I would like to ask your attention for an observation which thrilled me the first time I made it. (In retrospect it is pretty obvious and that is exactly why it may be worth-while to be explicit about it.) With each pearl we associate "an independent design decision" and the ordering of the pearls along the necklace therefore implies an ordering of the design decisions. Can we change this order? Yes, we can, although we then have different pearls. By way of experiment I have followed the well-known advice: if you are faced with two primitives—in our case "build" and "print"—decide immediately upon their interface—in our example "image"—so that the two primitives can now be refined independently of each other. So I did, and I came to the following form of necklace

COMPFIRST

LINER'

CLEARFIRST'

ISCANNER'

COMPPOS'

SHORTREP

(the four middle pearls being primed to indicate that they refer to different pearls, although they embody the same decisions as the ones in the original set). The resulting program is much messier. Why?

Along the necklace we can indicate for each concept its range of validity: of course they overlap and we can view them as the individual threads from which the whole explanation is twined, as a kind of "logical rope". The messy version has a logical rope twined from more and sometimes longer individual threads: its logical rope is thicker, the whole construction is more tightly interconnected. The observation thrilled me because it gave a very convincing demonstration (at least for me!) that elegance, clarity and the like have indeed marked quantitative aspects (as Mozart knew: many of his compositions that make one catch one's breath are misleadingly simple, they seem to be made just out of practically nothing!).

We can phrase the observation in more technical terms. The primed version is messy because the image is explained away in terms of lines at too early a stage, thereby forcing us to explain "CLEARFIRST", "ISCANNER" and "COMPPOS" in terms of lines, while they could still be explained in terms of the image, i.e. independent of the representation to be chosen for it. Or, in other words, in the original version we have made a more judicious exploitation of our power of abstraction than in the primed one. The larger the number of pearls independent of the particular representation, the more adaptable one's program and the more easily understandable—because that set of pearls can be understood at a higher level of abstraction. The experience seems to indicate that the goals of adaptability and clarity have been given some substance and (what is more) go by their very nature hand in hand. This is very encouraging (although not surprising).

It also gives—me at least—a somewhat clearer picture of the scope of my present efforts. Whatever I shall develop, it will not be a General Problem Solver, not a mechanical one, not even one written for the benefit of the human problem solver. But it may give the human some appreciation for the various aspects of "elegance" of a solution when he succeeds in finding one. And as such it may give him a guide line.

15. ON GROUPING AND SEQUENCING

While we are considering a programming tool in which explicit recognition has been given to the hierarchy of levels of abstraction, the present section is also applicable to programming in programming languages as they are understood today, viz. on a constant semantic level. (And there is a fair chance that the current section has its morals outside the restricted field of programming, for it seems to be concerned with problem solving in general.)

I shall illustrate my point with two examples, both of which, again, I have used in viva voce examinations. I owe the first example to Niklaus Wirth.

The problem is to construct a program generating non-empty sequences of 0's, 1's and 2's without non-empty, element-wise equal, adjoining subsequences, generating these sequences in alphabetical order until a sequence of length 100 (i.e. of 100 digits) has been generated. The programmer may make use of the knowledge that a sequence of length 100 and satisfying the conditions actually exists. The start of the list of sequences to be generated is:

```
0
01
010
0102
01020
010201
0102010
0102012
........
```

Each solution (apart from the first one) is an extension (by one digit) of an earlier solution and the algorithm is therefore a straightforward backtracking one.

We are looking for the "good" sequences, we assume a primitive available for the investigation of whether a trial sequence is good. If it is good, the trial sequence is printed and extended with a zero to give the next trial sequence; if the trial sequence is no good, we perform on it the operation "increase" to get the next trial sequence, i.e. final digits $= 2$ are removed and then the last remaining digit is increased by 1. (The operations "extend with zero" and "increase" guarantee that trial sequences are generated in alphabetical order, the solutions, being a selection from them, will then be printed in alphabetical order as well.) The algorithm will start investigating the following trial sequences, those marked by an asterisk will be rejected as "no good":

```
    0
*   00
    01
    010
*   0100
*   0101
    0102
    01020
*   010200
    010201
    0102010
*   01020100
*   01020101
*   01020102
*   0102011
    0102012
........
```

I found the majority of my students inclined to make a program with the following structure:

"set trial sequence to single zero;

repeat if good **then**

    begin print trial sequence; extend trial sequence with zero **end**

    else

    increase trial sequence

until length = 101"

Although a program along these lines produces the correct output, objections can—and to my taste: should—be made against it. The first objections regards the stopping criterion: when a solution of length 100 has been printed, *we* (knowing the algorithm) can deduce that after that for the first time the trial sequence will have length = 101 and this is now the criterion to stop, but this is a rather indirect and tortuous way to establish the stopping criterion. (How tortuous it is was clearly demonstrated by those students who did not see that an unnecessary trial sequence was generated and declared for the trial sequence an array of 100 elements instead of 101.) The second objection is that the operation "increase trial sequence" never increases its length: after rejection of a trial sequence a superfluous test on the length is performed. (When I used this example for student examination examinations I had not stressed very explicitly in my lectures any problem solving principles, so my disappointment was not too severe. In a sense I am glad to have observed these examinations, for it was for me an incentive to stress problem solving principles as far as I could find, formulate and teach them.)

The program to which the above objections do not apply treats the empty sequence as a virtual solution, not to be printed. It has—to the same level of detail—the following structure:

"set trial sequence empty;

repeat extend trial sequence with zero;

    while no good **do** increase trial sequence;

    print trial sequence

until length = 100"

Here length is the length of the solution printed (if any), thus avoiding the tortuous reasoning for the stopping criterion. Also no superfluous last trial sequence (never to be investigated) will be generated, thanks to the fact that we have two loops inside each other, superfluous length testing no longer occurs. Those for whom efficiency is the main criterion will probably be most convinced by the last observation. I myself, who attach considerable importance to understandability, am attracted to the latter program because I can interpret it as a further refinement of the program structure

"set sequence empty;

repeat transform sequence to next solution;

print sequence

until length = 100"

This (more abstract) program is only concerned with sequences that are solutions: on this level of description one can ignore that the transition from one solution to the next takes place via a sequence of trial solutions that turn out to be failures.

I owe to Joe Weizenbaum the second example. Make a program that, for given positive integer n, determines the smallest number s that can be decomposed into the sum of two nth powers in at least two non-trivially different ways.

$$(\text{for } n = 1 \quad s = 2 = 0^1 + 2^1 = 1^1 + 1^1$$
$$n = 2 \quad s = 25 = 0^2 + 5^2 = 3^2 + 4^2$$
$$n = 3 \quad s = 1729 = 1^3 + 12^3 = 9^3 + 10^3$$
$$n = 4 \quad s = 635318657 = 59^4 + 158^4 = 133^4 + 134^4)$$

When I first used this example in an oral examination, it took the student twenty minutes to get somewhat familiar with the problem and he then sketched a searching algorithm which—when patched up—could indeed find a number that allowed multiple decompositions into sums of two nth powers, but he could not prove that when his algorithm produced a value s that it would be the minimum value. (As a matter of fact he had, up till then, ignored that part of the problem statement.)

He then regrouped his forces and made a program of the following form:

"**integer** s, k;

$s := 1$;

repeat $s := s + 1$;

$k :=$ "the number of ways in which s can be decomposed as the sum of two nth powers"

until $k > 1$

thus arriving at a hopelessly inefficient algorithm. The error he made was the decision at too early a stage to investigate the natural numbers in succession, the overwhelming majority of which are not decomposable at all. Reasoning that the value we are looking for is the smallest decomposable number satisfying an additional property, one comes to an algorithm whose first sketch could be "**integer** k, s, t;

$t := 1$ (and further initialisation);

repeat $s :=$ "smallest decomposable value larger than t";

$\quad k :=$ "the number of ways the above minimum is obtained"

$\quad t := s$

until $k > 1$"

By storing a collection of triples (number pairs with their corresponding s-value), among which each time the pair(s) with minimum s-value exceeding t will occur and adjusting this collection each time t is increased, a program emerges that is orders of magnitude more efficient, t jumping from decomposable value to the next decomposable value. Programming (or problem solving in general?) as the judicious postponement of decisions and commitments!

16. DESIGN CONSIDERATIONS IN MORE DETAIL

Preceding sections—in particular "A first example of step-wise program composition." have evoked the criticism that I have oversimplified the design process almost to the extent of dishonesty; I don't think this criticism fully unjustified and to remedy the situation I shall treat two examples in greater detail. The first example is my own invention; I have tried it out in a few oral examinations and finally I have used it at the end of my course "An introduction into the Art of Programming" in the classroom. I posed the problem to an audience of fifty students and together, with me as leader of the discussion, they solved the problem in 90 minutes.

We consider a character set consisting of letters, a space(sp) and a point(pnt). Words consist of one or more, but at most twenty letters. An input text consists of one or more words, separated from each other by one or more spaces and terminated by zero or more spaces followed by a point. With the character valued function RNC (Read Next Character) the input text should be read from and including the first letter of the first words up to and including the terminating point. An output text has to be produced using the primitive PNC(x) (i.e. Print Next Character) with a character valued parameter. If the function of the program were to copy the text, the following program would do (assuming character valued variables at our disposal)

char x;

repeat $x := $ RNC; PNC(x) **until** $x = $ pnt

In this example, however, the text is to be subjected to the following transformation:

(1) in the output text, successive words have to be separated by a single space

(2) in the output text, the last word has to be followed by a single point

(3) when we number the words 0, 1, 2, 3, ... in the order from left to right (i.e. in which they are scanned by repeated evaluation of RNC), the words with an even ordinal number have to be copied, while the letters of the words with an odd ordinal number have to be printed in the reverse order.

For instance (using "–" to represent a space) the input text

"this——is—a-silly—program—."

has to be transformed into

"this-si-a-yllis-program."

My reader is cordially invited to try this program himself, before reading on and to record his considerations so as to enable himself to compare them with the sequel. (It should take an experienced programmer much less than 90 minutes!)

The unknown length of the non-empty input text suggested a program of the structure

prelude;

repeat something **until** ready;

coda

but immediately this question turned up: "With how much do we deal during a single execution of "something"?". Four suggestions turned up:

(1) a single character of the input text

(2) a single character of the output text

(3) a word (of both texts)

(4) two successive words (of both texts)

The first two suggestions were rejected very quickly and without much explicit motivation, although—or because?—it is not too difficult to provide it. (The first one is unattractive because the amount of output that can be produced on account of the next character of the input text varies wildly; for the second suggestion a similar objection holds. Apart from that, a program with a loop in a loop is in general cleaner: this suggests to look for larger portions.) The audience rejected the fourth suggestion on account of the remark that the terminating point could come equally well after an even number of words as after an odd number of words. To make the selection of the third suggestion explicit, we wrote on the blackboard:

```
prelude;
repeat process next word until point read;
coda
```

Everyone was satisfied in as far as this program expresses neatly that the output words are dealt with in exactly the same order as the corresponding input words are read, but it does not express that half of the words are to be printed in reverse order. When this was pointed out to them, they quickly introduced a state variable for the purpose. A first suggestion was to count the number of words processed and to make the processing dependent on the odd/eveness of this count, but a minor hesitation from my side was enough for the discovery that a boolean variable would meet the situation. It was decided that the "prelude" should include

$$\text{"forward}:= \textbf{true"}$$

while in "process next word" the printing in the order dependent on the current value of "forward" should be followed by

$$\text{"forward}:= \textbf{non}\ \text{forward"}$$

For me it was very gratifying to see that they introduced the variable "forward" before bothering about the details of word separation, which then became their next worry. It took them more time to realise that a further refinement of "process next word" required exact specification of which characters of the input text were going to be read and which characters of the output text were going to be printed at each execution of the repeatable statement. In fact, I had to pose the question to them and, after having done so, I asked them in which of the two texts the grouping presented itself most naturally. They selected the output text and chose the following grouping (indicating separation with a vertical bar):

| this–| si–| a–| yllis–| program. |

i.e. in units of a word followed by a proper terminator. I then asked for the corresponding grouping of the input characters. When their attention had been brought to the terminators, they suggested (from right to left!) the following separation of the input characters:

| this——i | s—a | –s | illy—p | rogram—. | ,

as soon as one of them had remarked that the program could only "know" that an output word should be followed by a space after having "seen" the first letter of the next input word. I then remained silent, leaving them gazing at their grouping of the symbols until one of them discovered that the exceptional grouping of the characters of the first input word was inelegant, that the grouping should be

t | his——i | s—a | –s | illy—p | rogram—. | ,

i.e. that the first character of the first word should be read in the prelude

Another variable was introduced and we arrived at

> **boolean** forward; **char** x;
>
> forward:= **true**; x:= RNC;
>
> **repeat** process next word;
>
> > forward:= **non** forward
>
> **until** x = pnt

in which the second line represents the prelude; in the meantime it had been decided that the coda could be empty.

The above stage had been reached after the first 45 minutes and we had our interval for coffee. Personally I felt that the problem had been solved, that from now onwards it was just a matter of routine; as it turned out, my audience was not practised enough and it took another 45 minutes to complete the program.

Unanimously they decided to introduce a

> **char array** $c[1{:}20]$

to store the letters of the word. (No one discovered that reading the letters and printing them in the reverse order could be done by a recursive routine!) Essentially, four things have to be done: the letters of the word have to be read, the letters of the word have to be printed, enough has to be read to decide which terminator is to be printed and the terminator has to be printed. I did not list these four actions, I did not ask for an explicit decision on how to group and/or combine them. The audience decided that first all reading should be done and thereafter all printing. (From their side this was hardly a conscious decision.)

Trying to refine the reading and the printing process they hit an unsuspected barrier: they were—at least for me, surprisingly—slow in discovering that they still had to define an interface between reading and printing through which to transmit the word to be processed, no matter how obvious this interface was. It took a long time before anyone formulated that $c[i]$ should equal the ith character of the word when read from left to right. Perhaps half of the audience was wondering what all the fuss was about, but it took an equally long time to discover that the length of the word needed some form of representation as well. No one suggested to do this by storing a terminator, they introduced a separate integer "l", counting the number of letters of the word. They decided that the first word "this" should be represented by

$$c[1] = \text{``}t\text{''},\ c[2] = \text{``}h\text{''},\ c[3] = \text{``}i\text{''},\ c[4] = \text{``}s\text{''} \text{ and } l = 4$$

They still had difficulty in arriving at the reading cycle and it was only when I had said repeatedly "so we have decided that "l" is going to represent the number of letter of the word stored in the array" that they arrived for the beginning of the reading process at

$l := 0$;

repeat $l := l + 1$; $c[l] := x$; $x := $ RNC **until** $x = $ sp **or** $x = $ pnt .

(In the first draft "**or** $x = $ pnt" was missing, but this was remedied quickly.) Once this was on the blackboard they completed the reading process without much hesitation:

while $x = $ sp **do** $x := $ RNC   .

When we turned our attention to the printing process, they were more productive. Clearly the reading process had shown them the purpose of the interface and suggestions came from various sides. I had never described the dilemma to them (see page 24), whether to code an alternative clause selecting between two repetitions or a repetitive clause repeating an alternative statement. I was waiting for the dilemma to turn up, it came and I showed it to them. Then I had a surprise, for one of the students suggested to map the two loops on each other with the aid of more variables. We introduced three integers "k. inc, term" and the printing of the letters became

if forward **then begin** $k := 0$; inc := $+1$; term := l **end**

        else begin $k := l + 1$; inc := -1; term := 1 **end**;

repeat $k := k + $ inc; PNC($c[k]$) **until** $k = $ term

followed by

if $x = $ pnt **then** PNC(pnt) **else** PNC(sp).

Thus we arrived at the following program:

boolean forward; **char** x; **char array** c[1:20]; **integer** l, k, inc, term;

forward := **true**; $x := $ RNC;

repeat $l := 0$;

   repeat $l := l + 1$; $c[l] := x$; $x := $ RNC **until** $x = $ sp **or** $x = $ pnt;

   while $x = sp$ **do** $x := $ RNC;

   if forward **then begin** $k := 0$; inc := $+1$; term := l **end**

     else begin $k := l + 1$; inc := -1; term := 1 **end**;

   repeat $k := k + $ inc; PNC($c[k]$) **until** $k = $ term;

   if $x = $ pnt **then** PNC(pnt) **else** PNC(sp);

   forward := **non** forward

until $x = $ pnt

This section has not been included because the problem tackled in it is very exciting. On the contrary, I feel tempted to remark that the problem is perhaps too trivial to act as a good testing ground for an orderly approach to the problem of program composition. This section has been included because it contains a true eye-witness account of what happened in the classroom. It should be interpreted as a partial answer to the question that is often posed to me, viz. to what extent I can teach programming style. (I never used the "Notes on Structured Programming"—mainly addressed to myself and perhaps to my colleagues—in teaching. The classroom experiment described in this section took place at the end of a course entitled "Introduction into the Art of Programming", for which separate lecture notes—with exercises and all that—were written. As at the moment of writing the students that followed this course have still to pass their examination, it is for me still an open question how successful I have been. They liked the course, I have heard that they described my programs as "logical poems", so I have the best of hopes.)

17. THE PROBLEM OF THE EIGHT QUEENS

This last section is adapted from my lecture notes "Introduction into the Art of Programming". I owe the example—as many other good ones—to Niklaus Wirth. This last section is added for two reasons.

Firstly, it is a second effort to do more justice to the process of invention. (As a matter of fact I start where the student is not familiar with the concept of backtracking and aim at discovering it as I go along.)

Secondly, and that is more important, it deals with recursion as a programming technique. In preceding sections (particularly in "On a program model") I have reviewed the subroutine concept; there it emerged as an embodiment of what I have also called "operational abstraction". In the relation between main program and subroutine we can distinguish quite clearly two different semantic levels. On the level of the main program the subroutine represents a primitive action; on that level it is used on account of "what it does for us" and on that same level it is irrelevant "how it works". On the level of the subroutine body we are concerned with how it works but can—and should—abstract from how it is used. This clear separation of the two semantic levels "what it does" and "how it works" is denied to the designer of a recursive procedure. As a result of this circumstance the design of a recursive routine requires a different mental skill, justifying the inclusion of the current section in this manuscript. The recursive procedure has to be understood and conceived on a single semantic level: as such it is more like a sequencing device, comparable to the repetitive clauses.

It is requested to make a program generating all configurations of eight queens on a chessboard of 8*8 squares such that no queen can take any of the others. This means that in the configurations sought, no two queens may be on the same row, on the same column or on the same diagonal.

We don't have an operator generating all these configurations, this operator is precisely what we have to make. Now there is a very general way (cf. "On grouping and sequencing") of tackling such a problem, which is as follows.

Call the set of configurations to be generated: set A. Look for a set B of configurations with the following properties:

(1) set A is a subset of set B

(2) given an element of set B it is not too difficult to decide whether it belongs to set A as well

(3) we can make an operator generating all elements of set B.

With the aid of the generator (3) for the elements of set B, all elements of set B can then be generated in turn; they will be subjected to the decision criterion (2) which decides whether they have to be skipped or handed over, thus generating elements of set A. Thanks to (1) this algorithm will produce *all* elements of set A.

Three remarks are in order.

(1) If the whole approach is to make sense, set B is not identical to set A, and as it must contain set A as a (true) subset, it must be larger than set A. For reasons of efficiency, however, it is advisable to choose set B "as small as possible": the more elements it has, the more elements of it have to be skipped on account of the decision criterion (2).

(2) We should look for a decision criterion that is cheap to apply, at least the discovery that an element of B does *not* belong to A should (on the average) be cheap. Also this is dictated by efficiency considerations, as we may expect set B to be an order of magnitude larger than set A, i.e. the majority of the elements of B will have to be rejected.

(3) The assumption is that the generation of the elements of set B is easier than a direct generation of the elements of set A. If, nevertheless, the generation of the elements of set B still presents difficulties, we can repeat our pattern of thinking, re-apply the trick and look for a still larger set C of configurations that contains B as a subset etc. (And, as the careful reader will observe, we shall do so in the course of this example.)

Above, we have sketched a very general approach, applicable to many, very different problems. Faced with a particular problem, i.e. faced with a specific set A, the problem of course is what to select for our set B.

In a moment of optimism one could think that this is an easy matter, as we might consider the following technique. We list all the mutually independent conditions that our elements of set *A* must satisfy and omit one of them. Sometimes this works but as a general technique it is too naïve: its shortcomings become apparent when we apply it blindly to the problem of the eight queens. We can characterise our solutions by the two conditions

(1) there are 8 queens on the board

(2) no two of the queens can take each other.

Omitting either of them gives for set *B* the alternatives

B1: all configurations with *N* queens on the board such that no two queens can take eachother

B2: all configurations of 8 queens on the board.

But both sets are so ludicrously huge that they lead to utterly impractical algorithms. So we have to be smarter. The burning question is: "How?".

Well, at this stage of our considerations, being slightly at a loss, we are not so much concerned with the efficiency of our final program as with the efficiency of our own thought processes! So, if we decide to make a list of properties of solutions, in the hope of finding a useful clue, this is a rather undirected search and therefore we should not invest too much mental energy in such a search, that is: for a start we should restrict ourselves to their *obvious* properties.

(I gave the puzzle as a sobering exercise to one of the staff members of the Department of Mathematics at my University, because he expressed the opinion that programming was easy. He violated the above rule and, being, apart from a pure, perhaps also a poor mathematician, he started to look for interesting, non-obvious properties. He conjectured that if the chessboard were divided in four squares of 4*4 fields, each square should contain two queens, and then he started to prove this conjecture without having convinced himself that he could make good use of it. He still has not solved the problem and, as far as I know, has not yet discovered that his conjecture is false.)

Well, let us go ahead and let us list the obvious properties we can think of.

(a) No row may contain more than one queen, 8 queens are to be placed and the chessboard has exactly 8 rows. As a result we conclude that each row will contain precisely one queen.

(b) Similarly we conclude that each column will contain precisely on queen.

(c) There are 15 "upward" diagonals, each of them containing at most one queen, i.e. 8 upward diagonals contain precisely one queen and 7 upward diagonals are empty.

(d) Similarly we conclude that 8 downward diagonals contain precisely one queen and 7 are empty.

(e) Given any non-empty configuration of queens such that no two of them can take each other, removal of any one of these queens will result in a configuration sharing that property.

Now the last property is very important. (To be quite honest: here I feel unable to buffer the shock of invention!) In our earlier terminology it tells us something about any non-empty configuration from set B1. If we start with a solution (which is an 8-queen configuration from set B1) and take away one queen we get a 7-queen configuration from set B1; taking away a next queen will leave again a configuration from set B1 and we can repeat this process until the chessboard is empty. We could have taken a motion picture of this process: playing it back backwards it would show how, starting from an empty board, via configurations from set B1 that solution can be built up by adding one queen at a time. (Whether the trick of the motion picture played backwards is of any assistance for my readers is not for me to judge; I only mention it because I know that such devices help me.) When making the picture, any solution could be reduced to the empty board in many ways, in exactly the same number of ways—while playing it back-wards—each solution can be built up. Can we exploit this freedom? We have rejected set B1 because it is too large, but maybe we can find a suitable subset of it, such that each non-empty configuration of the subset is a one-queen extension of only one other configuration of the subset. The "extension property" suggests that we are willing to consider configurations with less than 8 queens on the board and that we would like to form new configurations by adding a queen to an existing configuration—a relatively simple operation presumably. Well, this draws our attention immediately to the *generation* of the elements of the (still mysterious) set B. For instance, in what order? And this again raises a question to which, as yet, we have not paid the slightest attention: in what order are we to generate the solutions, i.e. the elements of set A? Can we make a reasonable suggestion in the hope of deriving a clue from it? (In my experience such a question about order is usually very illuminating. It is not only that we have to make a sequential program that by definition will generate the solutions in some order, so that the decision about the order will have to be taken at some stage of the game. The decision about the order usually provides the clue to the proof that the program will generate *all* solutions and each solution only *once*.)

Prior to that we should ask ourselves: how do we characterise solutions once we have them? To characterise a solution we must give the positions of 8 queens. The queens themselves are unordered, but the rows and the columns are not: we may assume them to be numbered from 0 through 7.

Thanks to property (a) which tells us that each row contains precisely one queen, we can order the queens according to the number of the row they occupy. Then each configuration of 8 queens can be given by the value of the **integer array** x [0:7], where

$x[i]$ = the number of the column occupied by the queen in the ith row.

Each solution is then a "8-digit word" $(x[0]\ldots x[7])$ and the only sensible order in which to generate these words that I can think of is the alphabetical order.

Note. As a consequence we open the way to algorithms in which rows and columns are treated differently, while the original problem was symmetrical in rows and columns! To consider asymmetric algorithms is precisely what the above considerations have taught us!

Returning to the alphabetical order: now we are approaching familiar ground. If the elements of set A are to be generated in alphabetical order and they have to be generated by selection from a larger set B, then the standard technique is to generate the elements of set B in alphabetical order as well and to produce the elements of the subset in the order in which they occur in set B.

First we have to generate all solutions with $x[0] = 0$ (if any), then those with $x[0] = 1$ (if any) etc.; of the solutions with $x[0]$ fixed, those with $x[1] = 0$ (if any) have to be generated first, followed by those with $x[1] = 1$ (if any) etc. In other words: the queen of row 0 is placed in column 0—say the square in the bottom left corner—and remains there until all elements of A (and B) with queen 0 in that position have been generated and only then is she moved one square to the right to the next column. For each position of queen 0, queen 1 will walk from left to right in row 1—skipping the squares that are covered by queen 0—for each combined position of the first two queens, queen 2 walks along row 2 from left to right, skipping all squares covered by the preceding queens, etc.

But now we have found set B! It is indeed a subset of $B1$, set B consists of all configurations with one queen in each of the first N rows, such that no two queens can take each other.

The criterion deciding whether an element of B belongs to A as well is that $N = 8$.

Having established our choice for set B, we find ourselves faced with the task of generating its elements in alphabetical order. We could try to do this via an operator "GENERATE NEXT ELEMENT OF B" with a program of the form

INITIALISE EMPTY BOARD;

repeat GENERATE NEXT ELEMENT OF B;

  if $N = 8$ **then** PRINT CONFIGURATION

until B EXHAUSTED .

(Here we have used the fact that the empty board belongs to B, but not to A, and is not B's only element. We have made no assumptions about the existence of solutions.)

But for two reasons a program of the above structure is less attractive. Firstly, we don't have a ready-made criterion to recognise the last element of B when we meet it and in all probability we have to generalise the operator "GENERATE NEXT ELEMENT OF B" in such a way that it will produce the indication "B EXHAUSTED" when it is applied to the last "true" element of B. Secondly, it is not too obvious how to make the operator "GENERATE NEXT ELEMENT OF B": the number of queens on the board may remain constant, it may decrease and it may increase.

So that is not too attractive. What can we do about it? As long as we regard the sequence of configurations of set B as a single, monotonous sequence, not subdivided into a succession of subsequences, the corresponding program structure will be a single loop as in the program just sketched. If we are looking for an alternative program structure, we must *therefore* ask ourselves "How can we group the sequence of configurations from set B into a succession of subsequences?".

Realising that the sequence of configurations from set B have to be generated in alphabetical order and thinking about the main subdivision in a dictionary—viz. by first letter—the first grouping is obvious: by position of queen 0.

Generating all elements of set B—for the moment we forget about the printing of those configurations that belong to set A as well—then presents itself as

INITIALISE EMPTY BOARD;

$h := 0$;

repeat SET QUEEN ON SQUARE$[0,h]$;

      GENERATE ALL CONFIGURATIONS WITH QUEEN 0

      FIXED;

      REMOVE QUEEN FROM SQUARE$[0,h]$;

      $h := h + 1$

until $h = 8$.

But now the question repeats itself: how do we group all configurations with queen 0 fixed? We have already given the answer: in order of increasing column number of queen 1, i.e.

$h1 := 0;$

repeat if SQUARE[1, $h1$] FREE **do**

    begin SET QUEEN ON SQUARE[1,$h1$];

        GENERATE ALL CONFIGURATIONS WITH FIRST

        2 QUEENS FIXED;

        REMOVE QUEEN FROM SQUARE[1,$h1$]

    end;

    $h1 := h1 + 1$

until $h1 = 8$.

For "GENERATE ALL CONFIGURATIONS WITH FIRST 2 QUEENS FIXED" we could write a similar piece of program and so on; inserting them inside each other would result in a correct program with eight nested loops, but they would all be very, very similar. To do so has two disadvantages

(1) it takes a cumbersome amount of writing

(2) it gives a program solving the problem for a chessboard of 8*8 squares, but to solve the same puzzle for a board of, say, 10*10 squares would require a new, still longer program.

We are looking for a way in which all the loops can be executed under control of the same program text. Can we make the text of the loops identical? Can we exploit their identity?

Well, to start with, we observe that the outermost and the innermost loops are exceptional.

The outermost loop is exceptional in the sense that it does not test whether square[0,h] is free because we know it is free. But because we know it is free, there is no harm in inserting the conditional clause

    if SQUARE[0,h] FREE **do**

and this gives the outermost loop the same pattern as the next six loops.

The innermost loop is exceptional in the sense that as soon as 8 queens have been placed on the board, there is no point in generating all configurations with those queens fixed, because we have a full board. Instead the configuration should be printed, because we have found an element of set B that is also an element of set A. We can map the innermost cycle and the embracing seven upon each other by replacing the line "GENERATE" by

if BOARD FULL **then** PRINT CONFIGURATION

 else GENERATE ALL CONFIGURATIONS EXTENDING THE CURRENT ONE

For this purpose we introduce a global variable, "*n*" say, counting the number of queens currently on the board. The test "BOARD FULL" becomes "*n* = 8" and the operations on squares can then have "*n*" as first subscript.

By now the only difference between the eight cycles is that each has "its private *h*". By the time that we have reached this stage, we can give an affirmative answer to the question whether we can exploit the identity of the loops. The sequencing through the eight nested loops can be evoked with the aid of a recursive procedure, "generate" say, which describes the cycle once. Using it, the program itself collapses into

 INITIALISE EMPTY BOARD; $n := 0$;

 generate

while "generate" is recursively defined as follows:

procedure generate;

begin integer h;

 $h := 0$;

 repeat if SQUARE[n,h] FREE **do**

 begin SET QUEEN ON SQUARE[n,h]; $n := n + 1$;

 if $n = 8$ **then** PRINT CONFIGURATION

 else generate;

 $n := n - 1$; REMOVE QUEEN FROM SQUARE[n,h]

 end;

 $h := h + 1$

 until $h = 8$

end

Each activation of "generate" will introduce its private local variable h, thus catering for h, $h1$, ... , $h8$ that we would need when writing eight nested loops.

Our program—although correct to this level of detail—is not yet complete, i.e. it has not been refined up to the standard degree of detail that is required by our programming language. In our next refinement we should decide upon the conventions according to which we represent the configurations on the board. We have already decided more or less that we shall use the

 integer array $x[0:7]$

giving in order the column numbers occupied by the queens, and also that

integer n

should be used to represent the number of queens on the board. More precisely

n = the number of queens on the board

$x[i]$ for $0 \leqslant i < n$ = the number of the column occupied by the queen in the ith row.

The array x and the scalar n are together sufficient to fix any configuration of the set B and those will be the only ones on the chessboard. As a result we have no *logical* need for more variables; yet we shall introduce a few more, because from a practical point of view we can make good use of them. The problem is that with only the above material the (frequent) analysis whether a given square in the next free row is uncovered is rather painful and time-consuming. It is here that we look for the standard technique as described in the section "On trading storage space for computation speed" (see page 42). The role of the stored argument is here played by the configuration of queens on the board, but this value does not change wildly— oh no; the only thing we do is to add or remove a queen. And we are looking for additional tables (whose contents are a function of the current configuration) such that they will assist us in deciding whether a square is free, and also such that they can be updated easily when a queen is added to or removed from a configuration.

How? Well, we might think of a boolean array of 8*8, indicating for each square whether it is free or not. If we do this for the full board, adding a queen might imply dealing with 28 squares. Removing a queen, however, is then a painful process, because it does not follow that all squares no longer covered by *her* are indeed free: they might be covered by one or more of the other queens that remain in the configuration. There is a remedy (again standard) for this, viz. associating with each square not a boolean variable, but an integer counter, counting the number of queens covering the square. Adding a queen then means increasing up to 28 counters by 1, removing a queen means decreasing them by 1 and a square is free when its associated counter equals zero. We could do it that way, but the question is whether this is not overdoing it: 28 adjustments is indeed quite a heavy overhead on setting or removing a queen.

Each square in the freedom of which we are interested covers a row (which is free by definition, so we need not bother about that), covers one of the 8 columns (which must still be empty), covers one of the 15 upward diagonals (which must still be empty) and one of the 15 downward diagonals (which must still be empty). This suggests that we should keep track of

(1) the columns that are free

(2) the upward diagonals that are free

(3) the downward diagonals that are free.

As each column or diagonal is covered only once we do not need a counter for each, a boolean variable is sufficient. The columns are readily identified by their column number and for the columns we introduce

boolean array col[0:7]

where "col[i]" means that the ith column is still free.

How do we identify the diagonals? Well, along an upward diagonal the difference between row number and column number is constant; along a downward diagonal their sum is constant. As a result, difference and sum respectively are the easiest index by which to distinguish the diagonals and we introduce therefore

boolean array up[$-7:+7$], down[0:14]

to keep track of which diagonals are free.

The question whether square[n,h] is free becomes

col[h] **and** up[$n-h$] **and** down[$n+h$] ,

setting and removing a queen both imply the adjustment of three booleans, one in each array.

In the final program the variable "k" is introduced for general counting purposes, statements and expressions are labeled (in capital letters). Note that we have merged two levels of description: what were statements and functions on the upper level, now appear as explanatory labels.

With the final program we come to the end of the last section. We have attempted to show the pattern of reasoning by which one could discover backtracking as a technique, and also the pattern of reasoning by which one could discover a recursive procedure describing it. The most important moral of this section is perhaps that all that analysis and synthesis could be carried out before we had decided how (and how redundantly) a configuration would be represented inside the machine. It is true that such considerations only bear fruit when eventually a convenient representation for configurations can be found. Yet the mental isolation of a level of abstraction in which we allow ourselves not to bother about it seems crucial.

Finally, I would like to thank the reader that has followed me up till here for his patience.

```
begin integer n, k; integer array x[0:7]; boolean array col[0:7], up[−7:+7], down[0:14];
  procedure generate;
    begin integer h;
      h:= 0;
      repeat if SQUARE[n,h] FREE: (col[h] and up[n−h] and down[n+h]) do
        begin SET QUEEN ON SQUARE[n,h]:
          x[n]:= h; col[h]:= false; up[n−h]:= false; down[n+h]:= false; n:= n + 1;
          if BOARD FULL: (n = 8) then
            begin PRINT CONFIGURATION:
              k:= 0; repeat print(x[k]); k:= k + 1 until k = 8; newline
            end
          else generate;
          n:= n − 1; REMOVE QUEEN FROM SQUARE[n,h]:
              down[n+h]:= true; up[n−h]:= true; col[h]:= true
        end;
        h:= h + 1
      until h = 8
    end;
  INITIALISE EMPTY BOARD:
  n:= 0;
  k:= 0; repeat col[k]:= true; k:= k + 1 until k = 8;
  k:= 0; repeat up[k−7]:= true; down[k]:= true; k:= k + 1 until k = 15;
  generate
end
```

II. Notes on Data Structuring *

C. A. R. Hoare

1. Introduction

In the development of our understanding of complex phenomena, the most powerful tool available to the human intellect is abstraction. Abstraction arises from a recognition of similarities between certain objects, situations, or processes in the real world, and the decision to concentrate on these similarities, and to ignore for the time being the differences. As soon as we have discovered which similarities are relevant to the prediction and control of future events, we will tend to regard the similarities as fundamental and the differences as trivial. We may then be said to have developed an abstract concept to cover the set of objects or situations in question. At this stage, we will usually introduce a word or picture to symbolise the abstract concept; and any particular spoken or written occurrence of the word or picture may be used to *represent* a particular or general instance of the corresponding situation.

The primary use for representations is to convey information about important aspects of the real world to others, and to record this information in written form, partly as an aid to memory and partly to pass it on to future generations. However, in primitive societies the representations were sometimes believed to be useful in their own right, because it was supposed that manipulation of representations might in itself cause corresponding changes in the real world; and thus we hear of such practices as sticking pins into wax models of enemies in order to cause pain to the corresponding part of the real person. This type of activity is characteristic of magic and witchcraft. The modern scientist on the other hand, believes that the manipulation of representations could be used to predict events and the results of changes in the real world, although not to cause them. For example, by manipulation of symbolic representations of certain functions and equations,

---

*This monograph is based on a series of lectures delivered at a Nato Summer School, Marktoberdorf, 1970.

he can predict the speed at which a falling object will hit the ground, although he knows that this will not either cause it to fall, or soften the final impact when it does.

The last stage in the process of abstraction is very much more sophisticated; it is the attempt to summarise the most general facts about situations and objects covered under an abstraction by means of brief but powerful *axioms*, and to prove rigorously (on condition that these axioms correctly describe the real world) that the results obtained by manipulation of representations can also successfully be applied to the real world. Thus the axioms of Euclidean geometry correspond sufficiently closely to the real and measurable world to justify the application of geometrical constructions and theorems to the practical business of land measurement and surveying the surface of the earth.

The process of abstraction may thus be summarised in four stages:

(1) Abstraction: the decision to concentrate on properties which are shared by many objects or situations in the real world, and to ignore the differences between them.

(2) Representation: the choice of a set of symbols to stand for the abstraction; this may be used as a means of communication.

(3) Manipulation: the rules for transformation of the symbolic representations as a means of predicting the effect of similar manipulation of the real world.

(4) Axiomatisation: the rigorous statement of those properties which have been abstracted from the real world, and which are shared by manipulations of the real world and of the symbols which represent it.

1.1. NUMBERS AND NUMERALS

Let us illustrate this rather abstract description by means of a relatively concrete example—the number four. In the real world, it is noticed that objects can be grouped together in collections, for example four apples. This already requires a certain act of abstraction, that is a decision to ignore (for the time being) the differences between the individual apples in the collection—for example, one of them is bad, two of them unripe, and the fourth already partly eaten by birds.

Now one may consider several different collections, each of them with four items; for example, four oranges, four pears, four bananas, etc. If we choose to ignore the differences between these collections and concentrate on their similarity, then we can form a relatively abstract concept of the number four. The same process could lead to the concept of the number 3, 15, and so on; and a yet further stage of abstraction would lead to the development of the concept of a natural number.

Now we come to the representation of this concept, for example scratched on parchment, or carved in stone. The representation of a number is called a numeral. The early Roman numeral was clearly pictorial, just four strokes carved in stone: IIII. An alternative more convenient representation was IV. The arabic (decimal) representations are less pictorial, but again there is some choice: both 4 and 04 (and indeed 004 and so on) are all recognised as valid numerals, representing the same number.

We come next to a representation which is extremely convenient for processing, providing that the processor is an electronic digital computer. Here the number four is represented by the varying directions of magnetisation of a group of ferrite cores. These magnetisations are sometimes represented by sequences of zeros and ones on line printer paper; i.e., the binary representation of the number in question.

A simple example of the manipulation of numerals is addition, which can be used to predict the result of adjoining of two collections of objects in the real world. The addition rules for Roman numerals are very simple and obvious, and are simple to apply. The addition rules for arabic numerals up to ten are quite unobvious, and must be learnt; but for numbers much larger than ten they are more convenient than the Roman techniques. Addition of binary representations is not a task fit for human beings; but for a computer this is the simplest and best representation. Thus we see that choice between many representations can be made in the light of ease of manipulation in each particular environment.

Finally we reach the stage of axiomatisation; the most widely known axiom set for natural numbers is that of Peano, which was first formulated at the end of the last century, long after natural numbers had been in general use. In the present day, the axiomatisation of abstract mathematical ideas usually follows far more closely upon their development; and in fact may assist in the clarification of the concept by guarding against confusion and error, and by explaining the essential features of the concept to others. It is possible that a rigorous formulation of presuppositions and axioms on which a program is based may reduce the confusion and error so characteristic of present day programming practice, and assist in the documentation and explanation of programs and programming concepts to others.

1.2. ABSTRACTION AND COMPUTER PROGRAMMING

It is my belief that the process of abstraction, which underlies attempts to apply mathematics to the real world, is exactly the process which underlies the application of computers in the real world. The first requirement in designing a program is to concentrate on relevant features of the situation, and to ignore factors which are believed irrelevant. For example, in analysing the flutter characteristics of a proposed wing design of an aircraft, its elasticity is what is considered relevant; its colour, shape, and production technique are considered to be irrelevant except in so far as they have contributed to its elasticity. To take a commercial example, the employees working for a Company have many characteristics, both physical and mental, which will be ignored when devising a payroll program for the Company.

The next stage in program design is the decision of the manner in which the abstracted information is to be represented in the computer. An elasticity function may be represented by its values at a suitable number of discrete points; and these may be represented in a variety of ways as a two-dimensional array. Alternatively, the elasticity might be given by a computed function, and the data be held as a vector of polynomial or chebyshev coefficients for the function. A payroll file on a computer consists of a number of records, one relating to each employee. The choice of representation within the record of each relevant attribute must be made as part of the design of the program.

The stage of axiomatisation is not usually regarded as a separate stage in programming; and is often left implicit. In the case of aircraft flutter, the axiomatisation is the formulation of the differential equations which are presumed to describe the reaction of the real wing to certain kinds of stresses, and which (it is hoped) also describe the process of approximate solution on the computer. In the case of a payroll, the axioms correspond to the descriptions of various aspects of the real world which need to be embodied in the program—for example, the fact that net pay equals gross pay minus deductions.

Finally there comes the task of programming the computer to get it to carry out those manipulations on the representation of the data that correspond to the manipulations in the real world in which we are interested. The success of a program is dependent on three basic conditions:

(1) The axiomatisation is a correct description of those aspects of the real world with which it is concerned.

(2) The axiomatisation is a correct description of the behaviour of the program, i.e., that the program contains no errors.

(3) The choice of representation and the method of manipulation are such that the cost of running the program on the computer is acceptable.

In order to simplify the task of designing and developing a computer program, it is very helpful to be able to keep these three stages reasonably separate and to carry them out in the appropriate sequence. Thus the first stage (axiomatisation) would culminate in a rigorous logical statement of presuppositions about the real world, and a formulation of the desired objectives which are to be achieved by the program. The second stage would culminate in an algorithm, or abstract program, which is demonstrably capable of carrying out the stated task on the given presuppositions. The third stage would be the decision on how the various items of data are to be represented and manipulated in the store of the computer in order to achieve acceptable efficiency. Only when these three stages have been satisfactorily concluded will there begin the final phase of coding and testing the program, which embodies the chosen algorithm operating upon the chosen data representation.

Of course, this is a somewhat idealised picture of the intellectual task of programming as a steady progression from the abstract formulation of the problem to the more and more concrete aspects of its solution. In practice, even in the formulation of a problem, the programmer must have some intuition about the possibility of a solution; while he is designing his abstract program, he must have some feeling that an adequately efficient representation is available. Quite frequently these intuitions and feelings will be mistaken, and a deeper investigation of representation, or even the final coding, will require a return to an earlier stage in the process, and perhaps even a radical recasting of the direction of attack. But this exercise of intuitive forethought, together with a risk of failure, is characteristic of all inventive and constructive intellectual processes, and does not detract from the merits of at least starting out in an orderly fashion, with more or less clearly separated stages.

One of the most important features of the progression is that the actual coding of the program has been postponed until after it is (almost) certain that all other aspects of the design have been successfully completed. Since coding and program testing is generally the most expensive stage in program development, it is undesirable to have to make changes after this stage has started. Thus it is advantageous to ensure beforehand that nothing further can go wrong at this final stage; for example, that the program tackles the right problem, that the algorithm is correct, that the various parts of the program cooperate harmoniously in the overall task, and that the data representations are adequately efficient. It is the purpose of this monograph to explore methods of achieving this confidence.

1.3. ABSTRACTION IN HIGH-LEVEL PROGRAMMING LANGUAGES

The role of abstraction in the design and development of computer programs may be reinforced by the use of a suitable high-level programming language. Indeed, the benefits of using a high-level language instead of machine code may be largely due to their incorporation of successful abstractions, particularly for data. To the hardware of a computer, and to a machine code programmer, every item of data is regarded as a mere collection of bits. However, to the programmer in ALGOL 60 or FORTRAN an item of data is regarded as an integer, a real number, a vector, or a matrix, which are the same abstractions that underlie the numerical application areas for which these languages were primarily designed. Of course, these abstract concepts have been mapped by the implementor of the language onto particular bit-pattern representations on a particular computer. But in the design of his algorithm, the programmer is freed from concern about such details, which for his purpose are largely irrelevant; and his task is thereby considerably simplified.

Another major advantage of the use of high-level programming languages, namely machine-independence, is also attributable to the success of their abstractions. Abstraction can be applied to express the important characteristics not only of differing real-life situations, but also of different computer representations of them. As a result, each implementor can select a representation which ensures maximum efficiency of manipulation on his particular computer.

A third major advantage of the use of a high-level language is that it significantly reduces the scope for programming error. In machine code programming it is all too easy to make stupid mistakes, such as using fixed point addition on floating point numbers, performing arithmetic operations on Boolean markers, or allowing modified addresses to go out of range. When using a high-level language, such errors may be prevented by three means:

(1) Errors involving the use of the wrong arithmetic instructions are logically impossible; no program expressed, for example in ALGOL, could ever cause such erroneous code to be generated.

(2) Errors like performing arithmetic operations on Boolean markers will be immediately detected by a compiler, and can never cause trouble in an executable program.

(3) Errors like the use of a subscript out of range can be detected by runtime checks on the ranges of array subscripts.

Runtime checks, although often necessary, are almost unavoidably more expensive and less convenient than checks of the previous two kinds; and high-level languages should be designed to extend the range of programming errors which logically cannot be made, or if made can be detected by a compiler. In fact, skilful language design can enable most subscripts to be checked without loss of runtime efficiency.

The automatic prevention and detection of programming errors may again be attributed to a successful appeal to abstraction. A high-level programming language permits the programmer to declare his intentions about the types of the values of the variables he uses, and thereby specify the meanings of the operations valid for values of that type. It is now relatively easy for a compiler to check the consistency of the program, and prevent errors from reaching the execution stage.

1.4. NOTATIONS

In presenting a theory of data structuring, it is necessary to introduce some convenient notation for expressing the abstractions involved. These notations are based to a large extent on those already familiar to mathematicians, logicians and programmers. They have also been designed for direct expression of computer algorithms, and to minimise the scope for programming error in running programs. Finally, the notations are designed to ensure the existence of efficient data representations on digital computers.

Since the notations are intended to be used (among other things) for the expression of algorithms, it would be natural to conclude that they constitute a form of programming language, and that an automatic translator should be written for converting programs expressed in the language into the machine code of a computer, thereby eliminating the expensive and error-prone coding stage in the development of programs.

But this conclusion would be a complete misunderstanding of the reason for introducing the notations, and could have some very undesirable consequences. The worst of them is that it could lead to the rejection of the main benefits of the programming methodology expounded in this monograph, on the grounds that no compiler is available for the language, nor likely to be widely accepted if it were.

But there are sound reasons why these notations must not be regarded as a programming language. Some of the operations (e.g., concatenation of sequences), although very helpful in the design of abstract programs and the description of their properties, are grotesquely inefficient when applied to large data objects in a computer; and it is an essential part of the program design process to eliminate such operations in the transition between an abstract and a concrete program. This elimination will sometimes involve quite radical changes to both algorithm and representation, and could not in general be made by an automatic translator. If such expensive operators were part of a language intended for automatic compilation, it is probable that many programmers would fail to realise their obligation to eliminate them before approaching the computer; and even if they wanted to, they would have little feeling for what alternative representations and operations would be more economic. In taking such vital decisions, it is actually helpful if a programming language is rather close to the eventual machine, in the sense that the efficiency of the machine code is directly predictable from the form and length of the corresponding source language code.

There is a more subtle danger which would be involved in the automatic implementation of the notations: that the good programmer would soon learn that some of them are significantly less efficient than others, and he will avoid their use even in his abstract programs; and this will result in a form of mental block which might have serious consequences on his inventive capacity. Equally serious, the implementation of a fixed set of notations might well inhibit the user from introducing his own notations and concepts as required by his understanding of a particular problem.

Thus there is a most important distinction to be drawn between an algorithmic language intended to assist in the definition, design, development and documentation of a program, and the programming language in which the program is eventually conveyed to a computer. In this monograph we shall be concerned solely with the former kind of language. All example algorithms will be expressed in this language, and the actual coding of these programs is left as an exercise to the reader, who may choose for this purpose any language familiar to him, ALGOL, FORTRAN, COBOL, PL/I, assembly language, or any available combination of them. It is essential to a realisation of the relative merits of various representations of data to realise what their implications on the resulting code will be.

In spite of this vigorous disclaimer that I am not embarking on the design of yet another programming language, I must admit the advantages that can follow if the programming language used for coding an algorithm is actually a *subset* of the language in which it has been designed. I must also confess that there exists a large subset of the proposed algorithmic language which can be implemented with extremely high efficiency, both at compile time and at run time, on standard computers of the present day; and the challenge of designing computers which can efficiently implement even larger subsets may be taken up in the future. But the non-availability of such a subset implementation in no way invalidates the benefits of using the full set of notations as an abstract programming tool.

1.5. SUMMARY

This introduction has given a general description of the motivation and general approach taken hereafter. As is quite usual, it may be read again with more profit on completion of the rest of the monograph.

The second section explains the concept of type, which is essential to the theory of data structuring; and relates it to the operations and representations which are relevant to the practice of computer programming.

Subsequent sections deal with particular methods of structuring data, progressing from the simpler to the more elaborate structures.

Each structure is explained informally with the aid of examples. Then the manipulation of the structure is defined by specifying the set of basic operations which may be validly applied to the structure. Finally, a range of possible computer representations is given, together with the criteria which should influence the selection of a suitable representation on each occasion.

Section 11 is devoted to an example, a program for constructing an examination timetable. The last section puts the whole exposition on a rigorous theoretical basis by formulating the axioms which express the basic properties of data structures. This section may be used as a summary of the theory, as a reference to refine the understanding, or as a basis for the proof of correctness of programs.

2. THE CONCEPT OF TYPE

The theory of data structuring here propounded is strongly dependent on the concept of type. This concept is familiar to mathematicians, logicians, and programmers.

(1) In mathematical reasoning, it is customary to make a rather sharp distinction between individuals, sets of individuals, families of sets, and so on; to distinguish between real functions, complex functions, functionals, sets of functions, etc. In fact for each new variable introduced in his reasoning, a mathematician usually states immediately what type of object the variable can stand for, e.g.

"Let f be a real function of two real variables"

"Let S be a family of sets of integers".

Sometimes in mathematical texts a general rule is given which relates the type of a symbol with a particular printer's type font, for example:

"We use small Roman letters to stand for individuals, capitals to stand for sets of individuals, and script capitals to denote families of sets".

In general, mathematicians do not use type conventions of this sort to make distinctions of an arbitrary kind; for example, they would not be generally used to distinguish prime numbers from non-primes or Abelian groups from general groups. In practice, the type conventions adopted by mathematicians are very similar to those which would be of interest to logicians and programmers.

(2) Logicians on the whole prefer to work without typed variables. However without types it is possible to formulate within set theory certain paradoxes which would lead to inescapable contradiction and collapse of logical and mathematical reasoning. The most famous of these is the Russell paradox:

"let s be the set of all sets which are *not* members of themselves. Is s a member of itself or not?"

It turns out that whether you answer yes or no, you can be immediately proved wrong.

Russell's solution to the paradox is to associate with each logical or mathematical variable a *type*, which defines whether it is an individual, a set, a set of sets, etc. Then he states that any proposition of the form "*x* is a member of *y*" is grammatically meaningful only if *x* is a variable of type individual and *y* a variable of type set, or if *x* is of type set and *y* is of type set of sets, and so on. Any proposition that violates this rule is regarded as meaningless—the question of its truth or falsity just does not arise, it is just a jumble of letters. Thus any proposition involving sets that are or are not members of themselves can simply be ruled out.

Russell's theory of types leads to certain complexities in the foundation of mathematics, which are not relevant to describe here. Its interesting features for our purposes are that types are used to prevent certain erroneous expressions from being used in logical and mathematical formulae; and that a check against violation of type constraints can be made merely by scanning the text, without any knowledge of the value which a particular symbol might happen to stand for.

(3) In a high-level programming language the concept of a type is of central importance. Again, each variable, constant and expression has a unique type associated with it. In ALGOL 60 the association of a type with a variable is made by its declaration; in FORTRAN it is deduced from the initial letter of the variable. In the implementation of the language, the type information determines the representation of the values of the variable, and the amount of computer storage which must be allocated to it. Type information also determines the manner in which arithmetic operators are to be interpreted; and enables a compiler to reject as meaningless those programs which invoke inappropriate operations.

Thus there is a high degree of commonality in the use of the concept of type by mathematicians, logicians and programmers. The salient characteristics of the concept of type may be summarised:

(1) A type determines the class of values which may be assumed by a variable or expression.

(2) Every value belongs to one and only one type.

(3) The type of a value denoted by any constant, variable, or expression may be deduced from its form or context, without any knowledge of its value as computed at run time.

(4) Each operator expects operands of some fixed type, and delivers a result of some fixed type (usually the same). Where the same symbol is applied to several different types (e.g. + for addition of integers as well as reals),

this symbol may be regarded as ambiguous, denoting several different actual operators. The resolution of such systematic ambiguity can always be made at compile time.

(5) The properties of the values of a type and of the primitive operations defined over them are specified by means of a set of axioms.

(6) Type information is used in a high-level language both to prevent or detect meaningless constructions in a program, and to determine the method of representing and manipulating data on a computer.

(7) The types in which we are interested are those already familiar to mathematicians; namely, Cartesian Products, Discriminated Unions, Sets, Functions, Sequences, and Recursive Structures.

2.1. DATA TYPE DEFINITIONS

Our theory of data structuring specifies a number of standard methods of defining types, and of using them in the declaration of variables to specify the range of values which that variable may take in the course of execution of a program. In most cases, a new type is defined in terms of previously defined *constituent* types; the values of such a new type are data structures, which can be built up from *component* values of the constituent types, and from which the component values can subsequently be extracted. These component values will belong to the constituent types in terms of which the structured type was defined. If there is only one constituent type, it is known as the *base* type.

The number of different values of a data type is known as its *cardinality*. In many cases the cardinality of a type is finite; and for a structured type defined in terms of finite constituent types, the cardinality is also usually finite, and can be computed by a simple formula. In other cases, the cardinality of a data type is infinite, as in the case of integers; but it can never be more than denumerably infinite. The reason for this is that each value of the type must be constructible by a finite number of computer operations, and must be representable in a finite amount of store. Arbitrary real numbers, functions with infinite domains, and other classes of non-denumerable cardinality can never be represented as stored data within a computer, though in some cases they can be represented by procedures, functions, or other program structures.

Obviously, the ultimate components of a structure must be unstructured, and the ultimate constituents of a structured type must be unstructured types. One method of defining an unstructured type is by simple enumeration of its values, as described in the next section. But in certain cases it is better to regard the properties of unstructured types as defined by axioms, and assume them to be provided as *primitive* types by the hardware of a computer or the implementation of a high-level programming language. For example, the primitive types of ALGOL 60 are **integer, real,** and **Boolean,** and these will be assumed available.

2.2. DATA MANIPULATION

The most important practical aspect of data is the manner in which that data can be manipulated, and the range of basic operators available for this purpose. We therefore associate with each type a set of *basic* operators which are intended to be useful in the design of programs, and yet which have at least one reasonably efficient implementation on a computer. Of course the selection of basic operators is to some extent arbitrary, and could have been either larger or smaller. The guiding principle has been to choose a set large enough to ensure that any additional operation required by the programmer can be defined in terms of the basic set, and be efficiently implemented in this way also; so an operator is regarded as basic if its method of efficient implementation depends heavily on the chosen method of data representation.

The most important and general operations defined for data of any type are assignment and test of equality. Assignment involves conceptually a complete copy of a data value from one place to another in the store of the computer; and test of equality involves a complete scan of two values (usually stored at different places) to test their identity. These rules are those that apply to primitive data types and there is no reason to depart from them in the case of structured types. If the value of a structured type is very large, these operations may take a considerable amount of time; this can sometimes be reduced by an appropriate choice of representation; alternatively, such operations can be avoided or removed in the process of transforming an abstract program to a concrete one.

Another general class of operators consists in the *transfer* functions, which map values of one type into another. Of particular importance are the *constructors*, which permit the value of a structured type to be defined in terms of the values of the constituent types from which it is built. The converse transfer functions are known as *selectors*; they permit access to the component values of a structured type. In many cases, we use the name of a defined type as the name of the standard constructor or transfer function which ranges over the type.

Certain data types are conveniently regarded as ordered; and comparison operators are available to test the values of such types. But for many types, such an ordering would have no meaningful interpretation; and such types are best regarded from an abstract point of view as unordered. This will sometimes be of advantage in giving greater freedom in the choice of representation and sequencing strategies at a later state in the concrete design.

In the case of a large data structure, the standard method of operating efficiently on it is not by assigning a wholly new value to it, but rather by *selectively updating* some relatively small part of it. The usual notation for this is to write on the left of an assignment an expression (variable) which uses selectors to denote the place where the structure is to be changed. However, we also introduce special assignment operators, always beginning with colon, to denote other more general updating operations such as adding a member to a set, or appending an item to a sequence. For both kinds of selective updating, it must be remembered that, from a conceptual or abstract point of view, the entire value of the variable has been changed by updating the least part of it.

2.3. REPRESENTATIONS

It is fundamental to the design of a program to decide how far to store computed results as data for subsequent use, and how far to compute them as required. It is equally fundamental to decide how stored data should be represented in the computer. In many simple and relatively small cases there is an obvious *standard* way of representing data, which ensures that not too much storage is used, and not too much time expended on carrying out the basic operations. But if the volume of data (or the amount of processing) is large, it is often profitable (and sometimes necessary) to choose some non-standard representation, selected in accordance with the characteristics of the storage media used (drums, discs, or tapes), and also taking into account the relative frequencies of the various operations which will be performed upon it. Decisions on the details of representation must usually precede and influence the design of the code to manipulate the data, often at a time when the nature of the data and the processing required are relatively unknown. Thus it is quite common to make serious errors of judgement in the design of data representation, which do not come to light until shortly before, or even after, the program has been put into operation. By this time the error is extremely difficult to rectify. However, the use of abstraction in data structuring may help to postpone some of the decisions on data representation until more is known about the behaviour of the program and the characteristics of the data, and thus make such errors less frequent and easier to rectify.

An important decision to be taken is on the degree and manner in which data should be compressed in storage to save space; and also to save time on input/output, on copying operations, and on comparisons, usually at the expense of increasing the time and amount of code required to perform all other operations. Representations requiring less storage than the standard are usually known as *packed*; there are several degrees of packing, from loose to tight. Of theoretical interest is the *minimal* representation, which uses the least possible space. In this representation the values of the type are represented as binary integers in the range 0 to $N - 1$, where N is the cardinality of the type. In the case of a type of infinite cardinality, a minimal representation is one in which every possible bit pattern represents a value of the type. Minimal representations are not often used, owing to the great expense of processing them.

Another method of saving space is to use an *indirect* representation. In the standard direct representation of data, each variable of a type is allocated enough space to hold every value of the type. In the indirect representation, the variable is just large enough to contain a single machine address, which at any given time points to a group of one or more machine locations containing the current value. This technique is necessary when the type has infinite cardinality, since the amount of storage used will vary, and is not known when writing the code which accesses the variable. It can also be profitable when the actual amount of storage is variable, and during a large part of a program run is significantly less than the maximum. Finally, it can be used when it is believed that many different variables will tend to have the same values; since then only one copy of the value need be held, and the variables may just contain pointers to it; copying the value is also very cheap, since only the pointer need be copied. However, such shared copies must never be selectively updated.

Unfortunately, indirect representations often involve the additional expense and complexity of a dynamic storage allocation and garbage collection scheme; and they can cause some serious problems if data has to be copied between main and backing stores.

This chapter describes only a small but useful range of the possible representations of data, and the skilful programmer could readily add to the selection. In many cases, the representation of an abstract data type can be constructed by means of a more elaborate but more efficient data type definition; for instance a large set may be represented as a sequence of items of some suitable type. Examples of this are given in later sections.

3. UNSTRUCTURED DATA TYPES

All structured data must in the last analysis be built up from unstructured components, belonging to a primitive or unstructured type. Some of these unstructured types (for example, reals and integers) may be taken as given by a programming language or the hardware of the computer. Although these primitive types are theoretically adequate for all purposes, there are strong practical reasons for encouraging a programmer to define his own unstructured types, both to clarify his intentions about the potential range of values of a variable, and the interpretation of each such value; and to permit subsequent design of an efficient representation.

In particular, in many computer programs an integer is used to stand not for a numeric quantity, but for a particular choice from a relatively small number of alternatives. In such cases, the annotation of the program usually lists all the possible alternative values, and gives the intended interpretation of each of them. It is possible to regard such a quantity as belonging to a separate type, quite distinct from the integer type, and quite distinct from any other similar set of markers which have a different interpretation. Such a type is said to be an *enumeration*, and we suggest a standard notation for declaring the name of the type and associating a name with each of its alternative values:

type suit = (club, diamond, heart, spade);

ordered type rank = (two, three, four, five, six, seven, eight, nine, ten, Jack, Queen, King, Ace);

type primary colour = (red, yellow, blue);

ordered type day of week = (Monday, Tuesday, Wednesday, Thursday, Friday, Saturday, Sunday);

type day of month = 1..31;

ordered type month = (Jan, Feb, March, April, May, June, July, Aug, Sept, Oct, Nov, Dec);

type year = 1900..1969;

type Boolean = (false, true);

ordered type floor = (basement, ground, mezzanine, first, second);

type coordinate = 0..1023;

Our first two examples are drawn from the realm of playing cards. The first declaration states that club, diamond, heart, and spade are suits; in other words, that any variable or expression of type suit can only denote one of these four values; and that the identifiers "club" "heart" "diamond" and "spade" act as *constants* of this type. Similarly, the definition of the type *rank* displays the thirteen constants denoting the thirteen possible values of the type. In this case it is natural to regard the type as ordered. The next examples declare the names of the primary colours and of the days of the week. In considering the days of the month, it is inconvenient to write out the thirty-one possible values in full. We therefore introduce the convention that $a..b$ stands for the finite range of values between a and b inclusive. This is known as a *subrange* of the type to which a and b belong, in this case integers. This convention is used again in the declaration of year. Other examples of enumeration are:

The Boolean type, with only two values, false and true.

The Month type, with twelve values listed in the required order.

The coordinate type, taking values between 0 and 1023, representing perhaps a coordinate on a CRT display.

Having defined a type in a suitable fashion, the programmer will use the type name to specify the types of his variables. For this purpose it is useful to follow the current practice of mathematicians and to write the type name *after* the variable, separated from it by a colon:

trumps: suit; today: day of week;

pc: primary colour;

If several variables of the same type are to be declared at the same time, it is useful to adopt the abbreviation of listing the variable names without repeating the type name, thus:

arrival, departure: day of month;

x, y, z: coordinate.

If only a few variables of a given type are to be used, it is convenient to write the type definition itself in place of and instead of the type name:

answer: (yes, no, don't know);

The cardinality of a type defined by enumeration is obviously equal to the length of the defining list; and for a numeric subrange, it is one more than the difference between the end points of the subrange.

3.1. MANIPULATION

The operations required for successful manipulation of values of enumeration types and subranges are:

(1) test of equality, for example:

if arrival = departure **then go to** transit desk;
if trumps = spade **then**...

(2) assignment, for example·

pc: = yellow;
trumps: = club;

(3) case discrimination, for example:

case *pc* **of** (red: ....,
                yellow: ...,
                blue: ...)

where *pc* is a variable or expression of type primary colour, and the limbs of the discrimination are indicated by lacunae. A case discrimination may be either a statement, in which case the limbs must be statements; or it may be an expression, in which case the limbs must be all expressions of the same type.

The effect of a case discrimination is to select for execution (or evaluation) that single statement (or expression) which is prefixed by the constant equal to the current value of the case expression. In some cases, it may be convenient to prefix several constants to the same limb, or even to indicate a subrange of values which would select the corresponding limb; but of course each value must be mentioned exactly once:

> **case** digit **of** $(0..2:....,$
>
> $\qquad 3:7:....,$
>
> $\qquad 4..6:8:9:...).$

In this last case, it would be convenient to replace the labels of the last limb by the basic word **else**, to cover all the remaining cases not mentioned explicitly on the preceding limbs.

When the limbs of a discrimination are statements, we shall sometimes use braces instead of brackets to surround them.

(4) In the case of a type declared as ordered, it is possible to test the ordering relationships among the values:

> **if** May $\leqslant$ this month & this month $\leqslant$ September **then**
> adopt summer timetables.

In other cases, the ordering of the values is quite irrelevant, and has no meaning to the programmer.

(5) In conjunction with ordering, it is useful to introduce a successor and a predecessor function (succ and pred) to map each value of the type onto the next higher or lower value, if there is one. Also, if T is any ordered type, the notation T.min will denote the lowest value of the type, and T.max the highest value, if they exist. This helps in formulating programs, theorems, and axioms in a manner independent of the actual names of the constants.

(6) In a computer program we will frequently wish to cause a variable to range sequentially all through the values of a type. This may be denoted by a form of for statement or loop

> **for** a:alpha **do**...;
>
> **for** i:1..99 **do**...;

In this construction, the counting variable (a or i) is taken to belong to the type indicated, and to be declared locally to the construction, in the sense that its value does not exist before or after the loop, and its name is not accessible outside the loop. In addition, the value of the counting variable is not allowed to be changed inside the body of the loop, since this would frustrate the whole intention of declaring the variable by means of the **for** construction.

In the case of an ordered type, it is natural to assume that the counting variable sequences through the values of the type in the defined order, T.min, succ(T.min),..., T.max. But if the type is an unordered one, it is assumed that the sequence of the scan does not matter at the current level of abstraction, and will be defined at some later stage in the development of a concrete program.

(7) For subrange types, particularly integer subranges, it is sometimes required to perform operations which are defined for the original larger type. In principle, it is simple to accomplish this by first converting the subrange value to the corresponding value of the larger type, and then performing the operation, and finally converting back again if necessary. This requires a type transfer function; and for this purpose it is convenient to use the name of the destination type, for example:

$x$distance: = integer(x) − integer(y);

z: = coordinate(integer(z) + $x$distance);

where $x$distance is an integer variable. Of course, this is an excessively cumbersome notation, and one would certainly wish to adopt the convention of omitting the conversions, where the need for their re-insertion can be established from the context:

$x$distance: = x − y;

z: = z + $x$distance.

Exercise

Given m:month and y:year, write a case discrimination expression giving the number of days in month m.

3.2. REPRESENTATION

The standard representation of an enumeration type T is to map the values in the stated order onto the computer integers in the range 0 to $n - 1$, where n is the cardinality of the type. Thus in this case the standard representation is also minimal. The standard representation of a subrange is to give each value the same representation that it had in the original type; thus transfer between the types involves no actual operation; though of course conversion from the base type to the subrange type should involve a check to ensure that the value is within the specified range.

The minimal representation of a subrange value is obtained by subtracting from the standard form the integer representation of the least value of the subrange. In this case, conversion to a subrange involves subtraction as well as a check, and conversion in the opposite direction involves an addition.

Apart from these conversions, enumerations and subranges in either representation can be treated identically. Tests of ordering can be accomplished by normal integer instructions of the computer, and succ and pred involve addition or subtraction of unity, followed by a test that the result is still within range.

The case discrimination can be most efficiently carried out by a switch-jump. For example, in ALGOL 60 the first example quoted above (3.1.(3)) would be coded:

> **begin switch** *ss*: = red, yellow, blue;
>
> > **go to** *ss*[*pc* + 1];
> >
> > red: **begin** . . . . ; **go to** end **end**;
> >
> > yellow: **begin** . . . ; **go to** end **end**;
> >
> > blue: **begin** . . . . ; **go to** end **end**;
>
> end: **end**.

This can be efficiently represented in machine code, using an indexed jump and a switch table, indicating the starting addresses of the portions of code corresponding to the limbs of the discrimination.

The implementation of the for statement corresponds in an obvious way to the for statement of ALGOL 60, with a step length of unity. The conventions proposed above, which regard the counting variable as a local constant of the loop, not only contribute to clarity of documentation, but also assist in achieving efficiency on a computer, by taking advantage of registers, special count and test instructions, etc.

3.3. EXAMPLE

The character set of a computer peripheral is defined by enumeration:

> **type** character = (. . . .);

The set includes the subranges

> **type** digit = nought . . nine;
>
> **type** alphabet = *A* . . *Z*;

as well as individual symbols, point, equals, subten, colon, newline, space, as well as a number of other single-character operators and punctuation marks.

There is a variable

> buffer: character

which contains the most recently input character from the peripheral. A new value can be input to buffer from the input tape by the procedure "read next character".

In a certain representation of ALGOL 60, basic words are not singled out by underlining, and therefore look like identifiers. Consequently, if they are followed or preceded by an identifier or a number, they must be separated from it by one or more spaces or newline symbols.

In the first pass of an ALGOL translator it is desired to read in the individual characters, and assemble them into meaningful symbols of the language; thus, an identifier, a basic symbol, a number, and the ":=" becomes sign, each count as a single symbol, as do all the other punctuation marks. Space and newline, having performed their function of separating symbols, must be ignored. We assume that each meaningful symbol will be scanned by a routine designed for the purpose, and that each such routine will leave in the buffer the first input character which is *not* part of the symbol.

As an example of the analysis of the symbols of a program, input of the text

> *l*: beta1 : = beta × 12;

should be analysed into the following symbols:

> *l*
>
> :
>
> beta1
>
> : =
>
> beta
>
> ×
>
> 12
>
> ;

The general structure of the program is a case discrimination on the first character of the symbol, which determines to which class the symbol belongs.

> read first character;
>
> **repeat case** buffer **of**
>
>   (alphabet: scan identifier,
>
>   digit: point: subten: scan number,
>
>   space: newline: read next character,
>
>   colon: **begin** read next character;
>
>   **if** buffer = equals **then**
>
>   **begin** deal with "becomes"; read next character **end**

    else deal with single colon character

    end

  else begin deal with single character;

  read next character

    end

)

until end of tape

4. THE CARTESIAN PRODUCT

Defined enumerations and subranges, like primitive data types, are in principle unstructured. Of course, any particular representation of these types will be structured, for example, as a collection of consecutive binary digits; but from the abstract point of view, this structuring is essentially irrelevant. No operators are provided for accessing the individual bits, or for building up a value from them. In fact, it is essential to the successful use of an abstraction that such a possibility should be ignored; since it is only thus that detailed decisions can be postponed, and data representations can be decided in the light of the characteristics of the computer, as well as the manner in which the data is to be manipulated.

We now turn to deal with data types for which the structure is meaningful to the programmer, at least at some stage in the development of his program. The basis of our approach is that, as in the case of enumerations, the programmer should be able by declaration to introduce new data types; but for structured data, the definition of a new type will refer to other primitive or previously defined types, namely the types of the components of the structure. Thus the declaration of a new type will be somewhat similar to the declaration of a new function in a language such as ALGOL and FORTRAN. A function declaration defines the new function in terms of existing or previously declared functions and operations. Just as a declared function can be invoked on many occasions from within statements of the program or other function declarations, so the new type can be "invoked" many times from within other declarations of the program; these may be either declarations of variables specified to range over the newly declared type, or they may be declarations of yet another new type.

We will deal first with elementary data structures, Cartesian products and unions. These elementary structures are almost as simple and familiar to mathematicians and logicians as the natural numbers. Furthermore, from the point of view of the computer programmer, the properties of elementary data structures are very favourable, provided that the constituent types are also elementary.

(1) Firstly, each data item occupies a fixed finite, and usually modest amount of core store, which increases only linearly with the size of the definition.

(2) The store required to hold each value can efficiently be allocated either permanently in main storage or on a run-time stack. There is no need for more sophisticated dynamic storage allocation systems.

(3) The most useful manipulations of the data items can be performed with high efficiency on present-day computers by simple and compact sequences of machine-code instructions.

(4) The structures do not require pointers (references, addresses) for their representation, and thus there is no problem with the transfer of such data between main and backing storage.

(5) For any given structure, the choice of an appropriate representation usually presents no difficulty to the programmer.

The first data structuring method which we shall discuss is the Cartesian product. A familiar example of a Cartesian product is the space of complex numbers, each of which is constructed as a pair of floating point numbers, one considered as its real part and the other as its imaginary part. The declaration of the complex type might take the form

      type complex = (realpart:real;imagpart:real);

    or more briefly:

      type complex = (realpart, imagpart:real).

The names realpart and imagpart are introduced by this definition to provide a means of selecting the components of a complex number. For example, if n is of type complex defined above, n. realpart will denote its real part and n. imagpart its imaginary part.

A constant denoting a value from a Cartesian product type may be defined in terms of a list of constants denoting the values of the components. As mentioned before, the name of the type is used as a transfer function to indicate the type of the resulting structure, and it takes a list of parameters rather than a single one. Thus the complex number $13 + i$ may be written

    complex (13, +1).

Another example of a Cartesian product is the declaration of a type whose values represent playing cards. Each card can be specified by giving first its suit (for example, heart) and then its rank, say Jack. Both items of information are required uniquely to specify a given card. Thus the type cardface can be defined as the Cartesian product of the types suit and rank:

type cardface = (s:suit; r:rank).

Typical constants of this type are:

cardface (club, two), cardface (heart, Jack).

Another simple example of a Cartesian product, this time with three components, is the date. In the normal way, this can be specified by three values, the first selected from among the possible values of the type day of month, say the seventh; the second from among the possible values of the type month, say March; and the third from among the values of the type year, say 1908. This date can be written:

date (7, March, 1908).

It belongs to the type declared thus:

type date = (day:day of month; m:month; y:year);

The defining feature of the Cartesian product type is that it comprises every possible combination of values of its component types, even if some of them should never be encountered in practice. So date (31, Feb, 1931) is a normal value of type date, even though in the real world no such date exists. However date (28, Feb, 1899) is *not* a value of type date, since 1899 is not a value of type year, as defined above. Thus the definition of the type date does not correspond exactly to the real world situation, but the correspondence is close enough for most purposes; and it is the responsibility of the programmer to ensure that the manipulation of the variables of this type will never cause them to take values which he would regard as meaningless.

This example shows that the means provided for defining new types in terms of other types are simpler and less powerful than the general mathematical techniques for defining new sets in terms of other sets; for it certainly is possible to define a set which excludes all unwanted dates. In fact, when declaring a type or variable, it is good documentation practice to specify rigorously the properties which will be possessed by every meaningful value.

The last example shows how the set of point positions on a two-dimensional raster can be declared as the Cartesian product of one-dimensional coordinates:

type raster = (x, y:coordinate)

This is the standard method by which two-dimensional spaces are constructed out of a single-dimension by the method of Cartesian coordinates; for every point in two-dimensional space can be named as an ordered pair of simple one-dimensional numbers. This explains the use of the term "Cartesian product" to apply to the given method of defining types. If r is a variable of type raster, $r.x$ and $r.y$ are commonly known as the projections of r onto the x and y axes respectively; however, we shall refer to the functions x and y as selectors rather than projections.

The cardinality of a Cartesian product type is obtained by multiplying together the cardinalities of the constituent types. This is fairly obvious from the visualisation of a Cartesian product as a rectangle or box with sides equal in length to the cardinalities of the types which form the axes. Thus the cardinality of the card type is thirteen times four, i.e., fifty-two, which is, as you might expect, the number of cards in a standard pack. The number of dates is 26 040, which slightly overestimates the actual number of days in the interval, since as explained above, it includes a small number of invalid dates.

4.1 MANIPULATION

Apart from assignment and test of equality, which are common to all types, the main operations defined for a product type are just those of constructing a value in terms of component values, and of selecting the components. When constructing a value of a Cartesian product type, it is in principle necessary to quote the name of the type as a transfer function. However, it is often more convenient to follow the traditional mathematical practice, and leave the transfer function implicit in cases where no confusion would arise. This is in any case necessary when a type is not even given an explicit name. For example, one may write (heart, Jack) instead of cardface (heart, Jack).

For selection of a component, a dot-notation has been used, e.g., $n.$ imagpart. This is more convenient than the normal functional notation imagpart (n), since it avoids unnecessarily deep nesting of brackets.

Another most important operation is the selective updating of the components of a variable. This may be denoted by placing the component name on the left of an assignment

$$u.\text{imagpart}: = 0;$$

$$r.x: = a \times r.x + b \times r.y.$$

If a Cartesian product is declared as ordered, it is necessary that all the constituent types be ordered, and it is natural to define the ordering in a lexicographic manner, taking the earlier components as the more significant. Thus if suit and rank are ordered, the cardface type could be declared as ordered in the traditional ranking whereby all clubs precede all diamonds, and these are followed by all hearts and all spades; whereas within each suit, the cards are ordered in accordance with their rank.

In inspecting or processing a structured value, it is often required to make many references to its components within a single small region of code. In such a case it is convenient to use a **with** construction

with sv **do** S;

where sv names the structured variable (or expression) and S is a program statement defining what is to be done with it. Within the statement S, the components of sv will be referred to simply by their selector names, $s_1, \ldots, s_n$, instead of by the usual construction: $sv.s_1, sv.s_2, \ldots sv.s_n$. The reasons for using this construction are:

(1) To clarify the purpose of the section of program.

(2) To abbreviate its formulation.

(3) To indicate the possibility of improved efficiency of implementation.

Example: Given today: date, test whether it is a valid date or not.

> **with** today **do case** m **of**
> > {Sept: April: June: Nov:
> > > **if** day > 30 **then go to** invalid,
> > > Feb: **if** day $> \left(\textbf{if } (y \div 4) \times 4 = y \textbf{ then } 29 \textbf{ else } 28\right)$
> > > > **then go to** invalid,
> > > **else** do nothing}.

Exercise

Write functions to represent the four standard arithmetic operations on complex numbers.

4.2. REPRESENTATION

The standard method of representing a value of Cartesian product type is simply by juxtaposing the values of its components in a consecutive region of store, usually in the order indicated. However, there is considerable variation in the amount of packing and padding which may be involved in the juxtaposition. In the standard unpacked representation, each component value is made to occupy an integral number of words, where a word is the smallest conveniently addressable and efficiently accessible unit of storage on the computer.

If the values can fit into less storage than one word, there is the option of packing more than one component into a word. In a tightpacked representation, the bitpatterns of the components are directly juxtaposed. In a loosely packed representation, the components may be fitted within certain subdivisions of a word, which are "natural" in the sense that special machine code instructions are available for selecting or updating particular parts of a word—for example, character boundaries, or instruction fields of a word.

The sequence of the components may be rearranged to fit them conveniently within such boundaries; but such rearrangement is usually inadvisable if the type is ordered.

If a packed representation stretches over several words, there is a possibility that a single component value may overlap word boundaries. The selection or updating of such a component on many machines would be much more time-consuming than normal; and it is therefore a common practice to leave some unused space (padding) at the end of words to prevent such overlaps.

In order to construct a minimal representation of a structured value, it is necessary to use minimal representation of all the components. Then each component is multiplied by the product of the cardinalities of all the types of all subsequent components, and these results are summed to give a minimal representation in the Cartesian product type. For example, the representation of 7th, Mar, 1908 is $6 \times 12 \times 70 + 2 \times 70 + 8 = 5188$.

The choice between the various representations depends on the wider context within which the values are processed. If selection and selective updating are frequent, it pays to use an unpacked representation, so that the normal selection mechanism of word-addressed hardware may be used directly in these operations. However if copying and comparison of the value as a whole is comparatively frequent, then it pays to use a packed representation, so that these operations can be carried out with fewer instructions and fewer stores accesses. A particular case of copying which should be taken into consideration is that which takes place between the main store of the computer and a backing store. If such transfers are frequent, considerable efficiency may be gained if the volume of material transferred is reduced by judicious packing.

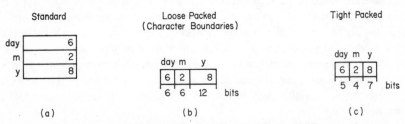

FIG. 1   Representations of date (7, March, 1908)

A second occasion for using packed representations is when data storage is scarce, either in main store or on external backing stores. However, care must be taken that space saved on data storage is not outweighed by the expansion of the code which results from having to unpack and repack the data whenever it is inspected or updated.

The minimal representation is not often used for data storage, since the small amount of extra space it saves (always less than one bit per component) is usually more than outweighed by the extra time taken by multiplying and dividing on every access to the components, as compared with the more usual shifting and masking. However, the technique can be useful, possibly in conjunction with more conventional packing, if there is no other way of fitting the value within convenient word boundaries. Also, if the value is to be used solely or primarily as an index to a multi-dimensional array, the minimal representation is to be preferred; since this will save a significant amount of space in the representation of the array (see Section 6.2).

In representing the **with** construction in machine code, it is sometimes convenient to compute the address of the structure being referenced and store it in a register; this may achieve shorter and faster code for accessing the components. If the components have been packed, it may pay to unpack them into separate words before starting to process them, so that they can be easily referenced or updated; and if they have been updated, they must be packed up again and stored in the structure when the processing is complete. On some machines, it is more economic to pack and unpack a whole structure at the same time, rather than to perform these operations one at a time on the components.

Exercise

Given a variable

> today: date;

write a program to assign the value of the next following date to the variable tomorrow: date. Translate this program into the machine code of your choice using a tightly packed representation. Rewrite the program using an unpacked and then a minimal representation. Compare the lengths of the code involved, and the time taken to execute them.

5. The Discriminated Union

In defining sets of objects, it is often useful to define one set as the union of two previously known sets. For example, when jokers are added to a standard pack of cards, the extended set may be described as the union of the standard set plus the set consisting of the "wild" cards, joker 1 and joker 2. A type whose values range over the members of this set may be declared as the union of two alternatives, the card type, and an enumeration type with two distinct values:

> **type** pokercard = (normal:(s:suit; r:rank),
>
> wild:(joker 1, joker 2)).

Each value of type pokercard corresponds either to an ordered pair with components indicating suit and rank; or else it corresponds to one of the two jokers in the enumeration type.

In specifying a constant of a discriminated union type, it is necessary to indicate to which of the alternative types the value denoted is intended to belong. This is done by writing the name of the alternative explicitly, for example:

pokercard (normal (heart, Jack))

denotes a value from the first alternative, whereas

pokercard (wild (joker 2))

denotes a value from the second alternative. In general, it is convenient to omit the type name, where the type can be inferred from context.

A second example of a discriminated union might be found in the maintenance of a register of all cars in a country. Cars may be distinguished as local cars owned by residents of the country, and visitor cars brought into the country temporarily by non-residents. The information required is rather different in the two cases. In both cases the number and the make of the car is considered relevant. However, for a local car, the name of the owner of the car is required, and the date on which the car was first registered in that owner's name. For visitor cars, this information is not relevant: all that is required is the standard three-letter abbreviation of the name of the country of origin. Thus the definition of the two alternative types of car might be:

type local car = (make: manufacturer; regnumber: carnumber;
                        owner: person; first registration: date);

type visitor car = (make: manufacturer; regnumber: carnumber;
                        origin: country);

Now it is possible to define a type covering both kinds of car:

type car = (local: local car,
                foreign: visitor car).

But here it is inconvenient to define the structure of local and foreign cars separately; and we would like to take advantage of the fact that several of their components are the same. This may be done by bringing the common components in front of both alternatives:

type car = (make: manufacturer;
                regnumber: carnumber;
                (local: (owner: person;
                first registration: date),
                foreign: (origin: country))
).

Every car has a make and regnumber but only local cars have an owner or first registration date; and only foreign cars have an origin.

A third example is the definition of geometric figures, which in some application might be categorised as either rectangles, triangles, or circles

type figure = (position:point; rect:R, tri:T, circ:C).

The method of specifying the figure varies in each case. For a rectangle, the angle of inclination of one of the sides is given, together with the two lengths of the sides:

type R = (inclination:angle; side 1, side 2:real).

A triangle is specified by the angle of inclination and length of one of its sides together with the angles formed between it and the other two sides:

type T = (inclination:angle; side:real; angle1, angle2:angle).

For a circle, all that is necessary is to specify the diameter as a real number.

type C = (diameter:real).

When a type is defined as the union of several other types, it is important to recognise that its values must be considered wholly distinct from those of any of the types in terms of which it is defined. Otherwise there would be an immediate violation of the rule that each value belongs to only one type. Thus the union of types must be clearly distinguished from the normal concept of set union. Furthermore, for each element of the union type, it is possible to determine from which of the constituent types it originated, even if the same type has been repeated several times. For example, a double pack of cards used for playing patience may be defined as the union of two packs, i.e.,

type patience card = (red:cardface, blue:cardface).

Each value of type patience card is clearly marked as having originated either from the red pack or from the blue pack, even if perhaps in the real world the colours of the backs are the same. This fact explains the use of the term "discriminated union" to apply to this form of type definition. It follows that the cardinality of a discriminated union is always the sum of the cardinalities of its constituent types.

5.1. MANIPULATION

Any value of a discriminated union carries with it a *tag* field indicating which of the particular constituent types it originated from; on assignment this is copied, and on a test of equality, the tag fields must be the same if the values are to be equal.

On constructing a value of a discriminated union type, it is necessary to name the alternative type from which the value originated:

> patience card (red (spade, Jack)).

This will automatically cause the value "red" to be assigned to the tag field of the result.

> A particular car may be denoted by
>
> car (Ford, "RUR157D",
>
> > local (me, date (1, Sept, 1968))).

In order to access and operate on the information encoded as a discriminated union, it is necessary to convert it back to its original type. This may be accomplished by the convention of using the label of this type as if it were a selector, e.g.:

> card1.wild   is of type (joker 1, joker 2)
>
> car1.foreign   is of type (origin:country)
>
> fig1.tri   is of type T

If the constituent type is a Cartesian product, its selectors may be validly applied to the resulting value, using the convention that the .operator associates to the left.

> card1.normal.r
>
> car1.local.owner
>
> fig1.circ.diameter

If the programmer attempts to convert a discriminated union value back to a type from which it did *not* originate, this is a serious programming error, which could lead to meaningless results. This error can be detected only by a runtime check, which tests the tag field whenever such a conversion is explicitly or implicitly invoked. Such a check is timeconsuming and when it fails, highly inconvenient. We therefore seek a notational technique which will guarantee that this error can never occur in a running program; and the guarantee is given by merely inspecting the text, without any knowledge of the runtime values being processed. Such a guarantee could be given by an automatic compiler, if available.

The proposed notational technique is a mixture between the **with** construction for Cartesian products and the case construction for discrimination. Suppose that a value *sv* of union type is to be processed in one of several ways in accordance with which of the alternative types it came from. Then one may write

with sv **do** $\{a_1 : S_1$
$\qquad a_2 : S_2,$

$\qquad\vdots$

$\qquad\vdots$

$\qquad a_n : S_n\};$

where S_i is the statement to be selected for execution whenever the value of the tag field of sv is a_i. Within S_i it is guaranteed safe to assume that the value came from the corresponding alternative type, provided that the value of sv remains unchanged. Consequently it is safe to use the component selectors which are defined for that alternative type by themselves to refer to the components of sv, just as in the case of a simple **with** statement described previously for a Cartesian product.

If it is desired to regard a union type as ordered, the most natural ordering is that defined by taking all values corresponding to earlier alternatives in the list before any of the values of the later alternatives.

Exercise
Write a function that will compute the area of a figure as defined above.

5.2. REPRESENTATION

In representing a value from a discriminated union it is necessary first to represent the tag as an integer between zero and $n - 1$, where n is the number of alternative types. The tag is followed directly by the representation of the value of the original type. As with the Cartesian product, there is a choice of the degree of packing used in a representation.

In the unpacked representation the tag occupies a complete word, and the space occupied by each value of a union type is one word more than that occupied by values from the largest alternative type. In a packed representation, this overhead can be reduced to a few bits. In the minimal representation, each value is obtained by adding its minimal representation in the original type to the sum of the cardinalities of all preceding types in the union. Thus a value originating from the first type, for example (diamond, four), has exactly the same value as it has in the original type, namely 16. But joker 1, with value zero in the original enumeration type, has added to it the cardinality of the card type.

The choice between unpacked, packed and tight packed representations is based on the same considerations as for Cartesian products; however the runtime speed penalty for the minimal representation is a great deal less, since recovery of the original value requires only subtraction rather than division.

In general the values of the different alternative types occupy different amounts of storage, so the shorter values have to be "padded out" to equalise the lengths, thus observing the convenient rule that elementary data types occupy a fixed amount of storage. In later chapters it will be seen that this padding can often be omitted when the value is a component of some larger structure.

A local car

Ford	make
RUR 157 D	regnumber
0	tag
CARH	owner
1 Sept 1968	first registration

A foreign car

Fiat	make
37-27-193	regnumber
1	tag
Italy	origin
	padding (sometimes omitted)

FIG. 2.   Representation of cars

In present-day programming practice, it is quite common to omit the tag field in the representation of unions. In order to operate correctly on such a representation, the programmer needs to "know" from other considerations what the interpretation of the value ought to be, since it is not possible to find out from the value itself. If his belief is mistaken, this is not detectable either by a runtime or compile-time check. Since the effect of such an error will depend on details of bitpattern representation, it will give rise to results unpredictable in terms of the abstractions with which the programmer is working. It would therefore in general seem advisable to use tag fields and compile-time checkable case discriminations as standard programming practice, to be bypassed only in exceptional circumstances.

5.3. EXAMPLE

We return to the context of the example in section 3.3, the analysis of language text into meaningful symbols. We wish to give a rigorous abstract definition of what these symbols are.

> **type** symbol =
>> (realconst:real,
>> integerconst:integer,
>> identifier:ident,
>> basic:delimiter);

where we will leave the type ident undefined for the time being, and assume that the delimiters are defined by enumeration.

6. THE ARRAY

The array is for many programmers the most familiar data structure, and in some programming languages it is the only structure explicitly available. From the abstract point of view, an array may be regarded as a mapping between a domain of one type (the subscript range) and a range of some possibly different type (the type of the array, or more accurately, the type of its elements).

The type of a mapping is normally specified by a mathematician using an arrow:

$M:D \rightarrow R;$

where D is the domain type and R is the range type. An alternative notation which will be more familiar to programmers is:

M:**array** D **of** R.

This notation is more expressive of the manner in which the data is represented, whereas the mathematical notation emphasises the abstract character of the structure, independent of its representation.

When a particular value M of a mapping type is applied to a value x of the domain type, it specifies some unique element of the range type, which is known as M of x, and is written using either round or square brackets

$M(x)$ or $M[x]$.

Another name for a mapping is a *function*: the term "mapping" is used to differentiate the data structure from a piece of program which actually computes a value in its range from an argument in its domain. The essence of the difference is that a mapping M is specified not by giving a computation method but by explicitly listing the value of $M(x)$ for each possible value x in its domain. Thus an array can be used only for functions defined at a finite set of points, whereas the domain of a computed function may be infinite.

An example of a finite mapping is a monthtable, which specifies for each month of the year the number of days it has:

type monthtable = **array** month **of** 28..31.

The domain is the month type and the range type consists of the integers between 28 and 31 inclusive. A typical value of this type may be simply specified by listing the values of $M(x)$ as x ranges over its domain. Thus if M:monthtable is specified as

monthtable (Jan:31, Feb:28, March:31, April:30,

May:31, June:30, July:31, Aug:31,

Sept:30, Oct:31, Nov:30, Dec:31)

then M[Jan] = 31, M[Feb] = 28, and so on.

The array provides a method of representing a particular arrangement of cards in a pack, since each arrangement may be regarded as a mapping which indicates for each of the fifty-two possible positions in a pack the value of the card which occupies that position. Thus each possible arrangement may be regarded as a value of the mapping type:

type cardpack = **array** 1..52 **of** cardface.

Of course, not all values of this type represent actual cardpacks, since there is nothing to prevent some value of the type from mapping two different positions onto the same card; which in real life is impossible.

Arrays with elements that are of Cartesian product type are sometimes known as *tables*.

A third example of an array is that which represents all possible configurations of character punching on a conventional punched card. This may be regarded as a mapping M which maps each column number into a character, namely the character punched in that column.

type punchcard = **array** 1..80 **of** character.

Any possible text punched into a card may be regarded as a single value of type punchcard.

A fourth example shows an array which represents a possible value of a page on a cathode ray tube display device. There are assumed to be 40 rows and 27 character positions in each row. The effect of two dimensions can be achieved by specifying the domain of the mapping as a Cartesian product of the possible rows and the possible character positions within each row. This is written as follows:

type spot = (row:1..40; column:1..27);

type display page = **array** spot **of** character.

An alternative method of dealing with a multidimensional array is to regard it as an array of rows, where each row is an array of characters:

type display page = **array** 1..40 **of** row;

type row = **array** 1..27 **of** character.

This is a more suitable abstract structure if the rows are to be processed separately and the columns are not.

The cardinality of an array type is computed by raising the cardinality of the range type to the power of the cardinality of the domain type, i.e.

$$\text{cardinality } (D \rightarrow R) = \text{cardinality } (R)^{\text{ cardinality } (D)}$$

This may be proved by considering the number of decisions which have to be made to specify completely a value of an array type. For each value of the domain we have to choose between cardinality (R) possible values of the range type. We have to make such a choice independently for each element of the array, that is cardinality (D) times.

6.1. MANIPULATION

A mapping which maps all values of its domain onto the same value of its range is known as a constant mapping. A natural constructor for arrays is one which takes as argument an arbitrary range value, and yields as result the constant array, all of whose elements are equal to the given range value. It is convenient to use the type name itself to denote this constructor, e.g.

$$M = \text{monthtable } (31)$$

is an array such that $M[m] = 31$ for all months m.

cardpack (cardface (heart, King))

is obviously a conjuror's pack.

The basic constructive operation on an array is that which defines a new value for one particular element of an array. If x is a value of an array type T, d a value from its domain type, and r a value from its range type, then we write:

$$T(x, d:r)$$

to denote a value of type T which is identical to x in all respects, except that it maps the value d into r. The T may be omitted if its existence can be inferred from context. Similarly, the constant array $T(x)$ may be denoted by all (x).

The basic selection operator on arrays is that of subscripting. This is effectively a binary operation on an array and a value from its domain type; and it yields the corresponding value of its range type.

The most common and efficient way of changing the value of an array is by selective updating of one of its components, which is accomplished by the usual notation of placing a subscripted array variable on the left of an assignment:

$$a[d] := r.$$

This means the same as

$$a := T(a, d:r).$$

Note that from an abstract point of view a new value is assigned to the whole array.

Normally an array type would be regarded as unordered; but in some cases, particularly character arrays, it is desirable to define an ordering corresponding to the normal lexicographic ordering; this is possible only when domain and range types are ordered. In this case the ordering of two arrays is determined by that of the lowest subscripted elements in which the two arrays differ. Thus

"BACK" < "BANK"

because the third letter is the first one in which they differ, and

$$"C" < "N"$$

A convenient method of specifying an array value is by means of a *for expression*, which is modelled on the for statement:

for $i:D$ **take** E

where E is an expression yielding a value of the range type, and containing the variable i. As i scans through the domain type D, evaluation of the expression E yields the value of the corresponding element of the array.

If certain operations are defined on the range type of an array, it is natural to extend these operations to apply to the array type as well. For example, if A and B are real arrays with the same domain, it is natural to write

$$A + B, A - B,$$

to denote arrays (with the same domain) whose elements are the sum and difference of the values of the corresponding elements of A and B. But the programmer must retain his awareness that these can be expensive operations if the arrays are large, and he should seek ways of eliminating the operations in progressing from an abstract to a more concrete program.

6.2. REPRESENTATION

The representation of arrays in a computer store is familiar to most programmers. The most usual representation is the unpacked representation, which allocates one or more whole words to each element of the array. In this case, the computer address of each element is simply computed: first, the value of the subscript is converted to a minimal representation; then this is multiplied by the number of words occupied by each element; and finally the result is added to the address of the first element of the array. The normal word-selection mechanism of the computer can be used to access and update this value independently of the other elements of the array.

An alternative representation involves packing of elements within word boundaries, so that each element occupies only a certain fixed number of bits within a word, although the array as a whole may stretch over several words. In the example of a monthtable, each element can take only four values, 28 to 31; therefore it can be accommodated in only two bits in the minimal representation; the whole array can therefore be accommodated in twenty-four consecutive bits.

When an array is packed in this way, the task of selecting the value of a subscripted variable is far more complicated. In order to select the right word, the subscript (in minimal form) must be divided by the number of elements in each word. The quotient is added to the address of the first word of the array, which is then accessed. The remainder is multiplied by the number of bits in each element, and the result is used as a shift-count, to shift the required value into a standard position within the word. The unwanted values of neighbouring elements of the array can then be masked off. The method of selectively updating an element of a packed array is even more laborious, since the new value must be inserted at the right position within the word, without disturbing the values of the neighbouring elements. The efficiency of both operations may be slightly increased if the number of elements per word is an exact power of two, since then the integer division of the subscript may be replaced by a shift to find the quotient, and a mask to find the remainder. On some machines, further efficiency may be gained if each element is stored in a single character position.

The minimal representation for an array is similar to that for a Cartesian product, except that the multiplier of each element value is equal to the cardinality of range type, raised to the power of the subscript value. The process of selecting or updating a value of an element of an array stored in minimal representation is even more laborious than that described above, unless the cardinality of the range type is an exact power of two. It would be prohibitive if the array were to stretch over more than one normal computer word. For this reason, the minimal representation for arrays is of mainly academic interest.

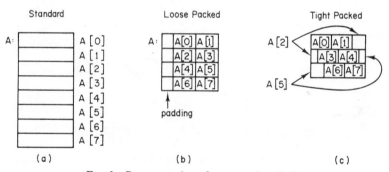

FIG. 3. Representation of A: **array** $0 .. 7$ **of** T

When the domain of a finite mapping is itself a data structure, for example, a Cartesian product, it is usual to represent this domain in the minimal representation, so as to avoid allocation of unused storage space. For example, the display page has a domain which is the Cartesian product of the integer ranges 1 to 40 and 1 to 27. In the minimal representation, this gives a range of integers between 0 and $40 \times 27 - 1 = 1079$. Consequently 1080 consecutive words are allocated to hold values of elements of the array. In order to access any element in a given row and character position, it is necessary first to construct a minimal representation for the subscript, in the manner described in Section 4.2.

An alternative method of representation of multidimensional arrays is sometimes known as a codeword or descriptor method, but we shall give it the title of "tree representation". The essence of the method is to allocate a single-dimensional *base* array with one element corresponding to each row of the array, and to place in it the address of a block of consecutive storage locations which holds the values of that row. These rows do not have to be contiguous. Now the process of accessing or updating each element does not have to be done by computing a minimal representation of the subscript. All that is necessary is to add the row-number to the address of the first element of the base of the tree, and thus access the address of the first element of the required row, to which the value of the next subscript is added to give the address of the required element.

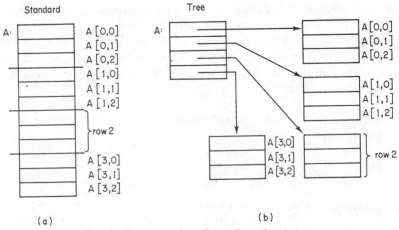

Fig. 4. Representation of two-dimensional arrays

The choice between unpacked and packed representations of arrays is made on grounds similar to the choice in the case of a Cartesian product. The unpacked representation is used when fast access and updating is required; it is also the obviously appropriate choice when the range type naturally fits within computer word boundaries, for example if the elements are floating point numbers. The packed representation is recommended if the size of the elements is considerably shorter than a single word, and if storage is short, or if copying and comparison of the arrays is frequent compared with subscripting and selective updating. A particularly common case of packed arrays is the representation of identifiers in a programming language, where it is acceptable in the interests of efficiency to truncate identifiers which are too long to fit into the standard array, and pad out those that are too short with blanks.

The choice between representations of multidimensional arrays is made on quite different grounds. The standard representation is more economical of storage, and gives good efficiency on sequencing through elements of the array by rows, columns, or both. Furthermore, it is more convenient when the arrays must be transferred as a whole between main and backing store. However, on a machine with slow multiplication, it will be faster to use the tree representation, and accept the extra storage required to hold the array of addresses, which is small provided that the rows are not too short. If each row contains only two words, there would be a fifty per cent overhead on data storage.

There are several other possible reasons for choosing the tree representation:

(1) In some computing environments, where dynamic storage allocation is standard, it may be difficult to obtain large consecutive areas, in which case a large two-dimensional array can be split up into a number of smaller rows which can be accommodated without trouble.

(2) It is possible to set up a scheme whereby some rows of the array are held on backing store while other rows are being processed, and then the backing store address of a row replaces the main store address in the base array when that row is absent from store. Thus it is hoped to be able to process arrays which are too large to be wholly accommodated in main store together with the program that processes them. However, the economics of this operation need to be carefully examined to ensure that the number of backing store transfers involved is acceptable.

(3) In some applications, it is known that several matrices share the same rows. In the tree representation it is possible to set up a single copy of such a shared row, and merely take copies of its address rather than its full value. But in such a case, the shared row must not be selectively updated.

(4) The tree representation is recommended even in the case of single-dimensional arrays if the size of the individual elements is highly variable; and on multidimensional arrays, if the length of the rows is highly variable.

Exercise
The character set of an input device includes only thirty characters, defined by enumeration; they include the characters space, newline, newpage. Characters may be read in one at a time from an input device to a buffer, using a procedure call

read next character.

They should be assembled line by line into an array

page: display page,

and on receipt of a newpage character, this should be output to a display device by the instruction

   outpage.

The display device does *not* recognise the characters newline or newpage; consequently the ends of lines and pages have to be filled up with spaces.

Write a program in a suitable language to perform this operation, using a selection of representations for the display page, e.g.

   unpacked

   loosely packed

   tightly packed

   indirect.

Rewrite the program, using different representations. Compare the lengths and speeds of the code and data involved in the different representations.

Write the corresponding programs to read a page from the display, and output the individual characters, taking care to eliminate redundant spaces at the ends of each line and blank lines at the end of each page wherever possible.

7. THE POWERSET

The powerset of a given set is defined as the set of all subsets of that set; and a powerset type is a type whose values are sets of values selected from some other type known as the *base* of the powerset. For example, the primary colours have been defined by enumeration as red, yellow and blue. The other main colours are made up as a mixture of two or three of these colours: orange is a mixture of red and yellow; brown is a mixture of all three primary colours. Thus each main colour (including the primary colours) can be specified as that subset of the primary colours out of which it can be mixed. For example, orange may be regarded as the set with just two members, red and yellow. Using the traditional notation for sets defined by enumeration, this may be written: {red, yellow}. The pure colour red may be regarded as the set whose only member is the primary colour red, i.e. {red}. In this way it is possible to represent the seven main colours, red, orange, yellow, green, blue, purple and brown. When no primary colour is present (i.e. the null or empty set) this may be regarded as denoting the absence of colour, i.e. perhaps white. The type whose values range over the colours may be declared as the power set of the type primary colour:

   type colour = **powerset** primary colour.

A second example is provided by considering a data structure required to represent the status of the request buttons in a lift. A simple variable of type floor (see Section 3) is capable of indicating one particular stop of a lift. But if we wish to record the status of the whole panel of buttons inside a lift, it would be necessary to represent this as a subset of all possible floors in the building, namely, the subset consisting of those floors for which a request button has been depressed. Thus the type liftcall may be defined as the powerset of the floor type:

type liftcall = **powerset** floor.

A third example is provided by a hand of cards in some card game, for example, poker or bridge. A hand is a subset of playing cards, without repetitions, and is therefore conveniently represented by a value from the powerset type:

type hand = **powerset** cardface;

This type covers all hands of up to fifty-two cards, even though for a particular game there may be standard size of a hand, or a limit less than fifty-two.

A final example expresses the status of a computer peripheral device, for example, a paper tape reader. There are a number of exception conditions which can arise on attempted input of a character:

(1) Device switched to "manual" by operator.

(2) No tape loaded.

(3) Parity error on last character read.

(4) Skew detected on last character read.

These conditions can be defined as an enumeration

type exception = (manual, unloaded, parity, skew);

and since several of these conditions can be detected simultaneously, the status of the reader can be specified as a value of a powerset type:

type statusword = **powerset** exception.

The cardinality of the powerset type is two raised to the power of the cardinality of the base type, i.e.

cardinality (**powerset** D) = $2^{\text{cardinality } (D)}$

This may be proved by considering the number of decisions which have to be made to specify completely a value of the type. For each value of the base type there are two alternatives, either it is in the set or it is not. This decision may be made independently cardinality (D) times.

7.1. MANIPULATION

The basic construction operation on sets is the one that takes a number of values from the domain type, and converts them into a set containing just those values as members. As in the case of the Cartesian Product, the type name is used as the transfer function, but for sets, the number of arguments is variable from zero upwards. For example:

primary colour (red, yellow)　　i.e. orange

liftcall (ground)　　　　　　　i.e. only a single button has been pressed

statusword ( )　　　　　　　　i.e. no exception condition.

The last two examples illustrate the concept of a *unit set* (which must be clearly distinguished from its only member) and the null or *empty set*, which contains no member at all. If the type name is omitted in this construction, curly brackets should be used instead of round ones in the normal way.

The converse of the null set is the universal set, which contains all values from the base type. This may be denoted

T.all.

However, this universal set exists as a storable data value only when the base type is finite.

The basic operations on sets are very familiar to mathematicians and logicians.

(1) Test of membership: If x is in the set s, the Boolean expression "x **in** s" yields the value true, otherwise the value false.

(2) Equality: two sets are equal if and only if they have the same members.

(3) Intersection: $s1 \wedge s2$ contains just those values which are in both $s1$ and $s2$.

(4) Unions: $s1 \vee s2$ contain just those values which are either in $s1$ or $s2$, or both.

(5) Relative complement: $s1 - s2$ contains just those members of $s1$ which are not in $s2$.

(6) Test of inclusion: $s1 \subset s2$ yields the value true whenever all members of $s1$ are also members of $s2$, and false otherwise.

(7) The size of a set tells how many members it has.

If the domain type of a set has certain operators defined upon it, it is often useful to construct corresponding operations on sets. In particular, if the domain type of a set is ordered, the following operators apply:

(8) min (s) the smallest member of s; undefined if s is empty.

(9) s **down** n is a set containing just those values whose nth successors are in s.

(10) s **up** n is a set containing just those values whose nth predecessors are in s.

(11) Range (a, b) is the set containing a, succ$(a), \ldots, b$ if $a \leqslant b$, and which is empty otherwise.

The most useful selective updating operations on sets are:

$x\!:\vee\; y;$	join the set y to x
$x\!:\vee\; T(a)$	add the member a to x
$x\!:\wedge\; y;$	exclude from x all members which are not also members of y
$x\!:- y$	exclude from x all members which are also members of y
$x\!:\mathbf{down}\; n$	subtract n from every member of x and exclude members for which this is not possible
$x\!:\mathbf{up}\; n$	add n to every member of x, and exclude members for which this is not possible

It is also sometimes useful to select some member from x and simultaneously remove it from x. This operation can be expressed by the notation:

a from x.

If the domain type of x is ordered, it is natural that the selected member should be the minimum member of x; otherwise the selection should be regarded as arbitrary.

It is often useful to define the value of a set by giving some condition B which is satisfied by just those values of the domain type which are intended to be members of the set. This may be denoted:

$$\{i\!:\!D \mid B\}$$

where i is a variable of type D regarded as local to B,

and B is a Boolean expression usually containing and depending on i.

In order for this expression to denote a value of the powerset type it is essential that the cardinality of D be finite, and that B is defined over all values of the type.

Finally, it is frequently required to perform some operation on each member of some set, that is to execute a loop with a counting variable which takes on successively all values in the set. A suitable notation for expressing this is:

for x in s do...

If the base type of s is an ordered type, it seems reasonable to postulate that the elements will be taken in the natural order, starting with the lowest. For an unordered base type, the programmer does not care in which order the members are taken, and he leaves open the option to choose an order that contributes best to efficiency.

7.2 REPRESENTATION

In choosing a computer representation for powersets, it is desirable to ensure that all the basic operations can be executed simply by single machine code instructions; and further, that the amount of store occupied is minimised. For most data structure storage methods, there is a fundamental conflict between these two objectives, and consequently a choice between representation methods must be made by the programmer; but in the case of powersets the two objectives can be fully reconciled, provided that the base type is not too large.

The recommended method of representation is to allocate as many bits in the store as there are potential members in the set. Thus to each value of the base type there is a single bit which takes the value one if it is in fact a member, or zero if it is not. For example, each value of type colour can be represented in three bits; the most significant corresponding to the primary colour red, and the least significant corresponding to blue. Thus the orange colour is represented as 110 and red as 100. Each set of size n is represented as a bitpattern with exactly n ones in the appropriate positions. The null set is accordingly represented as an all-zero bitpattern.

Another example is afforded by the "hand" type, which requires fifty-two bits for its representation, one corresponding to each value of type cardface. In this case, it is advisable to use the minimal representation of the base type, to avoid unused gaps in the bitpattern representation.

Since the number of values of a powerset type is always an exact power of two, for powersets of small base there can be no more economical method of utilising storage on a binary computer than that of the bitpattern representation. It remains to show that the operations defined over the powerset type can be executed with high efficiency.

(1) The unitset of x may be obtained by loading a single 1 into the signbit position, and shifting it right x places. On computers on which shifting is slow, the same effect may be obtained by table lookup. The construction of a set out of components may be achieved by taking the logical union of all the corresponding unit sets.

(2) A membership test x **in** s may be made by shifting s up x places and looking at the most significant bit: 1 stands for **true** and 0 for **false**.

(3) Logical intersection, union, and complementation are often available as single instructions on binary computers.

(4) The size of a set can sometimes be discovered by a builtin machine code instruction for counting the bits in a word. Otherwise the size can be determined by repeated standardisation, masking off the next-to-sign bit on

each occasion. A third method is to split the bitpattern into small parts, and use table lookup on each part, adding together the results.

(5) The **up** and **down** operations can obviously be accomplished by right or left shifts.

(6) The min of a set can be efficiently discovered by a standardise instruction, which automatically counts the number of shifts required to move the first one-bit into the position next to the sign.

(7) The for statement may also be efficiently constructed using standardisation, masking off each one-bit as it is reached.

(8) The range operation can be accomplished by two shifts, the first of which regenerates the sign bit.

Thus when the cardinality of the domain type is not greater than the number of bits in the largest computer word to which logical and shift operations can be applied, all these operations can be carried out with great efficiency. If significantly more than one such word is involved, it will usually pay to use selective updating operations rather than the normal result-producing operators. Furthermore, operations such as size and min can become rather inefficient, and it will often pay to store these values redundantly together with the set, and keep them up to date whenever the value of the set is updated, rather than recomputing them whenever they are required.

When it is known that the cardinality of the base type is very large (perhaps even infinite) compared with the size of the typical set, the bitpattern representation altogether loses its attraction, since it no longer pays to store and operate upon large areas of zeroes. The treatment of such sparse sets is postponed to Section 10.

7.3. EXAMPLE

Problem: Write a program to construct a set

primes:**powerset** $2..N$;

containing all prime numbers in its base type.
Use the method of Eratosthenes' sieve to avoid all multiplications and divisions.

The method of Eratosthenes is first to put all numbers in the "sieve" and repeat the following until the sieve is empty:
Select and remove the smallest number remaining in the sieve (necessarily a prime), and then step through the sieve, removing all multiples of that number.

The program can be written easily

```
begin n, next:2..N; sieve:powerset 2..N;
        sieve: = range (2, N);
        primes: = {  };
        while sieve ≠ empty do
                begin next: = min (sieve);
                primes: ∨ {next};
                    for n: = next step next until N do
                        sieve: − {n}
        end
end primefinder.
```

But if N is significantly large, say of the order of 10 000, this program cannot be directly executed with any acceptable degree of efficiency. The solution is to use this program as an abstract model of the algorithm, and rewrite it in a more efficient fashion, using only operations on sets not exceeding the word-length of the computer. We therefore need to declare an array of words to represent the two sets, assuming that "wordlength" is an environment enquiry giving the number of bits in a word:

primes, sieve:**array** 0..W **of powerset** 0..wordlength −1

where $W = (N + 1) ÷$ wordlength $+ 1$.

This means that the two sets may be slightly larger than N, but for convenience we shall accept that harmless extension.

In order to access an individual bit of these sets, it is necessary to know both the wordnumber and the bitnumber. Since we do not wish to use division to find these, we will represent the counting variables n and next as Cartesian products

n, next:(w, b:integer);

where w indicates the wordnumber and b indicates the bitnumber.

It is now as well to check the efficiency of this representation by recoding the innermost loop first.

for n: = next **step** next **until** N **do** sieve: − {n};

is recoded as:

```
n: = next;
while n.w ⩽ W do
    begin sieve [n.w]: − {n.b};
                n.b: = n.b + next.b;
```

$n.w := n.w + \text{next}.w;$

if $n.b \geqslant$ wordlength **then begin** $n.w := n.w + 1;$

$n.b := n.b -$ wordlength

end

end

Since this appears acceptably efficient we will code the other operations of the outer loop, starting with the most difficult:

next: = min (sieve);

Here we do not wish to start our search for the minimum at the beginning of the sieve set each time, since towards the end of the process this would involve scanning many empty words. We therefore take advantage of the fact that the new value of next must be larger than the old value.

The search consists of two parts, first finding a nonempty word, and then its first bit. But if the search for a word reaches the end of the array, the whole program is completed

while sieve [next.w] = { } **do** {next.w: = next.w +1;

if next.w > W **then exit** primefinder};

next.b: = min (sieve [next.w]);

The remaining operations are trivial. Since the outer loop is terminated by an exit, there is no need to test a separate while condition; and the statement

primes: ∨ {next};

can be coded as

primes [next.w]: ∨ {next.b}.

The whole program including initialisation is as follows:

primes, sieve:**array** 0..W **of powerset** 0..wordlength -1;

begin primefinder;

n, next:(w, b:integer);

for t:0..W **do begin** primes [t]: = { };

sieve [t]: = range (0..wordlength -1)

end;

sieve [0]: − {0, 1};

next.w: = 0;

while true **do**

begin while sieve [next.w] = { } **do**

$$\textbf{begin } next.w:= next.w +1;$$
$$\textbf{if } next.w > W \textbf{ then exit } primefinder$$
$$\textbf{end};$$
$$next.b:= \min (sieve\ [next.w]);$$
$$primes\ [next.w]: \lor \{next.b\};$$
$$n:= next;$$
$$\textbf{while } n.w \leqslant W \textbf{ do}$$
$$\textbf{begin } sieve\ [n.w]:- \{n.b\};$$
$$n.b:= n.b + next.b;$$
$$n.w:= n.w + next.w;$$
$$\textbf{if } n.b \geqslant wordlength \textbf{ then}$$
$$\textbf{begin } n.w:= n.w +1;$$
$$n.b:= n.b - wordlength$$
$$\textbf{end}$$
$$\textbf{end}$$
$$\textbf{end}$$

end primefinder

One feature of this program is that it uses an environment enquiry wordlength to achieve the full efficiency of which a machine is capable, and yet does so in a completely machine-independent fashion. The program will not only work, but work with high efficiency, on machines with widely varying word lengths.

But the most interesting feature about the program is the way in which it is related to the previous version. From an abstract point of view it expresses an identical algorithm; all that has changed is the manner in which the data has been represented on the computer. The original design acted as a framework or pattern, on which the more intricate coding of the second version was structured. By carrying out the design in two stages, we simplify the task of ensuring that each part of the final program works successfully in conjunction with the other parts.

Exercise

Rewrite the program using sets representing only the odd numbers. (Hint: rewrite the more abstract program first.)

8. The Sequence

The previous chapters have dealt with the topic of elementary data structures, which are of great importance in practical programming, and present very little problem for representation and manipulation on modern digital computers. Furthermore, they provide the essential basis on which all other more advanced structures are built.

The most important distinction between elementary structured types and types of advanced structure is that in the former case the cardinality of the type is strictly finite, provided that the cardinality of the constituent types is. The distinction between a finite and an infinite set is one of profound mathematical significance, and it has many consequences relating to methods of representation and manipulation.

(1) Since the number of potential values of the type may be infinite, the amount of storage allocated to hold a value of an advanced structure is not determinable from the declaration itself. It is normally only determined when the program is actually running, and in many cases, varies during the execution of the program. In the case of an elementary structure, the number of different potential values is finite, and the maximum amount of storage required to hold any value is fixed and determinable from the form of the declaration.

(2) When the size of a structured value is fairly large, it is more efficient to update individual components of the structure separately, rather than to assign a fresh value to the entire structure. Even for elementary types, it has been found sometimes more efficient to perform selective updating, particularly for unpacked representations of Cartesian products and for arrays. The increased efficiency of selective updating is usually even more pronounced in the case of advanced data structures.

(3) Advanced data structures, whose size varies dynamically, require some scheme of dynamic storage allocation and relinquishment. The units of storage which are required are usually linked together by pointers, sometimes known as references or addresses; and their release is accomplished either by explicitly programmed operations, or by some form of general garbage collection. The use of dynamic storage allocation and pointers leads to a significant complexity of processing, and the problems can be particularly severe when the data has to be transferred between the main and backing store of a computer. No problems of this kind need arise in the case of elementary data structures.

(4) The choice of a suitable representation for an advanced data structure is often far more difficult than for an elementary structure; the efficiency of the various primitive operations depends critically on the choice of representation, and therefore a sensible choice of representation requires a knowledge of the relative frequency with which these operations will be invoked. This knowledge is especially important when a part or all of the structure is held on a backing store; and in this case, the choice of repre-

sentation should take into account the characteristics of the hardware device; that is, arrangement of tracks and cylinders on a rotating medium, and times of head movement and rotational delay. In the case of elementary structures, the primitive operations are of roughly comparable efficiency for most representations.

Thus the differences between advanced and elementary structures are quite pronounced, and the problems involved are significantly greater in the advanced case. This suggests that the practical programmer would be well advised to confine himself to the use of elementary structures wherever possible, and to resort to the use of advanced structures only when the nature of his application forces him to do so.

The first and most familiar example of an advanced data structure is the sequence. This is regarded as nothing but a sequence of an arbitrary number of items of some given type. The use of the term "sequence" is intended to cover sequences on magnetic tapes, disc, or drum, or in the main store. Sequences in the main store have sometimes been known as streams, lists, strings, stacks, deques, queues, or even sets. The term file (or sequential file) is often used for sequences held on backing store. The concept of a sequence is an abstraction, and all these structures may be regarded as its various representations.

Our first example of a sequence is the string, familiar to programmers in ALGOL and SNOBOL. Since a string is constructed as a sequence of characters of arbitrary length, it may be defined:

type string = **sequence** character.

The next example is drawn from a data processing application; the maintenance of a file of data on cars. Each item of the file (sometimes known as a record) represents a single car, and is therefore of type car; an example of a possible definition of the car type has been given previously:

type car file = **sequence** car.

The third example gives an alternative method of dealing with a pack of cards. This may be regarded as just a sequence of cards, of length which perhaps varies as the cards are dealt:

type deck = **sequence** cardface;

Of course, not all card-sequences represent actual decks of cards in real life; for example, sequences which contain the same card twice are invalid, and should be avoided by the programmer. Thus the maximum length of a valid deck is 52, although this fact is not expressed in the declaration.

The next example is drawn from the processing of a particular class of symbolic expression, namely the polynomial. A polynomial

$$a_n x^n + a_{n-1} x^{n-1} \ldots . a_1 x + a_0$$

can be represented as the sequence of its coefficients a_i. If the degree n of the polynomial is unpredictable or variable during the course of a calculation, a sequence is the most appropriate method of defining it:

type polynomial = **sequence** integer.

Our final example shows how it is possible to represent the programming language concept of the identifier. Since in theory an identifier may be of arbitrary length, a sequence is required. The items of the sequence are either letters or digits. However, the first character is always alphabetic and may be separated from the rest. Thus an exact definition of a data structure corresponding to the identifier is:

type identifier = (first: letter; rest: **sequence** (l: letter, d: digit)).

8.1 MANIPULATION

The zero element of a sequence type T is the sequence that contains no items—this is known as the null or empty sequence, and is denoted by $T(\ )$. For each value v of the domain type, there is a sequence whose only item is v; this is known as the *unit sequence* of v and is denoted by $T(v)$. Finally, if $v_1, v_2, \ldots, v_n$ are values from the base type (possibly with repetition), $T(v_1, v_2, \ldots, v_n)$ denotes the sequence consisting of these values in the stated order. If for convenience the type name T is omitted, we will use square brackets to surround the sequence:

$$[v], \qquad [v_1, v_2, \ldots, v_n]$$

However, a sequence of characters is normally denoted by enclosing them in quotes.

The basic operation on sequences is concatenation, that is, adjoining two sequences one after the other. Thus if x is the sequence of characters "PARIS IN THE" and y is the sequence "THE SPRING", their concatenation $x \frown y$ is the sequence

$$z = \text{"PARIS IN THETHE SPRING"}$$

Unless the operands are exceptionally small, concatenation is very inefficient on a computer, since it usually involves making fresh copies of both operands. The programmer should therefore make every effort to replace concatenation by selective updating.

The basic operators for breaking down a sequence into its component parts are those that yield the first and last items of a non-empty sequence

$x.$first, $x.$last

and those that remove the last or first items of a non-empty sequence, yielding the initial or final segments.

initial (x), final (x).

An important relationship between sequences is that one sequence x is equal to some initial or final subsequence of a sequence y:

x **begins** y

or x **ends** y.

In our previous example, "PARIS" **begins** z and "RING" **ends** z. These two tests can be rather time-consuming in a running program, and should be avoided wherever possible.

A significant property of sequences is their length, i.e. the number of items they contain; this may be found for a sequence x by the function length (x).

For some purposes (e.g. the construction of a dictionary) it is useful to regard a sequence type as ordered in accordance with traditional lexicographic principles: as in the case of arrays, the order of two sequences is determined by the ordering of the first item in which they differ; or if there is no such item, a shorter sequence precedes the longer sequence which it begins, for example:

"ALPHA" < "ALPHABET".

In this ordering every sequence has a successor, but only a small proportion have predecessors.

A most important selective updating operation on sequences is the appending of a new value v to the end of an existing sequence x. This may be written:

$x\frown T(v)$;

and corresponds to the familiar concept of writing a value v to a sequential file x. The operation corresponding to reading the beginning of a file x is one which removes the first item of x and assigns its value to some variable v. This may be written:

v **from** x;

In some applications, it is useful to be able to read back the most recently written item from a sequence; this may be expressed

v **back from** x;

and it removes the last item from x. This operation can be used to "pop up" the top item of a stack which has been "pushed down" by an ordinary writing operation:

$x\frown T(v)$.

If desired, it is possible to define the fourth updating operation, that of attaching a new value to the beginning of a sequence. (putback (x, v)).

In some cases, it is more efficient to avoid the copying of an item which is involved in the **from** operation. These cases may be dealt with by merely omitting the left hand variable, e.g.

from x

back from x.

In this case, access to the items of the sequence will usually be made by the selectors x.first and/or x.last.

It is very common to wish to scan all the items of a sequence in succession; a suitable notation for this is modelled on the for statement:

for v **in** x **do** S;

If x is empty, the statement is omitted. Otherwise the variable v (regarded as local to S) takes in succession the values of all items from the sequence x, and S is executed once for each value. In this construction neither x nor v should be updated within S.

A similar construction can be used for defining a sequence as an item-by-item transformation $E(v)$ of items v in sequence s.

for v **in** s **take** $E(v)$.

In deciding a representation for a sequence, it is most important to know which of the selective updating operations are going to be carried out upon it.

(1) If the only operation is **from**, the sequence is known as an *input* sequence; obviously in order to have any value at all, an input sequence must be initialised to some value existing in the outer environment in which it is declared. The association of a sequence local to a program with some file existing more or less permanently on backing store is often known as "opening" the file for input, and we assume that this operation is invoked implicitly on declaration of a local input sequence. The reverse operation of "closing" the file is invoked implicitly on exit from the block to which the sequence is local.

(2) If the only operation is writing to the file, the sequence is known as an *output* sequence. An output sequence may be initialised from the environment in the same way as an input sequence; or more commonly, it may take an empty initial value. In either case, in order to serve any useful purpose, the final value of the sequence on exit from the block must be assigned to some variable existing in the outer environment in which the sequence is declared. The identity of this outer variable should be declared together with the sequence; if this outer variable is held more or less permanently on backing store, it is known as an output file; and the rules for implicit invocation of opening and closing of the file on entry and exit to the block are similar to those for input files.

(3) If the only operations are writing and reading back (push down and pop up), the sequence is known as a *stack*; the initial value of a stack is always empty, and the final value is not usually preserved.

(4) If the only operations are writing to the end and reading from the beginning, the sequence is known as a *queue*; again, the initial value is always empty, and the final value is not usually preserved.

(5) If reading and writing at both ends of a sequence are permitted, the sequence is sometimes known as a *deque* (double-ended queue). However, to make all four operations equally efficient requires some complexity of representation, so it is fortunate that most programs can get by without using deques.

8.2. REPRESENTATION

8.2.1. *Contiguous representation*

The simplest method of representing a sequence is to allocate to it a fixed contiguous area of storage, adequate to hold all items actually required. This method is suitable if the value (or at least the length) of the sequence is constant throughout the execution of the program—for example, a string of characters intended to be used as an output message or title.

In some cases, the length of the sequence is unknown at the time the program is written, but is known on entry to the block in which the sequence is declared, and this length remains constant throughout the existence of the sequence. In such cases, it is possible to allocate a contiguous area of storage in the local workspace of the block, using the standard stack method of store allocation and deallocation.

Even if the length of the sequence is subject to variation, it is sometimes possible to place an acceptably small upper bound on its length, and allocate permanently this maximum area. If the limit is exceeded during a run of the program, the programmer must be willing to accept its immediate termination. In addition to the fixed area, a pointer or count is required to indicate the current beginning and end of the sequence. In the case of a stack, the first item is always at the beginning, and only one pointer to the top of the stack is required. In the case of a queue, the sequence will at times overlap the end of the store area, and be continued again at the beginning. Such a representation is known as a cyclic buffer, and may be used in a parallel programming situation to communicate information between processes running in parallel. In this case, when a writing process finds the buffer full, it has to wait until a reading process reduces the size of the sequence again. Similarly, the reading process must wait when the buffer is empty.

Another case where the contiguous representation is the best is when the program requires only a single sequence, which may therefore occupy the whole of the remaining store available after allocation to other purposes; and if overflow occurs, the program could not have been run anyway. If two stacks are required, they can both be accommodated by arranging that one of them starts at one end of remaining available store and grows upwards, and the other starts at the other end and grows downwards. If the stacks meet, the program cannot continue.

If many sequences are to be represented, it is possible to set up a scheme in which they are spread through the remaining available store; and if any of them grows to meet its neighbour, it is possible to reshuffle some or all of the sequences, so that they all have sufficient room to grow again for a bit. For each sequence there must be a *base location* pointing to its beginning, through which that sequence is always addressed. In addition, the actual length of the sequence must be stored. The base location and length of the neighbouring sequence must always be inspected when the sequence is extended. When reshuffling takes place, the base locations of all moved sequences are updated to point to the new position of the sequence. This is quite a useful ad hoc scheme in cases where the reshuffling is known to be relatively infrequent; otherwise non-contiguous representations are to be preferred.

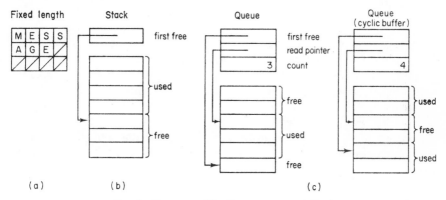

FIG. 5. Sequences (Contiguous representation)

When the individual items of a sequence are of variable length, there is usually no need to pad the shorter items out to the maximum length, since the use of the tag field, or other technique, will indicate the length of any given item, and this can be used to step the pointer by the right amount when the item is read. But this requires that the direction of reading be known at the time of writing, as in a stack or a queue. If reading is to be carried out from both ends, it will be necessary to ensure that the length of an item can be deduced from its bottom as well as its top, which will involve storing redundant information (e.g. length of previous item) between each item in the sequence.

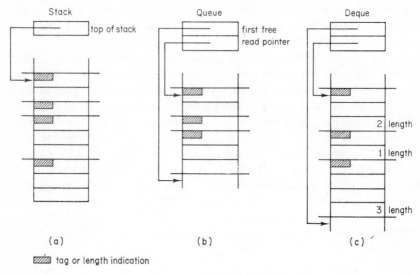

tag or length indication

FIG. 6. Sequences (variable length items)

When a sequence is itself a part of an item of some other sequence, the contiguous representation of the item-sequence may be used. This will normally be accompanied by a count giving the length of the sequence, so that the actual size of each item can be computed when the item is read.

8.2.2. *Chained Representation*

In order to avoid reshuffling problems mentioned in the previous section, it is usual to introduce indirect or chained methods of storage allocation, using either fixed length or variable length units of allocation. The available store is split into areas, some of which will be in use for storing items of some sequence, and others will be free. The free areas are also linked together as a chained sequence. Whenever a programmer's sequence requires extension, an area (or part of an area) is acquired from the free chain; and whenever a sequence is shortened by reading, an area can be returned to the free chain. In the case of fixed-length items, the administration of dynamic storage allocation with explicit deallocation presents no problems. The problems of variable length allocation will not be treated here; they are best avoided by the use of blocking (see next section).

The simplest form of chain is the single linked chain. Each item of the sequence has adjoined to it, in a link location, the address of the next item in the chain. The empty sequence is represented by a value which could not possibly be an address (say zero or minus one); and the link location of the last item in the sequence contains this value. The first item in the chain is pointed to by the base location of the sequence.

A single linked chain is useful when the direction in which the sequence will be read is known; for the links have to point in this direction. In the case of a stack they will point backwards, and in the case of input and output sequences and queues they will point forwards. In the case of an input or output sequence, the base location of the external variable which is to hold the initial and/or final value of the sequence points permanently at the beginning of the chain, while the base location of the sequence itself steps through the sequence. In the case of a queue, two base locations are used, to point to each end of the sequence.

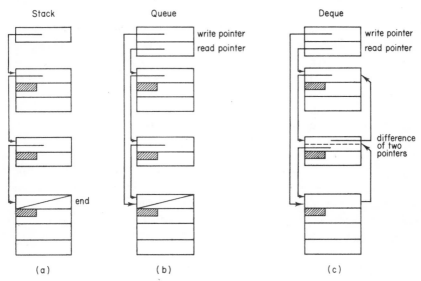

FIG. 7. Sequences (Chained Representation)

One possible advantage of the single-chained representation in the case of stacks is that several stacks can share the same initial segments, which may save space and time in some applications. However, when an item is popped up from such a stack, the storage space which it occupies cannot be immediately returned to the free chain, since it may be in use as part of another stack. One solution to this problem is never to return storage explicitly, but to wait until the free chain is exhausted. Then all currently allocated sequences are scanned, and all blocks currently in use are marked. Then all unmarked blocks are collected onto the free chain. This is known as a scan-

mark-collect garbage collection. Although it appears to relieve the programmer of the responsibility of explicit control of main store allocation and
deallocation, this can be dangerous in non-trivial computer applications
where the responsibility is one that cannot so lightly be evaded.

In the case of a deque, when reading is required in both directions, a single-
linked chain is no longer adequate; and the usual solution is to adjoin *two*
pointers to each item in the chain, one pointing to the previous item and one
pointing to the following item. In fact these two pointers can be compressed
into a single word containing only the difference between them. Since in
the first and last items one of the pointers is a standard null value, the value
of the other pointer from these items can always be obtained by subtraction.
On reading or writing, the value of the link location for the new first or last
item can be readily adjusted, since at this stage the address of the previous
first or last item is still known. The detailed working out of this scheme is
left as an exercise.

An alternative method of linking the items of a chain is to collect all links
together in a single contiguous table, preferably of fixed length. This gives a
form of tree representation for the sequence, and permits ready scanning
in both directions. But it places an upper bound on the number of items in
the sequence; and it means that the locations used for links must be permanently allocated, even at times when the sequence is relatively short.
This problem can be mitigated by the use of blocking.

8.2.3 *Blocked Representation*

One disadvantage of chaining is the amount of extra storage required to hold
the links, and the time taken to administer the free store chain on each
operation. These problems are particularly severe when the size of the
individual items of the sequence are small and the sequence is long. The
method of solving this problem is to use blocking; that is, a combination of
the contiguous and chained techniques.

In this technique, a fixed-length block of storage is allocated, sufficient to
hold perhaps between ten and a hundred items. When this block is filled, a
new block is chained to it, using any of the methods described in the previous
section. On input, a block is not released to free store until all the items it
contains have been scanned. Thus the amount of store used on links can be
reduced to negligible proportions. This can be of particular benefit in the
tree representation of the chain.

As mentioned above, the use of blocking can also avoid the
problems arising from variable-length dynamic storage allocation, since the
size of the block may be held constant for all sequences, independent of the
size of their items. Furthermore, in cases where part or all of the sequence
is to be held on backing store, the use of blocking is almost universally

indicated, since backing store transfers can be very inefficient if the unit of transfer is too small. The only (dubious) disadvantage of blocking is that it inhibits effective sharing of the tails of stacks.

The only remaining problem is to choose a size of block suitable for all purposes. It must obviously be large enough to accommodate the largest item of any sequence. In fact, it should be large enough to accommodate at least ten typical items; otherwise the space left over at the end of a block which is not large enough to accommodate the next item may reach significant proportions. Also, if the sequence is to be held partially or wholly on backing store, the block should be long enough to ensure that not too much space is wasted on interblock gaps, and the frequency of transfers is low enough to ensure that not too much time is spent in start-stop, latency, or head movement delays.

On the other hand, if the block size is too large, the space wasted at the beginning of the first block and/or the end of the last block will become significant; thus the block size should be small enough to ensure that the typical sequence occupies at least ten blocks.

In the presence of so many conflicting considerations, it is not easy to select a standard block size for sequences of differing length and item size, and all forms of backing store, with different methods of access. However, an acceptable compromise can often be made, and on present-day computer designs, a block size of between 128 and 1024 words will often be a suitable choice. Probably in most cases the size chosen is not critical within a factor of two either way.

8.2.4. *Backing Store Representation*

In processing a sequence, a program normally requires access to one of its ends, and all the material in the middle and other end is unused for relatively long periods of time. If main storage is at all scarce, it is very profitable to transfer this material to backing store, so that the space it occupies in main store may be used for other purposes. In the case of input and output sequences, which have a lifetime greater than the program which reads or writes them, the use of backing store for long-term storage is almost obligatory.

When using backing store, efficiency of processing and representation demands that transfers should occur in blocks of reasonable size. The block which contains an active end of a sequence is always held in main store; and to permit overlap of input/output with computing, the previous block (on writing) or the next block (on reading) also remains allocated during the transfer operation. This is known as double-buffering. It is possible to hold even more buffers in store to smooth out variations in the speed of processing and the speed of transfer; but the program designer must not fall into the trap of supposing that this will help when there is a basic mismatch in the speeds of processing and transfer. In general, if double or triple buffering is inadequate, it is not worth while filling the store with any further extra buffers.

In a machine which is endowed with an automatic paging scheme, the problems of representing sequences are very much reduced. As far as the programmer is concerned, he need only allocate the amount of storage required for the longest possible sequence, using the contiguous representation. This should not actually cause any waste of storage, since the paging system should delay allocation of store until it is first used. As the sequence expands, new blocks of store will be allocated, but the addressing of these blocks will appear contiguous to the programmer, so there is no problem of leaving unused space at the end of blocks which are not large enough to hold the next item. Shortly after a block has been filled, it will automatically migrate to backing store; and it will be brought back again automatically as soon as it is required. On input sequences, a block which has been scanned will also be removed shortly afterwards from main store; but this will not involve an unnecessary backing store transfer if the material has not been changed since the last input took place. The only operation which a paging system will not perform automatically is to read a block of an input sequence into store ahead of its actual requirement.

9. RECURSIVE DATA STRUCTURES

There are certain close analogies between the methods used for structuring data and the methods for structuring a program which processes that data. Thus, a Cartesian product corresponds to a compound statement, which assigns values to its components. Similarly, a discriminated union corresponds to a conditional or case construction, selecting an appropriate processing method for each alternative. Arrays and powersets correspond to **for** statements sequencing through their elements, with an essentially bounded number of iterations.

The sequence structure is the first that permits construction of types of infinite cardinality, with values of unbounded length; and it corresponds to the unbounded form of looping, with a **while** condition to control termination. The reason why the sequence is unbounded is that one of its components (i.e. the initial segment) from which it is built up belongs to the same type as itself, in the same way as the statement which remains to be obeyed after any iteration of a **while** loop is the same statement as before.

The question naturally arises whether the analogy can be extended to a data structure corresponding to recursive procedures. A value of such a type would be permitted to contain more than one component that belongs to the same data type as itself; in the same way that a recursive procedure can call itself recursively from more than one place in its own body. As in the case of recursive procedures such a structure can conveniently be defined by writing the name of the type being defined actually inside its own definition; or in the case of mutually recursive definition, in the definition of some preceding type.

The most obvious examples of recursive data structures are to be found in the description of arithmetic or logical expressions, programming languages, where the recursion reflects the possibility of nesting one expression inside another. For example, an arithmetic expression might be defined as follows:

"An expression is a series of terms, each of which consists of a sign (+ or −) followed by a sequence of factors. Each factor except the first consists of a sign (× or /) followed by a primary. A primary is either a constant, a variable, or an expression surrounded by brackets. An initial plus sign in an expression may be omitted."

A structured data type whose values comprise such expressions may be defined using only techniques already familiar, plus recursion:

> **type** expression = **sequence** term;
>
> **type** term = (addop: operator; f: **sequence** factor);
>
> **type** factor = (mulop: operator; p: primary);
>
> **type** primary = (const: (val: real),
>
>   var: (id: identifier),
>
>   bracketed: (e: expression));
>
> **type** operator = (plus, minus, times, div);

This definition expresses the abstract structure of an arithmetic expression, but not the details of its concrete representation as a string of characters. For example, it does not specify the symbols used for brackets or operators, nor does it state whether an infix, prefix or postfix notation is used for them. It does not state how the three kinds of primary are to be distinguished. It does not even represent the optional omission of plus on the first term of an expression, and the necessary omission of × on the first factor of a term. Apart from this degree of abstraction and representation-independence, this type definition would correspond to a set of BNF syntax equations:

> ⟨expression⟩:: = ⟨term⟩ | ⟨addop⟩⟨term⟩ |
>
>   ⟨expression⟩⟨addop⟩⟨term⟩
>
> ⟨term⟩:: = ⟨primary⟩ | ⟨term⟩⟨mulop⟩⟨primary⟩
>
> ⟨primary⟩:: = ⟨unsigned real number⟩ | ⟨variable⟩ |
>
>   (⟨expression⟩)

Note how we have used sequences to replace the recursion wherever possible. In fact this can be done whenever a type name occurs recursively only once at the beginning or at the end of its definition. For example:

type expression = **sequence** term;

might have been formulated recursively:

type expression =

(empty:( ), non-empty:(first:term; final:expression)).

A similar alternative formulation permits **while** loops to be expressed as recursive procedures.

The construction of values of a recursively defined type requires no new operators or transfer functions; all that is needed is recursive use of the methods defined for the other relevant structuring methods. For example, the expression

$$3/(b - 2)$$

could be specified by the cumbersome construction:

[term (plus,   [factor (times, primary (const (3))),

        factor (div, primary (bracketed (

           [term (plus, [factor (times, primary (var ("b")))]),

             term (minus, [factor (times, primary (const (2)))])])])))

      ])

].

An effective method of getting the computer itself to translate expressions into abstract structures will be given as an example in (9.2).

Another familiar example of recursively defined data is the family tree. A family tree (excluding information about marriage) can be defined by associating with each person the family trees of all his/her offspring. We assume that certain additional personal details are required to be held:

type family = (head:person; offspring:**sequence** family);

A person with no children is an ultimate component of the family tree, and may be represented:

family (Tom, [ ])

A family with three children may be represented:

family (Jill, [family (Tom, [ ]),

        family (Joanna, [ ]),

        family (Matthew, [ ])]).

The final example shows how the binary forking tree familiar to LISP programmers may be defined as a recursive data structure.

type list = (atom:**sequence** character, cons:(car, cdr:list)).

A list which in LISP dot-notation would be expressed

((A.(B.NIL)).NIL)

can be expressed as a value of type list in almost exactly the same way as it is in LISP:

cons (cons (atom ("A"),

      cons (atom ("B"), atom ("NIL")))),

    atom ("NIL")

    );

where the type transfer to list type is left implicit.

As an example of the processing of a list, we write a function to reverse a complete tree, so that every "left fork" in it becomes a "right fork" and vice-versa.

function reverse (*l*:list):list;

    with *l* **do**

        {atom:reverse: = *l*,

        cons:reverse: = cons (reverse (cdr), reverse (car))}

9.1. REPRESENTATION

The standard representation of a recursive type is also very similar to that of a similarly structured non-recursive type, with the exception that each component specified as belonging to the recursive type itself is represented by a location containing a pointer to its value, rather than the value itself. This use of a pointer is motivated by the fact that the component value may be of arbitrary size; and it is not possible to allocate any fixed amount of storage to contain it. This is known as the "tree representation", and is similar to the tree representation of an array or sequence, except that the branches may grow to arbitrary and varying heights.

An alternative method of representation is the linear sequence or *bitstream*. In this representation it is possible to avoid the use of pointers, and place the values of recursive substructures contiguous with the rest of the information, just as they are in the familiar bracketed character representations of expressions. However instead of using brackets, we can reestablish the bracketing structure by context, and if necessary by scanning the tag of union values. This method is usually associated with packed representations of the other components, and a very significant reduction in storage may be achieved, at the expense of enforcing serial access to the components of the structure. In many circumstances, a bitstream representation is some ten times more compact than the tree representation.

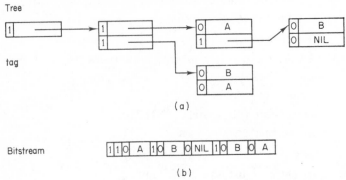

(a)

(b)

FIG. 8.   Representation of $((A \,.\, (B.NIL)) \,.\, (B \,.\, A))$

The choice between tree and linear representation is usually obvious. If the structure is being processed by the program, usually by means of recursive procedures, the needs of ready access to any component of the structure dictate a tree representation. In addition, some of the space lost may be regained by sharing common branches among several trees; such commonality of branches is a feature of the processing of symbolic expressions. However, if the structure has to be output and subsequently re-input, the linear structure is vastly preferable. Not only does the reduction in volume reduce transfer time, but the linearisation avoids a number of tricky problems of representing pointers in backing store. In many cases, a structure which passes through several phases of processing and input–output will be translated between the two representations at each phase; and this is standard practice in a multipass translator for a high-level programming language.

It is important to note that the sharing of the recursive sub-structure is nothing but a means of saving time and storage, and has no effect on the running of the program. This means that the sharing must be avoided whenever there is any danger that the shared sub-structure might be selectively updated as part of one of its owners. In principle, all values are entirely disjoint from all other values, and there is no way in which the programmer could either know or care how far his structures are shared. Furthermore, there is no way whatsoever in which a pointer can be made to point back to a structure of which it is a component; since this would mean that the structure was identical to one of its own components. Only an infinite structure can have this property; and infinite structures do not satisfy the axiom of exclusion on which the important principle of induction for recursive structures is based.

9.2. EXAMPLE

A source text for an expression in a programming language is presented as a sequence of symbols defined:

> **type** symbol = (constant:(value:real), variable:(identifier:ident),
>
> op:operator, leftbracket, rightbracket);

Write a program operating on an input variable

> source:**sequence** symbol,

which reads from its beginning the longest possible legitimate expression, delivers the corresponding abstract expression as a result, and exits to the label error if this is impossible. The structure of the result and the syntax of the source are as specified earlier in this chapter.

The structure of the program closely follows that of the desired result. There are three functions:

> compile expression
>
> compile term (sign)
>
> compile primary

each of which removes from the source the longest expression in its syntactic category, and delivers the corresponding abstract structure as a result. The main irregularity of the process is that the first term of an expression may be unsigned; this is why the sign is provided as a parameter for compile term, instead of being read from source by compile term itself. Each function has the side-effect of shortening the source sequence if successful, and jumping to error if not.

function compile expression:expression;

> **begin** sign:operator;
>
> > **if** source.first = plus ∨ source.first = minus **then** sign **from** source
> >
> > **else** sign: = plus;
> >
> > compile expression: = [compile term (sign)];
> >
> > **while** source.first = plus ∨ source.first = minus **do**
> >
> > > **begin** sign **from** source;
> > >
> > > compile expression: [compile term (sign)]
> > >
> > > **end**
>
> **end**;

function compile term (s:operator):term;

> **begin** p:primary; sign:operator; fs:**sequence** factor;

$p := $ compile primary;   ◐

$fs := $ [factor (times, p)];

while source.first $=$ times $\vee$ source.first $=$ div **do**

   begin sign **from** source;

      $p := $ compile primary;

      $\overset{\frown}{fs:}$ [factor (sign, p)]

   end;

   compile term$:= $ term (s, fs)

end;

function compile primary:primary;

   begin s:symbol;

      s **from** source;

      with s **do** {constant:compile primary$:= $ const (value),

               variable:compile primary$:= $ var (identifier),

               leftbracket:

               begin from source;

               compile primary$:= $ bracketed (compile expression);

               s **from** source;

               if $s \neq$ rightbracket **then go to** error

               end,

            else go to error}

   end;

Exercise

Write programs to convert an expression from tree representation to bitstream and back again.

10. Sparse Data Structures

In dealing with representations of arrays and powersets, we have hitherto assumed that the base type of a powerset and the domain type of an array is reasonably small, so that it is possible to allocate a bit or larger area of store to hold the value of every potential element of the structure. The examples also were confined to such cases. In this chapter we investigate the consequences and problems which arise when the base or domain types are very large or infinite, and when the standard representations are therefore impossible.

The representation and manipulation of powersets and mappings with infinite domains can be accomplished, provided that consideration is restricted to sets with only a finite number of members, and mappings in which only a finite number of elements take significant values; where "significant" is defined as different from some specified null or default value. The powerset of an infinite set is obviously also infinite; but since each value of the powerset type contains only a finite number of elements, each value can be specified simply by listing those elements in a finite period of time, and the list will occupy only a finite amount of storage. Similarly, each value of a mapping type with infinite domain can be finitely specified by listing all elements of the domain which map onto significant values of the range type, together with the value mapped in each case. A type which is restricted in this way is known as *sparse*.

In fact the concept of sparsity is not confined to infinite bases and domains; it may also be applied to very large but finite powersets, when the programmer knows that each actual set in which he is interested will contain only a very small proportion of the potential members. For example, the base type may contain hundreds of millions of values, but the programmer may know that he only has to deal with sets of less than a hundred in size, and perhaps most of them less than ten. It would be impossible to use the bitpattern representation, since this requires hundreds of millions of bits; but since each value actually used in a program contains only a few members, these members can readily be listed in a comparatively small amount of store. A powerset type of this sort is known as *sparse*. Similarly, arrays with a very large domain, nearly all of which map onto the same default value of the range, are said to belong to a *sparse array* type.

Sparse sets and arrays are frequently encountered in advanced data processing applications, and their representation and manipulation present a number of familiar problems. Our first example is the definition of a type whose values are sets of car numbers. The cardinality of the carnumber type is perhaps something like four thousand million; but the programmer wishes only to deal with sets of cars owned by a single person; most of these will have only one member, and very few will have more than ten. The carset type may therefore be declared as sparse powerset:

type carset = **sparse powerset** carnumber;

As an example of a sparse array, we may take the type of mappings between car owners and the set of cars they own. Each owner is represented by name and address; since these are of arbitrary length, the owner type may be defined:

type owner = **sequence** character;

and has infinite cardinality. The required type is therefore declared as sparse:

type carfile = **sparse array** owner **of** carset.

In a data processing application, a variable of carfile type would be known as a *random access* file, and the owner would be known as the *key* element of the file.

The next two examples are drawn from numerical applications. A vector is a mapping from integers onto floating point numbers. A sparse vector is one in which most of the elements are zero; consequently its initial value will be the zero constant function, and all elements will remain zero unless an explicit assignment is made of a different value:

type sparsevector = **sparse array** integer **of** real.

A sparse complex matrix may be defined in a similar way:

type irregular matrix = **sparse array** (row, column:integer)

of complex.

The next example is taken from the field of the translation of programming languages to machine code. During the process of translation, the translator needs to know certain information about each identifier declared in the program, such as machine address allocated to the variable, its length and type, etc. This information is assumed to belong to a type decode. The type of an array which associates a decode with each identifier is given the name dictionary and is declared:

type dictionary = **sparse array** ident **of** decode

Of course, the translator is interested in the decode only of those identifiers actually declared in the source program. For the vast majority of possible identifiers, the value given by any dictionary of this type will be that value of the decode type which indicates that the identifier was undeclared.

The final example is of a type that causes familiar problems in a commercial filing system and in real life—that of multidimensional cross-classification. The customers of a firm are split up into a number of geographical areas; they are also classified in a number of classes, in accordance with the kind of product they purchase. On occasions it is required to access all customers in an area, sequencing through all classes; on other occasions to access all customers in a class, sequencing through the areas; and finally, it is sometimes required to process all customers of a given class in a given area. The abstract structure required to deal with this situation is a two-dimensional sparse array of sparse sets:

sparse array (c:class; a:area) **of sparse powerset** customer.

A similar example may arise in the description of family relationship among persons:

type children = **sparse array** (mother, father: person) **of**

sparse powerset person:

This array caters for multiple marriages better than the more tree-like representations of a family, which can be defined as a recursive structure.

In the case of sparse arrays, it is sometimes useful to regard them as partial rather than total mappings. A partial mapping is one which does not necessarily give a value for each member of its domain type. In other words, the actual domain over which it is defined is a subset of the domain type. For such an array type it is necessary to introduce an additional constant omega, denoting a mapping which is everywhere undefined. It is also useful to introduce a function

domain (x)

which delivers as result the set of subscripts for elements of x which are actually defined. Thus the programmer can sequence through all the defined elements, or test whether a particular element is defined or not. Many of the examples quoted above might well have been declared as partial instead of sparse. In the case of a partial mapping, the default value does not have to be recorded.

10.1 REPRESENTATION

Sparse sets and arrays are usually represented by simply keeping a record of the default value and those members or elements which are significant; thus the representation borrows techniques which are used in the case of the sequence type to deal with structures of changeable size. A sparse set may be regarded as a special case of a sparse mapping, which maps all its members onto the Boolean value **true**, and all its non-members onto the default value **false**. Thus their representations are closely similar to those of sparse arrays, and do not require separate treatment.

A sparse mapping consists of a number of elements. Each element of the mapping is represented as the Cartesian product of its subscript and its value; in this case the subscript is known as the *key*, and the value is known as the *information* associated with the element, and the juxtaposition of the two will be known as an *entry*. In the case of a set which is sparse, there is no need to record any information, since the presence of the key itself is sufficient to indicate that this value is a member of the set. Thus an entry for a sparse set consists only of a key.

10.1.1. *Sequential Representation*

The simplest representation of a sparse array type is as a sequence of entries; i.e.

sparse array D **of** R

is represented as if it had been declared

(default: R; s:**sequence** (key: D; information: R)).

One of the possible sequence representations must now be chosen, in accordance with the same criteria that are used in the case of a sequence. But when a sequence is used to represent a sparse array, the order of the entries is immaterial, and does not have to reflect the relative times at which the entries were made. Thus the entries are often sorted into order of their key-value, particularly if this is the order in which they are going to be scanned.

The chief disadvantage of the sequential representation is the length of time taken to access the element corresponding to a random subscript. In the case of structures of any great size, the program designer usually goes to considerable trouble to ensure that entries are accessed in the same standard order that they are stored in the sequence; and that if new entries are to be inserted, these are also sorted and then merged with the original sequence. Thus the standard commercial practice of batch processing and updating of sequential files may be regarded as a practical implementation of the abstract concept of a sparse array on the rather unsympathetic medium of magnetic tape.

10.1.2. *Tabular Representation*

If there is an acceptably low upper limit N to the number of entries in a sparse mapping, a great increase in speed of lookup can be achieved by the tabular representation, in which the sparse mapping

sparse array D **of** R

is represented as a nonsparse array:

(default: R; occupied: **powerset** $0..N$;

array $0..N$ **of** (key: D; information: R)).

If all the significant entries are collected before they are used, the table can be sorted, and then the entry with a given key can be rapidly located by logarithmic search.

If access to the elements of the array is interleaved with addition of new entries, some form of hash-table technique is indicated. For this an arbitrary "hashing" function is chosen, which maps the domain type D into an integer in the range $0..N$. When the entry is inserted, it is placed at this position in the table; so whenever that entry is accessed, use of the same hashing function will find it there. If that position is already occupied by an entry with a different key, some other vacant position in the table must be found. It is quite usual to search for such a vacant position in the next following locations of the table; but when the table is nearly full, this may cause undesirable bunching around an area of the table which happens to be popular. A solution to this problem is to choose $N + 1$ as a prime number, and to use a second hashing function to compute an arbitrary step length from any given key. The next position to try when any given position is full is obtained by adding the step length (modulo $N + 1$) to the previous position.

10.1.3. *Indexed Representation*

The tabular method of storage is suitable only when the whole table can be accommodated in the main store of the computer. In the common case when this is not possible, a mixture of the tabular and sequential methods is often used. In this a sparse array is represented as a table, each of whose entries is a sequence:

(default: R; table: **array** 1 .. N **of**

(max: D; seq: **sequence** (key: D; information: R))).

Every entry is placed on that sequence i such that its key fails between table $[i - 1]$. max (or D. min if $i = 1$) and table $[i]$. max. The table is sorted so that the appropriate sequence can be quickly located. This technique may be likened to the organisation of a multivolume encyclopaedia, in which the keys of the first and last entries of each volume are indicated on the spine, so that the right volume can be quickly identified, without extracting the volumes from the shelf.

When using this representation, it is desirable to ensure that all sequences are of roughly the same length. Indeed, if disc backing store is used, it is very advantageous to ensure that each of them is fitted onto a single cylinder, so that a random access will not involve more than a single head movement. Thus, when one sequence gets too long, it must exchange material with the adjacent sequence. This involves extracting the entries with the largest and/or smallest keys, and is best done when all the sequences are sorted into order of key-value. The sorting and reshuffling is often carried out as a separate operation at regular intervals; and the general method of file organisation is known as "indexed sequential".

Naturally in this method of representation, it is an advantage to keep the sequences as short as possible, say less than a single track on disk. Consequently, the table itself may get so large that it will no longer fit in main store. In this case the table itself is split up into sections, and a second-level table may be set up to point to its sections, using the same principle again. Thus at least two accesses to backing store will in general be required for each access to an element of the array, and it is strongly recommended to ensure that the sizes and location of the sequences and sections be chosen to correspond closely with the access characteristics of the storage medium.

10.1.4. *Locally Dense Representation*

A special case of a sparse array encountered in numerical computer applications is the sparse matrix. Quite frequently a sparse matrix can be split into submatrices, only a few of which contain significant non-zero entries. In this case, the matrix may be said to be locally dense, and should be represented and processed in a manner which takes advantage of this fact.

One method of achieving this is to store with each significant submatrix its position and size, and to represent the whole matrix as a table or sequence of such submatrices, where each submatrix is stored contiguously in the usual way, using multiplicative address calculation. However, the submatrices will in general be of different sizes, and if the size varies during the processing of the matrix, the problems will be quite severe. A possible way of dealing with sparse matrices is to split them into submatrices of standard size, say sixteen by sixteen, and set up a table of pointers to each of these submatrices. A submatrix that is wholly zero is represented by a null pointer and occupies no additional storage; otherwise, the submatrix is stored in the usual way, using the following method of address calculation.

Each access to the array involves first "interleaving" the bit values of the two subscripts, so that the least significant part of the result contains the least significant part of both subscripts. The more significant part of the result is then used to consult the table of addresses, to locate the desired submatrix, and the less significant part to find the position of the required element within the submatrix. This technique of interleaving subscripts may on some machines be more efficient than general multiplication. If some of the submatrices have to be held on backing store, this method of address calculation is particularly recommended, since it is equally efficient at processing the matrix by rows as by columns; and the method can then be recommended for all large arrays, whether sparse or not, particularly on a paged computer. The inventor of this method is Professor E. W. Dijkstra.

10.1.5. *Grid Representation*

The phenomenon of cross-classification of files causes as many problems in a computer as it does in real life. It is usually solved by standardising on one of the classifications which is most convenient, and accepting the extra cost of processing in accordance with the other classification, even if this involves resorting the file. Thus the sparse mapping

  sparse array $(i : D_1 ; j : D_2)$ **of** R
is represented as:
  sparse array D_1 **of** (**sparse array** D_2 **of** R)

However, it is also possible to deal with the two dimensions in a more symmetric fashion, using a method based on the chained representation of sequences. In this representation, each actually used value of D_1 is placed in one chain, and each actually used value of D_2 is placed in another. These are called *border chains*. Each element of either border chain contains a base location pointing to a chained sequence of all elements with key values which fall into the class. Now each actual entry of the array has *two* addresses attached; one points to the next item of the sequence which has the same classification according to D_1, and the other to the next item which has the same classification according to D_2. Thus each item may be pictured as residing on an intersection of the lines of a two-dimensional grid, with pointers leading across and downwards to the next item on the same row or the same column.

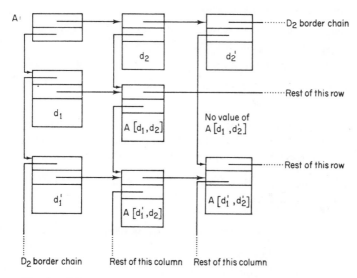

FIG. 9.   Grid Representation of A : **sparse array** $(d_1;D_1;d_2:D_2)$ **of** T

This grid representation is unfortunately suitable only when the entire structure will fit into main store. If the main part of the sequences have to be held on backing store, some sort of blocking of adjacent elements would be desirable in the interests of efficiency.

11. EXAMPLE: EXAMINATION TIMETABLES

In an educational establishment which offers students a wide choice of course combinations, there arises the problem of designing an examination time-table in which each examination is conducted in a single session, and yet each student can attend the examination for each course that he has taken. This can always be arranged by allocating a separate session for each examination; but the interests of examiner and student alike dictate that the total examination period be as short as possible. This means that each session should contain as many examinations as possible, subject to some limit k. An additional constraint is imposed by the size of the examination hall, which can only accommodate a certain maximum number of students.

Before designing the program, it is desirable to confirm our understanding of the problem by making a more rigorous formalisation in terms of the structure of the various items of data, both given and required. The types "student" and "exam" are obviously unstructured and need no further definition at this stage. The load of exams to be taken by each student is given by a mapping:

> load: **array** student **of powerset** exam.

A timetable is a set of sessions, where each session consists of a set of exams:

> **type** session = **powerset** exam;
>
> timetable: **powerset** session.

We next attempt to formalise the properties which the input and output data are required to possess.

(1) We choose not to formalise the condition that the number of sessions be minimised, since in fact we do not want an absolute minimum if this turns out to be too expensive to compute.

(2) Each exam is scheduled for one of the sessions

$$\bigcup_{s \text{ in timetable}} s = \text{exam.all}$$

(3) No exam is scheduled for more than one session:

$$(s1 \wedge s2 = \{ \}) \text{ or } (s1 = s2)$$

Conditions (2) and (3) effectively state that the timetable is a partitioning of the set of all exams into exhaustive and exclusive subsets.

(4) No session includes more than k exams

> s **in** timetable $\supset$ size $(s) \leqslant k$

(5) No session involves more than hallsize students. To formalise this, we need to count the number of students taking each exam:

> examcount $(e : \text{exam}) = \text{size } \{st : \text{student} \mid e \text{ in load } (st)\}$.

Now the number of students involved in a session is

$$\text{session count } (s : \text{session}) = \sum_{e \text{ in } s} \text{examcount } (e)$$

The condition may be formalised:

s **in** timetable $\supset$ sessioncount $(s) \leqslant$ hallsize.

(6) No student takes more than one exam in a session. To formalise this we introduce the concept of incompatibility of exams: two exams are incompatible if some student is taking both of them. For each exam $e1$ there is a set incompat $(e1)$ of exams which are incompatible with it:

$$\text{incompat}\,(e1) = \{e2:\text{exam} \mid e2 \neq e1 \,\&\, \exists\, st:\text{student}\,(e1 \text{ in load }(st)$$
$$\&\ e2 \text{ in load }(st))\}$$

Now we can define that every pair of exams in a session must be compatible:

s **in** timetable $\&\ e1, e2$ **in** $s \supset \neg e1$ **in** incompat $(e2)$.

These six conditions, defined in terms of load, hallsize, and k, must be possessed by any successful timetable in the real world, and by any successful computer representation of the timetable. They serve to define the objectives and criterion of correctness of our timetabling program.

11.1 THE ABSTRACT PROGRAM

Inspection of the conditions reveals that construction of the timetable does not require full knowledge of the load of each student. All that is needed is the examcount of each exam, and for each exam the set of other exams which are incompatible with it:

examcount:**array** exam **of** integer;

incompat:**array** exam **of powerset** exam.

These two arrays embody an abstraction from the real life data, which concentrate attention on exactly those features which are for the present purpose relevant, and permitting us to ignore for the time being the other features of the situation. It is plain that these two arrays can be readily constructed from a single scan of the student load data:

examcount: $=$ all (0);

incompat: $=$ all $(\ \{\ \}\ )$;

for st:student **do**

  for e **in** load (st) **do**

    begin examcount (e): $+1$;

      incompat (e): $\vee$ (load $(st) - \{e\}$)

  end;

One of the simplifying factors in the search for a solution to the given problem is that the conditions fall readily into two classes: (1) (2) and (3) relate to the timetable as a whole, whereas (4) (5) and (6) relate only to individual sessions, and do not mention the timetable at all. This suggests that the program can be structured as an inner part which selects a suitable session satisfying (4) (5) and (6), and an outer loop which constructs the timetable out of such suitable sessions.

The objective of the outer loop is to achieve satisfaction of conditions (2) and (3) on its completion. We therefore choose one of these conditions as a terminating condition of the loop, and design the body of the loop in such a way that is preserves the truth of the other condition (that is, the invariant of the loop); furthermore we ensure that the invariant is true before starting the loop.

The obvious choice of invariant is exclusiveness (condition (3)), leaving exhaustiveness as the terminating condition towards which each execution of the body of the loop will progress. The empty timetable obviously satisfies the invariant. This leads to an algorithm of the following structure:

> timetable: = { };
>
> **while** timetable does not satisfy (2) **do**
>
> **begin** select a session satisfying (4), (5), (6);
>
> 　　　　add the session to the timetable
>
> **end**;
>
> print timetable.

In order for the addition of a new session to preserve the truth of the invariant, it is necessary that the exams of the session shall be selected from exams which do not yet appear in the timetable. We therefore introduce a new variable to hold these remaining exams:

> remaining: **powerset** exam;

which is defined by the invariant relation:

$$\text{remaining} = \text{exam.all} - \bigcup_{s \text{ in timetable}} s.$$

The structure of the program as a whole now takes the form:

> timetable: = { };
>
> remaining: = exam.all;
>
> **while** remaining ≠ { } **do**
>
> 　　**begin** s: = suitable;
>
> 　　　　　timetable: ∨ {s};
>
> 　　　　　remaining: − s
>
> 　　**end**;
>
> 　print timetable.

The problem now remains of selecting a suitable session at each stage. In principle, there is no reason to suppose that the "best" choice at each stage will lead to a "best" or even a "good" timetable in the end. However, it would seem that in general it will pay to select a combination of remaining exams that most nearly fills the hall, or most nearly approaches the limit k. This will probably mean that the majority of students and exams will be catered for in a reasonably compact set of sessions, even though there may in the end be a fairly long "tail" of small sessions, involving a minority of students. Although this will not minimise the number of sessions, it may be reasonably satisfactory to most students and most examiners.

The alternative to accepting an apparent best choice on each occasion is to attempt some more global optimisation, which will either involve astronomical numbers of trials, or some sophisticated considerations which are unlikely to become apparent until after practical experience of a simpler algorithm. So there is nothing else that can be done at this stage except hope for the best.

It remains to program the function:

function suitable: session,

which selects a suitable session from the remaining set cf exams. A possible method of doing this is to generate a number of trial session satisfying (4) (5) and (6), and to select the best one found. The best one will probably be the one with the largest sessioncount, but since we may wish to adjust the criterion of selection, it is advisable to define it as a separate subroutine, updating a variable

bestsofar: session;

in accordance with the current value of a variable:

trial: session;

procedure record

        if sessioncount (bestsofar) $<$ sessioncount (trial) **then**

                bestsofar: $=$ trial.

The result of suitable is going to be the final value of bestsofar:

suitable: $=$ bestsofar.

It still remains to write a procedure that will generate and record a sequence of trial sessions which satisfy (4) (5) and (6). Inspection of these conditions shows that if a trial *fails* to satisfy one of them, no larger trial will satisfy it. In other words, having found an *im*possible trial, there is no need to generate any further trials which contain it. This suggests that we organise the generation process to generate all supersets of each trial that has been found already to be possible, but excluding any exams which have already been tried. We therefore introduce a variable:

untried : **powerset** exam,

and a procedure

procedure gensupersets,

which generates and records all possible supersets of trial by adding one or more exams from untried to it. This procedure will be called from within "suitable".

function suitable : session;

> **begin** trial, bestsofar : session; e : exam; untried : **powerset** exam ;
>
> > e **from** remaining;
> >
> > trial : = bestsofar : = $\{e\}$;
> >
> > untried : = remaining − trial − incompat (e);
> >
> > gensupersets;
> >
> > suitable : = bestsofar
>
> **end**;

Note that the first value of the trial is the unitset of some exam chosen from the remainder according to some as yet undefined criterion. The justification for this is that the chosen exam must eventually feature in some session of the timetable, and it might as well be this one. If this prior choice were not made, gensupersets would keep on generating the same supersets on every cycle of the major loop of the timetabling program.

As another significant optimisation, we have removed from untried any exams which are incompatible with the exams in the trial, since there is no need to even consider the addition of any of these exams to the trial.

The generation of supersets of a given trial may proceed by selecting each exam from untried, and adding it to trial. If the result is still valid, it should be recorded, and the new value of trial is then a suitable session to act as a basis for further superset generation. This suggests a recursive program structure. Of course, the exam added to trials should also be subtracted from untried, to avoid unnecessary repetitions; and it is very advantageous to remove from untried any exams which are incompatible with the exam just added to the trial, so that these do not have to be considered again in future. Also, the values of trial and untried must be left unchanged by each call, so any change made to them must be recorded and restored in variables save 1 and save 2.

procedure gensupersets;

begin e:exam; save 1, save 2:**powerset** exam;

    record; save 1: = untried;

    if size (trial) < k **then**

    while untried $\neq$ { } **do**

        begin e **from** untried;

            save 2: = untried $\wedge$ incompat (e);

            untried: − save 2;

            trial: $\vee$ {e};

            if sessioncount (trial) < hallsize **then**

                    gensupersets;

            untried: $\vee$ save 2;

            trial: − {e}

    end;

        untried: = save 1

end gensupersets.

The validity of this program depends on the fact that trial invariantly satisfies all conditions (4) (5) and (6) for sessions of the timetable, as well as always being a subset of remaining.

The reasoning is as follows:

for (4): gensupersets never generates a superset except when the size of the trial is strictly less than k.

for (5): gensupersets is never entered when the sessioncount of trial is greater than the hall size (we assume that no examcount is greater than hallsize).

for (6): removal of incompatible sets from untried ensures that at all times all exams remaining in untried are compatible with all exams of trial. Therefore, transfer of an arbitrary exam from untried to trial can never cause (6) to be violated.

Finally, at the initial call of gensupersets, untried $\subset$ remaining. Untried is an essentially non-increasing quantity: every addition of members to it has always been preceded by removal of those very same members. Untried is therefore always a subset of remaining; and trial, which is constructed only from members of untried, must also always be a subset of remaining.

This completes our first version of an abstract program to construct examination timetables. Collecting all the material together, it looks like this:

hallsize, k:integer, initially given;

load:**array** student **of powerset** exam, initially given;

type session = **powerset** exam;

timetable:**powerset** session, initially { };

examcount:**array** exam **of** integer, initially all (0);

incompat:**array** exam **of powerset** exam, initially constant ({ });

function sessioncount (s:session):integer;

    begin sum: integer, initially 0;

        for e **in** s **do** sum: + examcount (e);

        sessioncount: = sum

    end;

remaining:**powerset** exam, initially exam.all;

function suitable:session;

  begin bestsofar, trial:session; untried:**powerset** exam;

    e:exam; e **from** remaining; bestsofar: = {e};

    trial: = {e}; untried: = remaining − trial − incompat (e);

    gensupersets;

    suitable: = bestsofar

  end;

The following two procedures are local to suitable:

  procedure record;

    if sessioncount (bestsofar) < sessioncount (trial) **then**

                           bestsofar: =trial;

  procedure gensupersets;

    begin e:exam; save 1, save 2:**powerset** exam;

    record; save 1: = untried;

    if size (trial) < k **then**

      while untried ≠ { } **do**

      begin e **from** untried;

        save 2: = untried ∧ incompat (e);

        untried:— save 2;

        trial: ∨ {e};

        if sessioncount (trial) < hallsize **then**

            gensupersets;

```
            untried: ∨ save 2;
            trial: − {e}
  end;
            untried: = save 1
  end gensupersets;
```

The main program is as follows:

```
      for st: student do
        for e in load (st) do
          begin examcount (e): + 1; incompat (e): ∨ (load (st) − {e}) end;
            while remaining ≠ { } do
              begin s: session;
                  s: = suitable;
                  timetable: ∨ {s};
                  remaining: − s
              end;
        print timetable
```

Before spending any more effort on developing this program, it would be advisable to subject it to a critical examination, to ensure that it will be successful. Now the most obvious reasons why the program might fail are:

(1) The size of the timetable turns out to be unacceptably large; we have agreed that nothing can be done about this, until we know more about the data.

(2) The amount of time taken to generate all trials at each step is excessive. This will be particularly serious when the remainder is still large at the beginning of the program, and if the untried set remains large on every recursion of gensupersets. The main way in which the untried set is reduced is by removing all exams incompatible with the trial. This suggests that we should always prefer to add first to the trial those exams which have the largest incompatible sets, so that untried is reduced as quickly as possible. Among sets equal according to this criterion, the exam with the largest examcount would be selected first. The exact weighting between these criteria may have to be adjusted later in the light of experience; meanwhile, the simplest implementation of this policy is to presort the exams in accordance with the criterion, and implement e **from** untried by selecting the first member.

If it turns out that this elementary strategy is insufficient we may have to artificially curtail the number of iterations of the loop in gensupersets. But we would probably need some practical experience in order to select a suitable strategy; and for the time being, let us hope it will not be necessary.

11.2. DATA REPRESENTATION

In order to design a successful data representation, it is necessary to know something of the likely size of the problem. In this example, we will make the following assumptions:

(1) There are not more than 500 exams, each taken by less than 1000 students (typically 50).

(2) There are about 5000 students.

(3) Each student takes less than ten exams, and typically five.

(4) The examination hall will take about 1000 students.

(5) An acceptable limit on the number of concurrent exams is 30, and the typical number is 10.

(6) Manual timetabling methods have succeeded in constructing timetables with not more than 50 sessions.

We will consider the individual items of data.

(1) **type** *exam*

The obvious representation is as an integer subrange: $0..500$.

(2) **type** *session*

There is obviously a choice between a bitpattern representation (500 bits), and an array of 30 nine-bit elements (+pointer) (270 bits + one word). The number of sessions to be stored is not great, so considerations of storage economy are not significant. The main operations on a session are the insertion of an exam which is known not to be in it already, and the removal of an exam, which is the most recently inserted. Thus the array method would be the best, since the insertion and removal of members can be accomplished by stack methods.

Since we frequently wish to know the session-count, it would pay to record this together with the session, and keep it up to date as members are inserted and removed.

This representation is used for trial and bestsofar.

(3) *timetable*

The only operation on the timetable is the insertion of new sessions. Since sessions are of variable length, the timetable could be organised as a sequence of variable-length sequences. Since each exam occurs exactly once in the timetable, the maximum size of the timetable is $500 \times$ nine bits, plus perhaps sixty words to indicate the separation of the sessions (if there are more than sixty sessions, the program will have failed anyway).

An alternative and much simpler representation is simply to record for each exam which session it occurs in. This requires only

array exam **of** 1..60

This representation is made possible only by the fact that the sessions of the timetable are mutually exclusive.

(4) *examcount*: **array** *exam* **of** *integer*

·A standard representation is the obvious choice.

(5) *remaining, untried, save* 1, *save* 2

These variables start rather full, and get emptier as the program progresses. Their average density is therefore about fifty percent, and there is no point in adopting a sparse representation. Furthermore, the frequency of standard set operations applied to them indicate a standard bitpattern representation.

(6) *incompat*

The most frequent use of elements of incompat is to subtract them from untried. They should therefore also use the bitpattern representation. This will require 500×500 bits, of the order of 10000 words. This is by far the largest data structure required, but its total size is probably fully justified by the extra speed which it imparts to the program, and since it is acceptable on most computers on which this program will run, it does not seem worth while to seek a more compact representation.

(7) *load*

The load of each student is the primary input data for the problem; it may also be extremely voluminous. It is therefore doubly fortunate that the program only needs to make a single scan of the data; for not only will this enable the data to be presented as an external sequence; it also means that the representation can be designed to be suitable for human reading, writing, and punching.

We therefore allocate one card for each student, and use ten columns of six characters each to hold the examination numbers. To save unnecessary punching, the first blank column will signify the end of the examination set. For identification purposes, each card should also contain the student number; fortunately this can be wholly ignored by the program, though it should probably be checked to avoid duplications or omissions.

Exercise
Code the abstract program described above using the recommended data representations.

12. AXIOMATISATION

The preceding sections have introduced a number of methods of constructing data spaces (types), and have explained some useful operations defined over these spaces. But the description has been essentially intuitive and informal, and the question arises whether all the relevant information about the data spaces has been communicated, or whether there remains some possibility of misunderstanding of the details.

In order to remove such misunderstanding, or check that it has not occurred, it is desirable to give a rigorous mathematical specification of each data space, and the operators defined over it; and we follow what is now a customary mathematical practice of defining rigorously the subject matter of our reasoning, not by traditional definitions, but by sets of axioms.

In view of the role which axioms play in the theory of data structuring, it may be helpful to summarise their intended properties.

(1) Axioms are a formal statement of those properties which are shared by the real world and by its representation inside a computer, in virtue of which manipulation of the representation by a computer program will yield results which can be successfully applied back to the real world.

(2) They establish a conceptual framework covering those aspects of the real world which are believed to be relevant to the programmer's task, and thereby assist in his constructive and inventive thinking.

(3) They state rigorously those assumptions about the real world on which the computer program will be based.

(4) They state the necessary properties which must be possessed by any computer representation of the data, in a manner free from detail which is in initial stages irrelevant.

(5) They offer a carefully circumscribed freedom to the programmer or high-level language implementor to choose a representation most suitable for his application and hardware available.

(6) They form the basis of any proof of correctness of a program.

The axioms given here are not intended to be used directly in the proof of non-trivial programs, since such proofs would be excessively long-winded. Rather they may be used to establish the familiar properties of the data spaces they describe, and these properties can then be used informally in proofs. Eventually it may be possible to get computers to check such proofs; but this will require the development of much more powerful formal languages for expressing proofs than are at present provided by logicians, and the use of powerful decision procedures for large subclasses of theorems, to assist in verification of the individual steps of a proof.

The axioms applicable to a given type depend on how that type has been defined. Thus it is not possible to give in each case a fixed set of axioms like those for integers; instead we give a pattern or schema which shows how a particular axiom set may be derived from the general form of the corresponding type definition.

12.1. ENUMERATIONS AND SUBRANGES

The following axioms are common to both enumerations and subranges. They are modelled on the familiar axioms for natural numbers. The type name is assumed to be T, and all variables are assumed to be of this type.

(1) T.min is a T

(2) If x is a T, and $x \neq T$.max

then succ (x) is a T

(3) The only elements of T are as specified in (1) and (2)

(4) succ $(x) =$ succ $(y) \supset x = y$

(5) succ $(x) \neq T$.min

(6) pred $($succ $(x)) = x$

The following three axioms apply only to ordered types

(7) T.min $\leqslant x$

(8) $x \leqslant T$.min $\supset x = T$.min

(9) succ $(x) \leqslant$ succ $(y) \equiv x \leqslant y$

Note: succ $(T$.max) and pred $(T$.min) are not defined.

The general form of definition of a type by enumeration is

type $T = (k_1, k_2, \ldots, k_n)$;

where T is the type name

and $k_1, k_2, \ldots, k_n$ are names of all values of the type.

The additional axiom for this type is:

(10) $k_1 = T$.min

  & $k_2 =$ succ (k_1)

  & $k_3 =$ succ (k_2)

    $\ldots$

  & $k_n =$ succ $(k_{n-1}) = T$.max.

The general form of a definition of a type as a subrange is

type $T = k..l$;

where k and l are of the base type T_0.

The additional axioms for this type are:

(10) $T.\min = k$

   & $T.\max = l$.

(11) $T(T_0(x)) = x$.

(12) $k \leqslant x_0 \ \& \ x_0 \leqslant l \supset T_0(T(x_0)) = x_0$.

(13) $x \leqslant y \equiv T_0(x) \leqslant T_0(y)$.

Using axioms (1) to (9) it is possible to prove the following properties of ordering:

(T1) $x \leqslant x$.

(T2) $x \leqslant \text{succ} \ (y) \supset x = \text{succ} \ (y) \vee x \leqslant y$.

(T3) $z \leqslant y \ \& \ y \leqslant x \supset z \leqslant x$.

(T4) $x \leqslant y \ \& \ y \leqslant x \supset x = y$.

Hint: Use induction on x. Proof of T3 requires T2.

Abbreviations:

If $\ominus$ is a monadic operator and $\oplus$ is a dyadic operator, both taking operands from the base type T_0, then the following abbreviations permit omission of the transfer function, if a is of type T_0 and x, y are of type T:

(14) $\ominus x$ stands for $\ominus T_0(x)$.

(15) $x \oplus y$,,   ,, $T_0(x) \oplus T_0(y)$.

(16) $x \oplus a$,,   ,, $T_0(x) \oplus a$.

(17) $a \oplus x$,,   ,, $a \oplus T_0(x)$.

(18) $a := x$,,   ,, $a := T_0(x)$.

12.2. CARTESIAN PRODUCTS

The general form of the definition of a type as a Cartesian product is

      type $T = (s_1 : T_1; s_2 : T_2; \ldots; s_n : T_n)$;

where $s_1, s_2, \ldots, s_n$ are the selectors of the components, and $T_1, T_2, \ldots, T_n$ are the types of the corresponding components.

(1) If x_1 is a T_1 and x_2 is a T_2 and ... and x_n is a T_n

        then $T(x_1, x_2, \ldots, x_n)$ is a T.

(2) The only elements of T are as specified in (1).

(3) If $x = T(x_1, x_2, \ldots, x_n)$ then

      $x.s_1 = x_1 \ \& \ x.s_2 = x_2 \ \& \ldots \& \ x.s_n = x_n$.

Abbreviations:

(4) $x.s_1 := x_1$ stands for $x := T(x_1, x.s_2, \ldots, x.s_n)$

$\qquad x.s_2 := x_2$,, ,, $x := T(x.s_1, x_2, \ldots, x.s_n)$

$\qquad \ldots\ldots$

$\qquad x.s_n := x_n$,, ,, $x := T(x.s_1, x.s_2, \ldots, x_n)$.

(5) If x is a T then

with x **do** S or **with** x **take** S stands for

$$S^{s_1, s_2, \ldots, s_n}_{x.s_1, x.s_2, \ldots, x.s_n}$$

which means that each of the subscripts of S replaces all free occurrences of the corresponding superscript in S.

(6) $(x_1, x_2, \ldots, x_n)$ stands for $T(x_1, x_2, \ldots, x_n)$ in those contexts where an expression of type T is expected.

The following axiom applies if the Cartesian product type is to be regarded as ordered:

(7) $x \leqslant y \equiv \quad x.s_1 < y.s_1$

$\qquad \lor\ x.s_1 = y.s_1 \ \& \ (x.s_2 < y.s_2$

$\qquad \lor\ x.s_2 = y.s_2 \ \& \ (x.s_3 < y.s_3$

$\qquad \lor \qquad \ldots \qquad \& \ (x.s_{n-1} < y.s_{n-1}$

$\qquad \lor\ x.s_{n-1} = y.s_{n-1} \ \& \ x.s_n \leqslant y.s_n) \ldots)).$

12.3. DISCRIMINATED UNIONS

The general form of the definition is:

$\qquad$ **type** $T = (s_1 : T_1; s_2 : T_2; \ldots; s_n : T_n; k_1 : T'_1, k_2 : T'_2, \ldots, k_m : T'_m)$

(1) if x_1 is a T_1, x_2 is a T_2, $\ldots$, x_n is a T_n

$\qquad$ and x'_1 is a T'_1, x_2 is a T'_2, $\ldots$, x'_m is a T'_m

$\qquad$ then the following are distinct elements of T

$\qquad T(x_1, x_2, \ldots, x_n, k_1(x'_1))$

$\qquad T(x_1, x_2, \ldots, x_n, k_2(x'_2))$

$\qquad \ldots\ldots$

$\qquad T(x_1, x_2, \ldots, x_n, k_n(x'_n))$

(2) The only elements of T are as specified in (1).

(3) If $x = T(x_1, x_2, \ldots, x_n, k_i(x'_i))$ for each i between 1 and m

$\qquad x.s_1 = x_1 \, \& \, x.s_2 = x_2 \, \& \, \ldots \, \& \, x.s_n = x_n$

$\qquad \& \, x.k_i = x'_i$

Note: $x.k_l$ is undefined for $l \neq i$.

Abbreviations:

(4) Under the same condition as (3)

$\qquad$ **with** x **do** $\{k_1:S_1, k_2:S_2, \ldots, k_n:S_n\}$ means

$\qquad$ **with** x'_i **do** $(S_i)_{x_1,x_2,\ldots,x_n}^{s_1,s_2,\ldots,s_n}$;

$\qquad$ and similarly with **take** instead of **do.**

(5) If $n = 0$, $k_i(x'_i)$ stands for $T(k_i(x'_i))$.

12.4. ARRAYS

The general form of an array definition is:

$\qquad$ **type** $T = $ **array** D **of** R

(1) If r is an R then $T(r)$ is a T

(2) If x is a T, d is a D, and r is an R

$\qquad\qquad\qquad$ then $T(x, d:r)$ is a T

(3) The only elements of T are as specified in (1) and (2).

(4) $T(T(x, d:r), d':r') =$

$\qquad$ **if** $d = d'$ **then** $T(x, d':r')$

$\qquad\qquad\qquad$ **else** $T(T(x, d':r'), d:r)$.

(5) $T(r)[d] = r$.

(6) $T(x, d:r)[d'] = $ **if** $d' = d$ **then** r **else** $x \, [d']$.

(7) (**for** $i:D$ **take** $E(i))[j] = E(j)$.

Abbreviations:

(8) $x[d] := r$ means $x := T(x, d:r)$.

(9) $T(x, d_1:r_1, d_2:r_2, \ldots, d_n:v_n)$ stands for
$\qquad T(T(\ldots T(T(x), d_1:v_1), d_2:v_2)\ldots), d_n:r_n)$.

(10) in (9), the x may be omitted, if $d_1, d_2, \ldots, d_n$ exhaust the domain type. Similarly, the T may be omitted in suitable contexts.

If the array type is ordered, the following axiom applies:

(11) $x \leqslant y \equiv \forall \, d:D(y[d] < x[d] \supset \exists \, d':D(d' < d \, \& \, x[d'] < y[d']))$

Theorem:

$\qquad x = y \equiv \forall \, d:D(x[d] = y[d])$

12.5 POWERSETS

The axioms given below for sets apply only to *finite* sets of hierarchically ordered type. It is therefore possible to avoid the paradoxes which endanger axiomatisations of more powerful versions of set theory.

The general form of a powerset definition is:

   type T = **powerset** T_0,

where T_0 is the base type.

let a, b, be values of type T_0.

(1) $T(\ )$ is a T

(2) If x is a T and a is a T_0 then
   $x \vee T(a)$ is a T

(3) The only members of T are as specified in (1) and (2).

(4) $\neg a$ **in** $T(\ )$

(5) a **in** $(y \vee T(a))$

(6) $a \neq b \supset (a$ **in** $(x \vee T(b))) \equiv (a$ **in** $x)$

(7) $T(\ ) \subset x$

(8) $(y \vee T(a)) \subset x \equiv (y \subset x \,\&\, a$ **in** $x)$

(9) $x = y \equiv (x \subset y) \,\&\, (y \subset x)$

(10) $x \vee T(\ ) = x$

(11) $x \vee (y \vee T(a)) = (x \vee T(a)) \vee y$

(12) $x \wedge T(\ ) = T(\ )$

(13) $x \wedge T(a) = $ **if** a **in** x **then** $T(a)$ **else** $T(\ )$

(14) $x \wedge (y \vee T(a)) = (x \wedge y) \vee (x \wedge T(a))$

(15) $T(\ ) - x = T(\ )$

(16) $T(a) - x = $ **if** a **in** x **then** $T(\ )$ **else** $T(a)$

(17) $(x \vee T(a)) - y = (x - y) \vee (T(a) - y)$

(18) size $(T(\ )) = 0$

(19) size $(x \vee T(a)) = $ *if* a **in** x **then** size (x) **else** succ $($size $(x))$

The following apply if the domain type T_0 is ordered:

(20) min $(T(a)) = T(a)$

(21) $x \neq T(\ ) \supset$ min $(x \vee T(a)) = $ **if** $a < $ min (x) **then** a **else** min (x)

Note: min $(T(\ ))$ is not defined

(22) x **down** $0 = x$ **up** $0 = x$

(23) x **down** succ $(n) = (x$ **down** $n)$ **down** 1

(24) $T(\ )$ **down** $1 = T(\ )$

(25) $(x \vee T(a))$ **down** $1 = (x$ **down** $1 \vee$
$$\qquad\qquad \textbf{if } a \neq T_0.\min \textbf{ then } T(\text{pred }(a)) \textbf{ else } T(\ )$$

(26)–(28) **up** is similarly defined, with succ for pred and max for min.

(29) $b < a \supset \text{range }(a, b) = T(\ )$

(30) $a \leqslant b \supset \text{range }(a, b) = T(a)$

(31) $a < b \supset \text{range }(a, b) = \text{range }(a, \text{pred }(b)) \vee T(b)$

(32) j **in** $\{i{:}D \mid B(i)\} \equiv B(j)$

Abbreviations:

(33) $T(a_1, a_2, \ldots, a_n)$ stands for $T(a_1) \vee T(a_2) \vee \ldots \vee T(a_n)$

(34) $\{a_1, a_2, \ldots, a_n\}$ stands for $T(a_1, a_2, \ldots, a_n)$

(35) $x{:} \wedge y$ stands for $x{:} = x \wedge y$

(36) $x{:} \vee y$,,   ,, $x{:} = x \vee y$

(37) a **from** x stands for $a{:} = \text{one of }(x); x{:} - \{a\}$

(38) if $x = \{a_1, a_2, \ldots, a_n\}$ **then**

> **for** a **in** x **do** S stands for
>
> $$S^a_{a_1}; S^a_{a_2}; \ldots; S^a_{a_n}$$

where the a_i are in natural order if the base type is ordered, and are in arbitrary order otherwise; and they do not contain repetitions.

(39) $x{:} - y$ stands for $x{:} = x - y$

Theorems:

$$x = y \equiv \forall\, a{:}T_0(a \ in \ x \equiv a \ in \ y)$$
$$a \textbf{ in } (x \vee y) \equiv (a \textbf{ in } x \vee a \textbf{ in } y)$$
$$a \textbf{ in } (x \wedge y) \equiv (a \textbf{ in } x \ \& \ a \textbf{ in } y)$$
$$a \textbf{ in } (x - y) \equiv (a \textbf{ in } x \ \& \ \neg\, a \textbf{ in } y)$$

12.6 SEQUENCES

The general form of a sequence definition is:

> **type** $T = $ **sequence** D;

(1) $T(\ )$ is a T

(2) If x is a T and d is a D

> then $x \frown T(d)$ is a T

(3) The only elements of T are as specified in (1) and (2)

(4) $(x \frown T(d)).\text{last} = d$

(5) initial $\left(x \frown T(d)\right) = x$

(6) $x \frown (y \frown z) = (x \frown y) \frown z$

(7) $T(d).\text{first} = d$

(8) $x \neq T(\ ) \supset \left(x \frown T(d)\right).\text{first} = x.\text{first}$

(9) final $\left(T(d)\right) = T(\ )$

(10) $x \neq T(\ ) \supset \text{final} \left(x \frown T(d)\right) = \text{final}\ (x) \frown T(d)$

Note: last, initial, first, and final are not defined for $T(\ )$

(11) $T(\ )$ **ends** y

(12) $x \frown T(d)$ **ends** $y \equiv y \neq T(\ )\ \&\ y.\text{last} = d\ \&\ x$ **ends** initial (y)

(13) x **begins** $T(\ ) \equiv x = T(\ )$

(14) x **begins** $y \frown T(d) \equiv x = y \frown T(d) \lor x$ **begins** y

(15) length $\left(T(\ )\right) = 0$

(16) length $\left(x \frown T(d)\right) = \text{succ}(\text{length}\ (x))$

For an ordered sequence type we have:

(17) $T(\ ) \leqslant y$

(18) $x \leqslant T(\ ) \supset x = T(\ )$

(19) $x, y \neq T(\ ) \supset \left(x \leqslant y \equiv x.\text{first} < y.\text{first} \lor (x.\text{first} = y.\text{first}\right.$
$\left. \&\ \text{final}\ (x) \leqslant \text{final}\ (y))\right)$

Abbreviations:

(20) $x: \frown T(d)$ means $x: = x \frown T(d)$

(21) d **from** x means $d: = x.\text{first};\ x: = \text{final}\ (x)$

(22) d **back from** x means $d: = x.\text{last};\ x: = \text{initial}\ (x)$

(23) **from** x means $x: = \text{final}\ (x)$

(24) **back from** x means $x: = \text{initial}\ (x)$

(25) $T(d_1, d_2, \ldots, d_n)$ stands for
$$\left(T(\ ) \frown T(d_1) \frown T(d_2) \frown \ldots \frown T(d_n)\right)$$

(26) $[d_1, d_2, \ldots, d_n]$ stands for $T(d_1, d_2, \ldots, d_n)$

(27) If $x = [d_1, d_2, \ldots, d_n]$ then

    for d **in** x **do** S stands for
$$S_{d_1}^d;\ S_{d_2}^d;\ \ldots;\ S_{dn}^d$$
    for d **in** x **take** E stands for
$$[E_{d_1}^d,\ E_{d_2}^d,\ \ldots,\ E_{dn}^d]$$

Theorems

$$x = y \equiv (x = y = T(\ ) \vee x.\text{first} = y.\text{first} \ \& \ x.\text{final} = y.\text{final})$$
$$\equiv (x = y = T(\ ) \vee x.\text{last} = y.\text{last} \ \& \ x.\text{initial} = y.\text{initial})$$

REFERENCES

The following works have acted as an inspiration and guide for this chapter, and they are recommended for further reading.

I am also deeply indebted to Professor N. Wirth for many fruitful discussions and suggestions, and for his willingness to test several of the ideas of the paper in his design and implementation of PASCAL; and to Professor E. W. Dijkstra for his perpetual inspiration.

Dijkstra, E. W. (1972). Notes on Structured Programming. "Structured Programming". pp. 1–82. Academic Press, London.

Knuth, D. E. (1968). "The Art of Computer Programming" Vol. 1, Chapter 2. Addison-Wesley, Reading, Mass.

McCarthy, J. (1963). "A Basis for a Mathemetical Theory of Computation in Computer Programming and Formal Systems" (eds. Braffort, P. & Hirschberg D.). North-Holland Publishing Company, Amsterdam.

Mealy, G. H. (1967). Another Look at Data. *A.F.I.P.S. Fall Joint Computer Conference Proceedings*. **31**, pp. 525–534.

Wirth, N. (1970). Programming and Programming Languages. Contribution to Conference of European Chapter of *A.C.M*, Bonn.

Wirth, N. (1971). Program Development by Stepwise Refinement. *Comm. A.C.M.* **14**, 4, pp. 221–227.

Wirth, N. (1971). The Programming Language PASCAL. *Acta Informatica*, **1**, 1, pp. 35–63.

III. Hierarchical Program Structures

OLE-JOHAN DAHL AND C. A. R. HOARE

1. INTRODUCTION

In this monograph we shall explore certain ways of program structuring and point out their relationship to concept modelling.

We shall make use of the programming language SIMULA 67 with particular emphasis on structuring mechanisms. SIMULA 67 is based on ALGOL 60 and contains a slightly restricted and modified version of ALGOL 60 as a subset. Additional language features are motivated and explained informally when introduced. The student should have a good knowledge of ALGOL 60 and preferably be acquainted with list processing techniques.

For a full exposition of the SIMULA language we refer to the "Simula 67 Common Base Language" [2]. Some of the linguistic mechanisms introduced in the monograph are currently outside the "Common Base"*.

The monograph is an extension and reworking of a series of lectures given by Dahl at the NATO Summer School on Programming, Marktoberdorf 1970. Some of the added material is based on programming examples that have occurred elsewhere [3, 4, 5].

2. PRELIMINARIES

2.1 BASIC CONCEPTS

Our subject matter as programmers is a special class of dynamic system, which we call computing processes or data processes. A programming

---

* The Simula 67 language was originally designed at the Norwegian Computing Center, Oslo. The Common Base defines those language features which are common to all implementations. The Common Base is continually being maintained and revised by the "Simula Standards Group", each of whose members represents an organisation responsible for an implementation. 8 organisations are currently represented on the SSG. (Summer 1971).

language provides us with basic concepts and composition rules for constructing and analysing computing processes.

The following are some of the basic concepts provided by ALGOL 60.

(1) A *type* is a class of *values*. Associated with each type there are a number of operations which apply to such values, e.g. arithmetic operations and relations for values of type **integer**.

(2) A *variable* is a class of values of a given type ordered in a time sequence. The associated operations are accessing and assigning its current value. Both can be understood as *copying* operations.

(3) An *array* is a class of variables ordered in a spatial pattern. Associated is the operation of *subscripting*.

Notice that each of the concepts includes a data structure as well as one or more associated operations.

As another example consider machine level programming. The fundamental data structure is a bit string, which is not itself a very meaningful thing. However, combined with an appropriate sensing mechanism it has the significance of a sequence of Boolean values. In connection with a binary adder the bit string has the meaning of a number in some range, each bit being a digit in the base two number system. An output channel coupled to a line printer turns the bit string into a sequence of characters, and so forth. Thus the meaning of the data structure critically depends on the kind of operations associated with it.

On the other hand, no data process is conceivable which does not involve some data. In short, data and operations on data seem to be so closely connected in our minds, that it takes elements of both kinds to make up any concept useful for understanding computing processes.

2.2. HIGHER LEVEL CONCEPTS

As the result of the large capacity of computing instruments, we have to deal with computing processes of such complexity that they can hardly be constructed and understood in terms of basic general purpose concepts. The limit is set by the nature of our own intellect: precise thinking is possible only in terms of a *small* number of elements at a time.

The only efficient way to deal with complicated systems is in a hierarchical fashion. The dynamic system is constructed and understood in terms of high level concepts, which are in turn constructed and understood in terms of lower level concepts, and so forth. This must be reflected in the *structure* of the program which defines the dynamic system; in some way or another the higher level concepts will correspond to program components.

The construction of concepts suitable in a given situation is a creative process which often requires insights obtained at later stages of the system construction. Therefore, as programmers are painfully aware, any software project tends to be a complicated iterative process involving reconstruction and revision at each stage.

Each concept necessarily concerns a limited aspect of the system and should correspond to a piece of program obtained by *decomposition* of the total program. Good decomposition means that each component may be programmed independently and revised with no, or reasonably few, implications for the rest of the system. Thereby the total iteration process may be speeded up.

Any useful concept has some degree of generality, i.e. it is a *class* of specialised instances. In other words one tries to group phenomena occurring in a dynamic system into *classes* of phenomena and to describe each class by a single piece of program.

As an obvious example consider the arithmetic operations involved in a matrix multiplication. They may all be classified as dynamic instances (executions) of the single statement

$$C[i, j]: = C[i, j] + A[i, k] \times B[k, j];$$

provided that the matrix coefficients are classified as elements of two-dimensional arrays A, B, and C, and that the variables i, j, and k are given values according to a certain pattern.

The above statement is not sufficiently well decomposed to be thought of as a "concept". The procedure declaration below, however, defines in a concise way the concept of matrix multiplication.

It is important that a concept may be classified as a *syntactic category* (e.g. $\langle$block$\rangle$, $\langle$procedure$\rangle$) in a general language framework. Structured thought in terms of given concepts implies the construction of sentences, where the concepts have syntactic and semantic relationships to one another. The procedure below is related to other program components through calling sequences (procedure statements).

```
procedure matmult (A, B, C, m, n, p);
    array A, B, C; integer m, n, p;
begin integer i, j, k;
        for i: = 1 step 1 until m do
        for j: = 1 step 1 until n do
        begin C[i, j]: = 0;
            for k: = 1 step 1 until p do
            C[i, j]: = C[i, j] + A[i, k] × B[k, i]
        end
    end;
```

The parameter mechanism of procedures in SIMULA deviates somewhat from that of ALGOL 60. The default transmission mode is by value for ordinary simple ⟨type⟩ parameters, and by "reference" for parameters of other kinds. This deviation is introduced for various pragmatic reasons, one of them being the compatibility with class declarations (cf. 3.1). Thus, in the above procedure the parameters i, j, and k are called by value, A, B, and C by reference.

2.3. BLOCKS AND BLOCK INSTANCES

One of the most powerful mechanisms for program structuring in ALGOL 60 is the block and procedure concept. It has the following useful properties from the standpoint of concept modelling.

(1) *Duality.* A block head and block tail together define an entity which *has properties* and *performs actions.* Furthermore the properties may include a data structure as well as associated operators (local procedures).

(2) *Decomposition.* A block where only local quantities are referenced is a completely selfcontained program component, which will function as specified in any context. Through a procedure heading a block (procedure) instance may interact with a calling sequence. Procedures which reference or change non-local variables represent a partial decomposition of the total task, which is useful for direct interaction with the program environment.

(3) *Class of instances.* In ALGOL 60 a sharp distinction is made between a block, which is a piece of program text, and a dynamic block instance, which is (a component of) a computing process. An immediate and useful consequence is that a block may be identified with the *class* of its potential activations. (Strictly speaking a "block" in this context means either the outermost block or a block immediately enclosed by a dynamic block instance.) Through the recursion mechanism of ALGOL 60 different instances of the same block may co-exist in a computing process at the same time.

(4) *Language element.* A block is itself a statement, which is a syntactic category of the language. Furthermore, through the procedure mechanism, reference to a block may be dissociated from its defining text.

Referring back to our earlier discussion it appears that the ALGOL block mechanism has all the properties required of a concept modelling mechanism. On closer inspection, however, it turns out that the composition rules and interaction mechanisms provided place certain restrictions on the range of concepts to be formulated.

In ALGOL 60, the rules of the language have been carefully designed to ensure that the lifetimes of block instances are nested, in the sense that those instances that are latest activated are the first to go out of existence. It is this feature that permits an ALGOL 60 implementation to take advantage of a stack as a method of dynamic storage allocation and relinquishment. But it has the disadvantage that a program which creates a new block instance can never interact with it as an object which exists and has attributes, since it has disappeared by the time the calling program regains control. Thus the calling program can observe only the results of the actions of the procedures it calls. Consequently, the operational aspects of a block are overemphasised; and algorithms (for example, matrix multiplication) are the only concepts that can be modelled.

In SIMULA 67, a block instance is permitted to outlive its calling statement, and to remain in existence for as long as the program needs to refer to it. It may even outlive the block instance that called it into existence. As a consequence, it is no longer possible to administer storage allocation as a simple stack; a general garbage-collector, including a scan-mark operation, is required to detect and reclaim those areas of store (local workspace of block instances) which can no longer be referenced by the running program. The reason for accepting this extra complexity is that it permits a wider range of concepts to be conveniently expressed. In particular, it clarifies the relationship between data and the operations which may be performed upon it, in a way which is awkward or impossible in ALGOL 60.

3. Object Classes

A procedure which is capable of giving rise to block instances which survive its call will be known as a *class*; and the instances will be known as *objects* of that class. A class may be declared, with or without parameters, in exactly the same way as a procedure:

⟨class declaration⟩:: = **class** ⟨class identifier⟩
⟨formal parameter part⟩; ⟨specification part⟩;
⟨class body⟩
⟨class body⟩:: = ⟨statement⟩

Any variables or procedures declared local to the class body are called *attributes* of that class; and so are the formal parameters, whether called by value or called by reference. If the class body is not a block, it is regarded as if it were surrounded by block brackets **begin...end**.

A call of a class generates a new object of that class. The initial values of those of its attributes corresponding to formal parameters are specified in the actual parameter part of the generator. A generator always appears as a function designator, returning as its value a *reference* to the newly generated object:

⟨object generator⟩:: = **new** ⟨class identifier⟩
⟨actual parameter part⟩

In order to be able to refer again to a generated object, it is necessary to store the reference to it in a variable. Variables used for this purpose should be declared as of *reference* type; and the declaration should also be *qualified* by stating the class of objects to which that variable will refer.

⟨reference variable declaration⟩∷=

ref (⟨qualification⟩) ⟨identifier list⟩

⟨qualification⟩∷= ⟨class identifier⟩

The notation **ref** (⟨qualification⟩) may also be used to declare reference arrays, procedures, and parameters. An analogous mechanism for "record handling" was first proposed by Hoare [6].

There is a neutral reference value **none** which does not refer to any object; and this is automatically assigned as initial value to every reference variable.

Reference values may be assigned, and tested for equality or inequality; but in SIMULA these operations are given special symbols, in order to emphasise the fact that they operate on references to objects, and not upon the current values contained in those objects.

Thus:

:−   denotes reference assignment

= =   denotes reference equality

=/=   denotes reference inequality.

Reference values may also be passed as parameters, and they may be returned as the result of a function designator. A special example of such a function designator is of course the object generator which brings the object into existence, and passes back a reference to it as result.

Example:

class $C(...)$; ... class body for $C...$;

ref $(C)X$;

. . . .

if $X = =$ **none then** X: − **new** $C(...)$;

The attributes of any object may be inspected or changed by the technique of *remote identification*. If X is a reference variable qualified by class C, and A is an attribute identifier (i.e. local quantity) of that class, then $X.A$ refers to the attribute A of the object currently referenced by X. If X has the value **none**, the remote access is erroneous. If A is a variable attribute, $X.A$ may appear to the left of an assignment, as an actual parameter, or in an expression. If A is a procedure attribute, $X.A$ may appear as an actual parameter, or as a procedure statement or function designator, in which case it will be immediately followed by an actual parameter part. In short, a remote identifier $X.A$ may appear in any context in which an ordinary identifier may appear, except for a defining occurrence in a declaration.

In addition to reference variables, every reference parameter, function or expression has a qualification associated with it. In every assignment to a reference variable, it is possible to check that the assignment is valid, by comparing the qualifications of the left hand and right hand sides. SIMULA 67 has been designed to ensure that this check can be carried out wholly at compile time, thus avoiding the inefficiency of run-time checking, and the inconvenience of run-time error. Furthermore all remote identifiers can be checked at compile time to ensure that the combination of reference variable and attribute identifier is valid, so that the only error that has to be detected at run-time is when the reference variable has the value **none**.

The following sections provide examples of concepts modelled by means of class declarations.

3.1. FREQUENCY HISTOGRAM

A frequency histogram of a real random variable with respect to given disjoint intervals can be represented by a table of integers $T_0, T_1, \ldots, T_n$, where T_i is the number of observations falling in the ith interval. A sequence of increasing numbers $X_1, X_2, \ldots, X_n$ partitions the real axis into the following $n + 1$ intervals:

$$\langle -\infty, X_1 \rangle, (X_1, X_2), \ldots, (X_n, \infty \rangle.$$

The ith relative frequency $(i = 0, 1, \ldots, n)$ is equal to T_i/N, where N is the total number of observations tabulated in the histogram.

We wish to represent the concept of a histogram as a self-contained piece of program, which can be incorporated in any subsequently written program which requires it. In a realistic program, it will be necessary to maintain several histograms to tabulate different random variables; for example, it may be necessary to record not only random lengths, but also random weights and random heights, and this will require three separate histograms, existing simultaneously with each other and with the main program which has generated them and which is using them. Furthermore, the numbers of the intervals and the partitioning values between them may be different in each case. This suggests that the histogram should be declared as a *class*, with two parameters:

class histogram (X, n); **array** X; **integer** n;

where X is a real array of n elements specifying the boundaries of the partitions. The main program will use this class in the following way:

begin ref (histogram) heights, weights, lengths;

    real array $A[1:7]$, $B[1:12]$;

    ...initialise A, B...;

    heights: $-$ **new** histogram $(A, 7)$;

weights: — **new** histogram $(B, 12)$;

lengths: — **new** histogram $(A, 7)$;

. . . . rest of program. . . .

end

In the rest of the program, the three histograms may be referred to by the names of the three reference variables. In order to record each new observation (say h or w) in the appropriate histogram, the program will contain the corresponding calls on a procedure tabulate:

weights.tabulate (w);

heights.tabulate (h);

The procedure "tabulate" must therefore be an attribute of the histogram class. Another attribute of the class must be the array T which counts the number of observations in each interval; and also a variable N to count the total number of observations recorded so far. Finally, a function frequency (i) is required so that the relative frequency of observations in the ith interval may be read out. The only action required of the class body is to initialise these variables.

The declaration of the histogram class may be given:

    class histogram (X, n); **array** X; **integer** n;

      begin integer N; **integer array** $T[0{:}n]$;

        procedure tabulate (Y); **real** Y;

          begin integer i; $i{:} = 0$;

            while (**if** $i < n$ **then** $Y < X[i + 1]$ **else false**)

              do $i{:} = i + 1$;

            $T[i]{:} = T[i] + 1$; $N{:} = N + 1$

        end of tabulate;

        real procedure frequency (i); **integer** i;

          frequency$: = T[i]/N$;

        integer i;

        for $i{:} = 0$ **step** 1 **until** n **do** $T[i]{:} = 0$; $N{:} = 0$

      end of histogram;

Note. (1) In SIMULA 67, all simple parameters of a class or a procedure are called by value, even if the value parts are omitted. Arrays and other parameters are called by name.

(2) In SIMULA 67 all variables are automatically initialised on declaration to neutral values, **false** for Booleans, 0 for numbers, **none** for references. Thus in the examples given above the statements $i{:} = 0$, $N{:} = 0$, and the loop initialising T could have been omitted.

It seems reasonable to claim that this piece of program adequately represents the concept of a histogram, in that it expresses the close relationship between the data items X, n, T and N, and the operation of tabulation which is to be performed on them. It would be possible, of course, to write the operation in ALGOL 60 as a separate procedure with many parameters:

procedure tabulate (X, n, T, N, y);

which records observation y in the histogram T in accordance with partitions defined by X, and also increments N. But this would be an artificial separation of the operational aspect of the histogram from the data storage aspect; and the failure in adequately representing the concept is evidenced by the complexity of the specification of the procedure and the awkwardness of its use.

It is worth while to explain the effect of creating a new object of class histogram by means of the statement

weights: − **new** histogram $(B, 12)$.

First, a new object is created, consisting of the variables brought into existence by execution of the declarations for T, N, i, and the parameters X and n, which are initialised to B and 12 respectively. The body of the class declaration is now executed to initialise the other variables. On exit from the body, the variables are *not* deallocated. Rather a reference (pointer, address) to them is passed back and assigned to the variable "weights". It is convenient to think of an object as a complete textual copy of the class body (including the specification part), in which the parameters and local variables and arrays correspond to actual storage locations. Thus an object may well contain local procedure (and even class −) declarations, as well as executable statements.

Subsequently, on execution of the procedure call weights.tabulate (w), it is the tabulate procedure local to the object referenced by "weights" that is actually executed, and causes updating of the local attributes T and N of that object and no other.

3.2. GAUSS-INTEGRATION

A definite integral may be approximated by an "n-point Gauss formula", which is a weighted sum of n function values computed at certain points in the integration interval.

$$\int_a^b f(x)dx \approx \sum_{i=1}^n w_i f(x_i)$$

The weights and abscissa values are chosen such as to give an exact result for the integral of any polynomial of degree less than $2n$. By a suitable transformation we find

$$w_i = (b - a)W_i \text{ and } x_i = a + (b - a)X_i,$$

where W_i and $X_i (i = 1, 2, \ldots, n)$ only depend on n, and not on a or b. The idea of Gauss-integration is expressed in the following partly informal class declaration.

class Gauss (n); **integer** n;

begin array $W, X[1:n]$;

      real procedure integral (f, a, b);

           real procedure f; **real** a, b;

$$\text{integral} := \sum_{i=1}^{n} W[i] \times f(a + (b - a) \times X[i]) \times (b - a);$$

      compute $W[1], \ldots, W[n], X[1], \ldots, X[n]$ as

      functions of n

end of Gauss;

. . . .

ref (Gauss) G5, G7;

. . . .

G5: – **new** Gauss (5); G7: – **new** Gauss (7);

. . . .

. . .   G5.integral (F, A, B). . . . . .G7.integral (F, A, B). . . . .

Comments. The variables G5 and G7 refer to the concepts "5-point" and "7-point Gauss-integration". Each of them is a *specialised instance* of the more general concept of "n-point Gauss-integration", represented by the class.

A Gauss object computes once and for all the values of its local array elements, after which control returns to the ⟨object generator⟩. The procedure "integral" is intended for repeated use from outside the object.

The example indicates that the *own*-concept of ALGOL is superfluous in this framework.

4. Coroutines

In ALGOL 60, a most powerful method of combining two pieces of program to accomplish some task is to declare one of them as a procedure, and to invoke it (possibly repeatedly) from within the other. However, in some cases the relationship between the two pieces of program is not fairly represented by this form of master/subordinate relationship; and it is better to regard them as *coroutines* operating in some sense at the same level.

A simple example of coroutine structuring is provided by a games-playing program, which calculates its own move and outputs it to its opponent, inputs the opponent's response, computes its next move, and so on until the game is complete. Suppose now that two different programs have been constructed to play the same game, and it is desired to see which of them is the stronger player. The complete program to play the game is very naturally structured from its two component players, but the structuring method is that of the coroutine rather than the subroutine.

Another example of coroutine structuring is provided in a two-pass compiler for a programming language. The first pass normally outputs a long sequence of messages which are subsequently input by the second pass. However, if sufficient main storage is available to accommodate the program for both passes simultaneously, it is possible to arrange for the whole trans-lation to be carried out apparently in a single pass, where the sequence of messages is transmitted *piecewise* from the first pass to the second pass. First, the second pass is executed until it reaches its first request for an input message. The first pass program is then executed until it produces its first output message. The message is then handed over to the second pass, and the process is repeated until the second pass is complete. In some circumstances it might be possible to restructure one of the passes as a subroutine to the other; but since the choice would be arbitrary, it is better to regard the two programs as coroutines.

This case may be distinguished from the games-playing example in that the flow of information is in one direction only, from the first pass program which "produces" it to the second pass program which "consumes" it. This suggests that a single coroutine may profitably be regarded as a complete selfcontained program whose input and output instructions have been replaced by calls upon other coroutines to produce and consume the data. Each time a coroutine passes control to another coroutine for this purpose, it will expect to resume at the next following instruction. The instruction which causes transfer of control to another coroutine is known as

$$\text{resume } (X)$$

where X refers to the coroutine being resumed.

In SIMULA, a coroutine is represented by an object of some class, co-operating by means of resume instructions with objects of the same or another class, which are named by means of reference variables. The communication of information may be accomplished in variables either global to all the objects or local to one of them; a producing coroutine assigns values to these variables, and the consuming coroutine accesses them. In the case of two-way communication, both coroutines may update the same global variables in turn.

When an object is first generated, it has a subordinate, procedurelike relationship to the block instance which generated it. This is evidenced by the fact that control automatically returns to the generator upon passage through the end of the object. The object does not in general know the identity of its generating block instance; it cannot therefore use a resume instruction to achieve the effect of a coroutine exit. A special, parameterless "detach" instruction is therefore provided by which a generated object can return control to the generator. The generator may then resume the detached object at the point following its (most recently executed) detach instruction by the statement

call (X)

where X is a reference to the detached object. Now the object is again in a subordinate position, with respect to the caller, and has an obligation to return to it either by a detach instruction or by going through its own **end**.

Thus a main program may establish a coroutine relationship with an object that it has generated, using the call/detach mechanism instead of the more symmetric resume/resume mechanism. In this case, the generated object remains subordinate to the main program, and for this reason is sometimes known as a *semicoroutine*. But a semicoroutine may also be a full coroutine with respect to a group of other generated objects, with which it communicates by means of resume statements. In this case, if any of the group issues a detach, control returns to the master program which originally called a particular member of the group. Thus a coroutine issuing a resume statement imposes on the resumed coroutine its own responsibility, eventually to pass control back to the original caller by means of a detach.

Let X and Y be objects, generated by a "master program" M. Assume that M issues a call (X), thereby invoking an "active phase" of X, terminated by a detach operation in X; and then issues a call (Y), and so forth. In this way M may act as a "supervisor" sequencing a pattern of active phases of X, Y, and other objects. Each object is a "slave", which responds with an active phase each time it is called for, whereas M has the responsibility to define the large scale pattern of the entire computation.

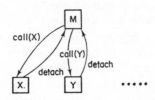

Alternatively the decision making may be "decentralised", allowing an object itself to determine its dynamic successor by a resume operation.

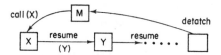

The operation resume (Y), executed by X, combines an exit out of X (by detach) and a subsequent call (Y), thereby bypassing M. Obligation to return to M is transferred to Y.

The history of a typical coroutine object may be summarised as follows:

(1) Upon generation, an object starts performing the operations of its class body, and is said to be *operating* and *attached* to (the block instance containing) the object generator which calls it into existence.

(2) The object issues a *detach* statement which returns control to the point at which the object was generated. The object is then said to be detached, but not yet terminated. The detach statement leaves a mark in the body of the object specifying where its operations will be continued. This mark is positioned at the end of the detach statement most recently executed by that object.

(3) Control returns to the object on execution of either a call statement or a resume statement specifying that object by means of its reference parameter. It is then *reattached* to the *calling* block instance if called, or to the original caller if resumed. The object may then temporarily relinquish control again, either by a detach or by a resume, in which case it becomes detached again.

(4) Alternatively, it may relinquish control finally by passing through its **end**, which has the same effect as a detach. But in this case it is said to be *terminated*, and it may not be reactivated either by a call or a resume. However, it remains in existence as an item of data, which may be referenced by remote identification of its attributes, including procedure and function attributes, as in the case of the histogram.

Note. The detach operation represents a coroutine exit out of an *object*, and is only available textually within objects, i.e. textually within class bodies. If issued in a subblock or in a procedure body, a detach instruction still represents an exit out of the (smallest) textually enclosing object. The same is true for the resume instruction (which includes a coroutine exit). The call instruction is, however, available at any point in a program.

4.1. TEXT TRANSFORMATION

As an example of the cooperation of coroutines we take a problem posed by Conway [7]. A text is to be read from cards and listed on a line printer. The cards each contain 80 characters, but the line printer prints 125 characters on each line. It is intended to pack as many characters as possible on each output line, marking the transition from one card to the next only by insertion of an extra space. In the text, any consecutive pair of asterisks is to be replaced by "↑". The end of the text is marked by a special character known as "end".

We assume the existence of a coroutine "incard", which on each resumption will fill the array $C[1:80]$ with characters read from the next card in the card hopper, and pass the card through to the stacker. Also, we are given a coroutine "lineout", which on each resumption will print on the next line of paper the characters from the array $L[1:125]$, and then throw the line.

The task is carried out by three coroutines, which will be known by reference as:

ref disassembler, squasher, assembler;

The disassembler inputs a card (through C) and outputs individual characters (through $c1$) to the squasher, after inserting a space between cards. The squasher performs the transformation on double asterisks, and outputs individual characters through $c2$ to the assembler. The assembler groups the characters into lines and outputs them; it also detects the "end" character and takes appropriate action.

The required class declarations are:

```
class pass 1;
begin detach;
    while true do
        begin integer i; resume (incard);
            for i: = 1 step 1 until 80 do
                begin c1: = C[i]; resume (squasher) end;
            c1: = blank; resume (squasher)
        end infinite loop;
end pass 1;
class pass 2;
begin detach;
    while true do
        begin if c1 = "*" then
```

```
          begin resume (disassembler);
            if c1 = "*" then c2: = "↑"
            else begin c2: = "*"; resume (assembler);
                  c2: = c1
              end;
        end
                    else c2: = c1;
          resume (assembler); resume (disassembler)
        end infinite loop;
    end pass 2;
    class pass 3;
    begin detach;
        while true do
          begin integer i;
            for i: = 1 step 1 until 125 do
              begin L[i]: = c2;
                if c2 = "end" then
                  begin for i: = i + 1 step 1 until 125 do
                    L[i]: = blank;
                    resume (lineout);
                    detach; comment back to main program;
                  end
                        else resume (squasher)
              end of this line;
          resume (lineout)
        end infinite loop
    end pass 3;
```

The main program generates one instance of each of the passes. Each pass immediately detaches itself from the main program. The system of coroutines is initiated by calling the disassembler. On detection of the end of the task, the assembler issues a detach instruction. Since the assembler obtained control (indirectly) by resume instructions from the disassembler, its detach has the same effect as it would have had if issued by the disassembler, and takes control back to the main program, which then immediately terminates.

The main program is:

> **begin** disassembler: — **new** pass 1;
>
> squasher: — **new** pass 2;
>
> assembler: — **new** pass 3;
>
> call (disassembler);
>
> **end**

The relationships between the five coroutines and the main program may be represented pictorially:

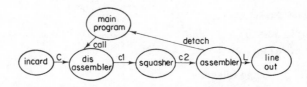

The horizontal arrows represent resume/resume relations. Their direction corresponds to the flow of information; and they are annotated by the name of the variable used to hold the communicated information.

In this example, it is intended that each class should only ever have one object in it; and therefore the full class/generation/reference mechanism is unnecessarily elaborate. The elaboration is inconvenient in that separate names have to be invented for the class and its unique object (e.g. pass 1 and disassembler). Furthermore, in the implementation it should be possible to take advantage of this special case to save both space and time. But SIMULA 67 provides no means of achieving this.

4.2. PERMUTATION GENERATOR

We wish to define a class "permuter" representing the concept of permutations. An object of this class should be capable of generating all permutations of the integers between 1 and n, where n is a parameter of the class. One of the attributes of the class will be an **integer array** $p[1:n]$, which is to be initialised to the value $(1, 2, \ldots, n)$ (representing the identity permutation) when an object of the class is generated. Every subsequent call of the object causes the array p to take a new permutation as value. When all permutations are exhausted, an attribute

Boolean more;

(initially true) will be assigned the value **false**, and the object will terminate.

A typical structure for a program which wishes to inspect all permutations of N numbers will be:

> **ref** (permuter)P;
>
> P: − **new** permuter (N);
>
> **while** P.more **do**
>
> > **begin**...inspect $P.p$...; call (P) **end**;

The structure of the permuter class will be a semicoroutine, which issues a detach instruction after each updating of p:

> **class** permuter (n); **integer** n;
>
> > **begin integer array** $p[1:n]$;
> >
> > **Boolean** more;
> >
> > **integer** q;
> >
> > **for** q: = 1 **step** 1 **until** n **do** $p[q]$: = q;
> >
> > more: = **true**;
> >
> > ...generate all permutations of p,
> >
> > issuing a "detach" after each of them...;
> >
> > more: = **false**
>
> **end**

It remains to find an algorithm to carry out all the permutations of $p[1]$, $p[2]$, ..., $p[n]$, and restore them to their original state. This algorithm may be recursively structured. Let us assume that we know how to generate *all* permutations of the numbers

$$p[1], p[2], \ldots, p[k-1],$$

and finally return these to their original state. This will be accomplished by a procedure call

> permute $(k-1)$.

Now all that need be done is to use this procedure to permute every *combination* of $k-1$ numbers from the original k numbers. Thus there must be k calls of permute $(k-1)$, and on each call, exactly one of the $p[i]$ for $1 \leqslant i \leqslant k$ must be excluded from the operation. A good way of excluding it is to exchange its value with that of $p[k]$, which remains untouched by permute $(k-1)$. In order to ensure that each of the k values is excluded exactly once, we may take advantage of the assumption that the procedure returns the given sequence unchanged. In that case $p[k]$ will be assigned each value once if we first swap $p[1]$ and $p[k]$, then $p[2]$ and $p[k]$, ..., and then $p[k - 1]$ and $p[k]$. Thus we are led to the following kernel:

> **integer** i;
>
> permute $(k - 1)$;
>
> **for** $i: = 1$ **step** 1 **until** $k - 1$ **do**
>
> > **begin** swap $(p[i], p[k])$; permute $(k - 1)$ **end**;

On the assumption that permute $(k - 1)$ leaves p unchanged, this kernel has the net effect of rotating the elements $p[1]$, $p[2]$, ..., $p[k]$ one place cyclically to the right. This can be seen from the example:

> original state: 1 2 3 4 5
>
> after swap $(p[1], p[5])$:   5 2 3 4 1
>
> after swap $(p[2], p[5])$:   5 1 3 4 2
>
> after swap $(p[3], p[5])$:   5 1 2 4 3
>
> after swap $(p[4], p[5])$:   5 1 2 3 4

Since the overall effect of the operation must be to leave the array p as it was before, the right rotation must be followed by a compensatory left rotation.

> $q: = p[1]$;
>
> **for** $i: = 1$ **step** 1 **until** $k - 1$ **do** $p[i]: = p[i + 1]$;
>
> $p[k]: = q$

Finally it is necessary to determine an appropriate action for the case where $k = 1$. Recall that the purpose of the procedure is to

"generate all permutations of k objects, issuing a detach command after each of them".

Since the only permutation of one number is that number itself, all that is necessary is to issue a single detach instruction.

The permute procedure must be written as an attribute of the permuter class, so that the detach which it issues relates to the relevant object. The whole class may now be declared:

> **class** permuter (n); **integer** n;
>
> **begin integer array** $p[1:n]$; **integer** q; **Boolean** more;
>
> > **procedure** permute (k); **integer** k;
> >
> > **if** $k = 1$ **then** detach **else**
> >
> > **begin integer** i; permute $(k - 1)$;
> >
> > > **for** $i: = 1$ **step** 1 **until** $k - 1$ **do**
> > >
> > > **begin** $q: = p[i]$; $p[i]: = p[k]$;
> > >
> > > > $p[k]: = q$; permute $(k - 1)$ **end**;

$q := p[1];$

for $i := 1$ **step** 1 **until** $k - 1$ **do** $p[i] := p[i + 1];$

$p[k] := q$

end of permute;

for $q := 1$ **step** 1 **until** n **do** $p[q] := q;$

more: = **true**; permute (n); more: = **false**

end of permuter;

Note. The detach issued by a permute procedure instance is *not* an exit out of the procedure instance, and does not return control to the call of the procedure. Rather, it is an intermediate exit out of the object as a whole (including the entire recursion process) and passes control back to the main program which generated or called the object. A subsequent call on the object will thus resume the recursion process exactly where it left off.

The decision (assumption) that the procedure permute should leave the sequence unchanged is really quite arbitrary. The reader is invited to convince himself of this fact by writing a procedure based on the same swapping strategy, which returns with the numbers in the reverse order.

5. LIST STRUCTURES

The facilities introduced above for declaration of classes and reference to objects may be used to represent recursive data structures such as stacks and trees, and even cyclic structures such as two-way lists. This is accomplished by declaring attributes of a class to be references to objects of the very same class.

5.1. BINARY SEARCH TREES

A binary tree may be defined as

either (i)   **none**

or (ii) a node,

where a node consists of

(a) a left component which is a tree

(b) a right component which is a tree

(c) a val which is an integer.

The val component may be regarded as being associated with each node of the tree. A node whose left and right subtrees are both **none** is a terminal element of the tree (leaf).

A binary search tree is defined as a binary tree which is either **none**, or else it is a node which has a val lying between all vals of its left subtree and all vals of its right subtree, which are themselves both binary search trees. The purpose of a binary search tree is to provide for any integer a swift access to the node which has val equal to that integer; and also to provide swift means of inserting a new node with any given val. Thus a class representing the concept of a binary search tree will have the form:

> **class** tree (val); **integer** val;
>> **begin ref** (tree) left, right;
>>> **procedure** insert (x); **integer** x;
>>>> $\ldots\ldots$;
>>
>> **ref** (tree) **procedure** find (x); **integer** x;
>>> $\ldots\ldots$;
>>
>> **end** of tree;

The bodies of the two procedure components are quite simple recursive procedures, matching the recursive structure of the tree:

> insert: **if** $x <$ val **then**
>> **begin if** left $= =$ **none then** left: $-$ **new** tree (x)
>>> **else** left . insert (x)
>>
>> **end**
>
>   **else if** right $= \rightleftharpoons$ **none then** right: $-$ **new** tree (x)
>> **else** right . insert (x);

> find: **if** $x =$ val **then this** tree
> **else if** $x <$ val **then**
>> (**if** left $= =$ **none then none**
>>> **else** left . find (x))
>
> **else if** right $= =$ **none then none**
>> **else** right . find (x);

In the body of "find" there occurs the expression

> **this** tree

which is intended to yield as value a reference to the current node, that is, the one which owns this particular instance of the find attribute. For example, if the find procedure of X is called by the function designator

> X . find (x)

and X . val $= x$, then the result of the function is the reference value of X itself.

Another operation which is meaningful for a binary search tree is that of scanning all its values in ascending order. This operation may be implemented by a "producing" semicoroutine, which on each call assigns to its attribute

integer current;

the next higher value of a node on the tree. On exhaustion of the tree, the attribute current will take the maximum integer value.

The scanning can be accomplished by a recursive procedure attribute, local to the relevant instance of the coroutine.

> **class** scanner (X); **ref** (tree) X;
>
> > **begin integer** current;
> >
> > > **procedure** traverse (X); **ref** (tree) X;
> > >
> > > > **if** $X =/=$ **none then**
> > > >
> > > > > **begin** traverse $(X.$left$)$;
> > > > >
> > > > > current$: = X.$val;
> > > > >
> > > > > detach;
> > > > >
> > > > > traverse $(X.$right$)$
> > > > >
> > > > **end** traverse;
> > >
> > > traverse (X);
> > >
> > > current$: =$ integer max
> >
> > **end** scanner;

As an example of the use of these concepts, we consider the task of merging values from several binary search trees, held in an array:

> **ref** (tree) **array** forest $[1:N]$;

and outputting the values in ascending order. In order to do this we will require N scanners, one operating on each tree of the forest:

> **ref** (scanner) **array** trav $[1:N]$;
>
> **for** $i: = 1$ **step** 1 **until** N **do** trav $[i]: -$ **new** scanner (forest $[i]$);

Each scanner has now detached with its own minimal val assigned to its own current. All that is now necessary is to locate the minimum of the N currents and output it. The corresponding scanner should then be reinvoked to produce its next higher val. When the minimum takes the maximum integer value, the merge is complete.

     integer min, j, i;

     min: = 0;

     while min < integer max **do**

        begin min: = trav [1].current; j: = 1;

          for i: = 2 **step** 1 **until** N **do**

            if min > trav [i].current **then**

              begin min: = trav [i].current;

                 j: = i

              end search for smallest current;

          if min < integer max **then**

            begin output (min);

              call (trav [j])

        end

     end of merge process;

5.2. SYNTAX ANALYSER

As a more substantial example of list processing, we take a general table-driven context-free syntax analyser. We shall use a top-down back-tracking algorithm, which will detect all possible analyses (more than one if the grammar is ambiguous), on condition that the grammar does not contain left recursion. The symbol string is represented by a "tape" with the following operators.

     procedure move right; ....;

     procedure move left; .....;

     integer procedure symbol; .....;

The "move" operations move a reading head one symbol to the right or left. The "symbol" procedure reads the symbol under the reading head, and converts it to an integer according to a one–one mapping.

    A given function "meta" determines whether a given integer represents a meta-symbol.

     Boolean procedure meta (S); **integer** S; ...;

For simplicity the grammar is represented by a three-dimensional array G

     integer array G[..., ..., ...];

where $G[i, j, k]$ contains the kth symbol of the jth alternative right hand side for the meta-symbol represented by i. There is an

     integer array jm[...];

where $jm[i]$ is the number of right hand sides for a given meta-symbol. Each right hand side is followed by a special symbol "⊥" outside the vocabulary of the grammar. If one of alternative definitions of the syntactic class is ⟨empty⟩, it will be represented by this symbol alone.

For example, consider a simple context-free grammar for a subclass of arithmetic expressions:

(1) ⟨exp⟩:: = ⟨term⟩|⟨term⟩⟨addop⟩⟨exp⟩

(2) ⟨term⟩:: = ⟨primary⟩|⟨primary⟩⟨mulop⟩⟨term⟩

(3) ⟨primary⟩:: = ⟨constant⟩|⟨variable⟩|(⟨exp⟩)

(4) ⟨addop⟩:: = +|−

(5) ⟨mulop⟩:: = X|/

(6) ⟨constant⟩:: = 1|2|3|4|5|6|7|8|9|0

(7) ⟨variable⟩:: = I|J|K|L|M|N

There are seven meta-symbols which may be given integer values 1 to 7. The 22 terminal symbols may be given values 8 to 29 inclusive, and the "⊥" terminating symbol may be given value 0.

The array G representing this grammar may now be declared:

integer array $G[1:7, 1:10, 1:4]$

The first plane of this array will take the value

$$G[1, ., .] = 2, 0, 0, 0 \quad \text{first alternative}$$
$$2, 4, 1, 0 \quad \text{second alternative}$$
$$0, 0, 0, 0 \quad \text{the other 8 rows}$$
$$...... \quad \text{are irrelevant.}$$
$$0, 0, 0, 0$$

Note also that:

$$jm[1] = 2, jm[6] = 10$$
$$\text{meta } (1) = \text{meta } (7) = \textbf{true}$$
$$\text{meta } (8) = \text{meta } (29) = \textbf{false}$$

The desired result obtained by generating an instance of the syntax analyser, with the first symbol of text under the reading head, will be a complete syntax tree representing the text; the character *after* the last character of the analysed text will be under the reading head, and a variable "good" will be set to **true**. Subsequent calls of the same instance will produce trees representing alternative analyses. When no further analyses are possible, the input text will be stepped back to the beginning, and the variable good will be set **false**. This will happen on first generation, if the input text contains a syntax error.

Note that the analyser will discover all successful analyses of any initial segment of the text.

The syntax tree output on each call of the analyser will contain a node for each phrase identified in the text. Each phrase has the following attributes:

    integer i: indicating the syntactic class of the phrase

    integer j: indicating which alternative of its class it belongs to

ref (phrase) sub: refers to the last subphrase of the given phrase

ref (phrase) left: refers to the phrase immediately preceding this phrase on the same level of analysis. The left of the first subphrase of any phrase is **none**.

Thus the expression

$$M \times N + 7$$

should give rise to a tree of the form shown in Fig. 1.

The syntax analyser will be recursively structured, as a class of phrase objects, each of which reproduces on a single phrase the intended behaviour of the analyser as a whole.

A phrase object accepts a meta-symbol i and a left neighbour as parameter, and is responsible for producing all possible syntax trees of the given syntax class which match a portion of text to the right of (and including) the current symbol. The input text will on each occasion be stepped on to the first symbol which does *not* match the stated analysis. When all possible analyses are complete, the tape is stepped back to the position it was before entry to the given phrase, a global variable good is set to **false**, and the phrase terminates.

We are now in a position to outline the general structure of the phrase class:

    class phrase (i, left); **integer** i; **ref** (phrase) left;

        begin integer j; **ref** (phrase) sub;

            for j: $= 1$ **step** 1 **until** $jm[i]$ **do**

                . . . match remainder of text in all possible

                    ways to alternative j of class i,

                    issuing a detach after each successful match . . . ;

            good: $=$ **false**

        end of phrase;

Assume that an object has successfully matched the first $k - 1(k > 0)$ symbols of a chosen alternative (j) for the given meta-symbol (i). We now formulate a piece of program for matching the kth symbol to the input in all possible ways. We assume that the remainder, if any, of the right hand side is

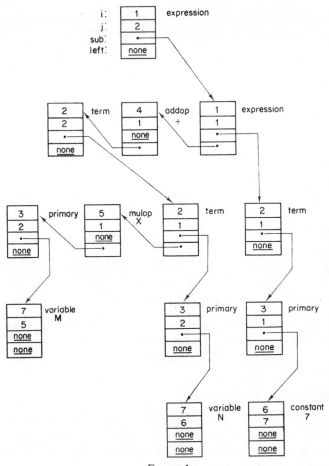

FIGURE 1

matched to the input in all possible ways by the statement "match remainder", and that this statement leaves unaltered the position of the reading head and the part of the syntax tree so far constructed. We make the latter assumption also for an object which has failed to identify (another) phrase.

1. **begin integer** g; $g := G[i, j, k]$;

2.   **if** g = "$\perp$" **then begin** good: = **true**; detach **end**

3.   **else if** g = symbol **then**

4.   **begin** move right; match remainder; move left **end**

5.   **else** if meta (g) **then**

6.   **begin** sub: − **new** phrase (g, sub);

7.　　　　**while** good **do**

8.　　　　**begin** match remainder; call (sub) **end**;

9.　　　　sub: − sub.left

10.　**end**

11. **end**

Comments.

Line 1.　The kth symbol of the right hand side number j is called g for brevity.

Line 2.　If g is the terminator symbol the whole right-hand side has been successfully matched to the input. The object reports back to its master. Line 2 does not alter the syntax tree or the position of the reading head.

Line 4.　Since we have a match the object moves the reading head to the next symbol. After having matched the remainder in all possible ways the object restores the position of the reading head. Thus, according to assumptions, line 4 has a null net effect.

Line 6.　Since g is a meta-symbol, a new phrase object is generated to identify sub-phrases of the syntax class g. It becomes the new rightmost sub-phrase. Its left neighbour phrase is the old rightmost sub-phrase.

Line 7.　We have assumed that an object when failing sets "good" to **false**.

Line 8.　Since "good" is **true**, a sub-phrase has been identified matching g. After having matched the remainder in all possible ways, "sub" is called to identify the next possible sub-phrase. Since we want to match g in all possible ways, line 8 is repeated until the sub-phrase object fails.

Line 9.　According to assumptions a phrase object which has failed, has had a null net effect. The total effect of lines 6–8 is thus to add an object to the syntax tree. Line 9 restores the syntax tree to its original state.

The comments show that the block above matches the symbol g followed by the remainder of the jth right-hand side of i in all possible ways and has a null net effect. Consequently the block itself satisfies the assumptions made for the "match remainder" statement. It follows that the whole matching algorithm may be expressed in a simple way by a recursive procedure. The whole computing process is described by the following class declaration.

```
class phrase (i, left); integer i; ref (phrase) left;
begin integer j; ref (phrase) sub;
    procedure match (k); integer k;
    begin integer g; g: = G[i, j, k];
        if g = "⊥" then begin good: = true; detach end
        else if g = symbol then
        begin move right; match (k + 1); move left end
        else if meta (g) then
        begin sub: − new phrase (g, sub);
                while good do
                begin match (k + 1); call(sub)end;
                sub: − sub.left

        end
    end of match;
    for j: = 1 step 1 until jm[i] do match (1);
    good: = false
end of phrase
```

A master program could have the following structure

```
ref (phrase) tree;

. . . . . . . . . . . . . . .

tree: − new phrase (start, none);

while good do begin found: . . . . . ; call(tree)end;
```

where "start" represents the start symbol of the grammar. At the label "found" a sentence has been identified and the variable "tree" refers to its syntax tree represented as described above. For each node its associated meta-symbol (i), the rhs alternative number (j), and the links to other nodes (sub, left) are available through remote identification, for example

tree.i, tree.sub.j, tree.sub.left.left.sub.

We must expect in general that the strings matched by different successful trials may be of unequal lengths, starting at the same location of the tape. This may be avoided by defining the language in such a way that no initial segment of a valid text is also valid. Alternatively, the whole text should be followed by some symbol outside the alphabet, say "⊥", and the master program might have the following structure

> **ref**(phrase)parse; **Boolean** good;
>
> parse: − **new** phrase (start, **none**);
>
> **while** good **do**
>
> **begin if** symbol = "⊥" **then** inspect successful parse;
>
> call(parse)
>
> **end**

It is a remarkable feature of the phrase class that the result it yields on each call is a tree whose nodes consist in phrase objects which have been activated recursively and not yet terminated. Each of these phrase objects plays a dual role, both as a part of the syntactic tree which is to be inspected by the master program, and as the set of local variables for the recursive activations of other phrase objects. It is this close association of data and procedure which permits the algorithm to be so simply and concisely formulated.

Notice that each phrase object is the nucleus of a separate stack of recursive activations of its local "match" procedure. At the time when a detach is issued on behalf of an object, signalling a successful (sub-) parse, its stack has attained a temporary maximum depth, one level for each symbol in the current right-hand side, plus one level corresponding to the rhs terminator ⊥, which issued the detach.

Thus the whole dynamic context of a successful parse is preserved. When an object is called to produce an alternative parse a backtracking process takes place, during which the "match" stack of the object is reduced. At a level corresponding to a meta-symbol in the rhs the match procedure calls on the corresponding phrase object to produce an alternative sub-parse (line 8) and so on. (cf. the row of officers in Chaplin's Great Dictator).

6. PROGRAM CONCATENATION

In the preceding sections we have seen how the *class* mechanism is capable of modelling certain simple concepts, by specifying data structures and defining operations over them. In this section, we develop a method by which more elaborate concepts can be constructed on the basis of simpler ones. This will establish potential hierarchies of concepts, with complex concepts subordinate to the more simple ones in terms of which they are defined. The structuring technique gives a new method of composing a program from its constituent parts, and is known as *concatenation*.

Concatenation is an operation defined between two classes A and B, or a class A and a block C, and results in formation of a new class or block. Concatenation consists in a merging of the attributes of both components, and the composition of their actions. The formal parameters of the con-catenated object consist of the formal parameters of the first component followed by formal parameters of the second component; and the same for specification parts, declarations and statements (if any).

A concatenated class B is defined by prefixing the name of a first com-ponent A to the declaration of B:

A **class** $B(b_1, b_2, \ldots)$; $\ldots$ specification of b's;

  begin$\ldots$attributes of $B\ldots$; $\ldots$actions of $B\ldots$**end**

Suppose the class A has been defined:

class $A(a_1, a_2, \ldots)$; $\ldots$specification of a's$\ldots$;

  begin$\ldots$attributes of $A\ldots$; $\ldots$actions of $A\ldots$**end.**

According to the concatenation rules, the effect of the prefixed declaration for class B is the same as if B had been declared without a prefix thus:

class $B(a_1, a_2, \ldots, b_1, b_2, \ldots)$; $\ldots$specification of a's$\ldots$

    specifications of b's$\ldots$;

  begin$\ldots$attributes of $A\ldots$; $\ldots$attributes of $B\ldots$;

  $\ldots$statements of $A\ldots$; $\ldots$statements of $B\ldots$**end**;

Note. If any local identifiers of A are the same as local identifiers of B, the collision of names is resolved by systematic change of B's identifiers. A block also may be prefixed by a class identifier:

A **begin**$\ldots$declarations$\ldots$; $\ldots$statements **end**,

and the effect is similar to that described above, except that the result of the concatenation is a block, not a class. (If the class A has parameters, the prefix must include an actual parameter part 1). The effect of prefixing a block is to make available within that block the library of procedures and related data (including even classes) declared within the class declaration for A.

A single class may be used as prefix to several different concatenated classes. For example, suppose a program requires to deal with trucks, buses, and private cars. These are three separate classes, and each has its own attributes. But there are certain attributes (for example license number) which are common to all of them, by virtue of the fact that they are all vehicles. The concept of vehicle is a more general one, and could be declared as a separate concept;

> **class** vehicle (license no); **integer** license no; ... ;

This class can now be used as a prefix in the remaining class declarations.

> vehicle **class** truck (load); **real** load; ... ;

> vehicle **class** bus (seating); **integer** seating; ... ;

> vehicle **class** car; ... ;

An object belonging to a prefixed class is a compound object, which has certain attributes and operations *in addition to* those defined in the prefix part. Thus a truck object has a license no and a load, and a bus object has a license no and a seating. It is reasonable to regard "truck" and "bus" and "car" as *subclasses* of the vehicle class; any object of a subclass also belongs to the prefix class "vehicle".

A reference variable may be qualified as belonging to a prefix class or to a concatenated class. If it belongs to the prefix class it may point to objects of *any* of the subclasses, and may be used in a remote identifier to access any of the attributes of the prefix class but not to access any attributes of the subclasses. A reference qualified by a subclass may point only to objects of the subclass, but may be used in a remote identifier to access all its attributes. Thus given the reference variables:

> **ref** (vehicle) V; **ref** (bus) B;

the following are valid remote identifiers:

> V.license no, B.license no, B.seating,

but V.seating is not valid.

Thus the subclass notion provides a useful flexibility of object referencing. A "weak" qualification permits a wide range of objects referencing, at the cost of inability to make remote access to attributes declared in a subclass.

Assignment of a subclass reference to a prefix class reference variable (e.g. $V: - B$) is always valid, and can be recognised as such at compile time. But assignment in the other direction (e.g. $B: - V$) may give rise to an error (detected only at run time), if the object referenced does not in fact belong to the expected subclass (bus).

6.1. BINARY SEARCH TREE

Suppose it is desired to set up a binary search tree to hold information about stock items in an inventory. Each node of the tree should contain not only a val (indicating the stock number of the item) but also certain other information about quantity on hand, price, reorder point, etc. The simplest way of achieving the required effect is to prefix the class "stock item" by the class tree, and then declare the additional attributes required, for example:

tree **class** stock item;

 begin integer *qoh*, price, reorder point;

  Boolean ordered;

  procedure reduce;

   begin if *qoh* = reorder point & ¬ordered **then**

    issue reorder;

    qoh: = *qoh* − **1**

   end of remove;

 end of stock item;

6.2. TWO WAY LIST

Taking advantage of the concatenation technique, it is possible to design classes which are intended solely or primarily to act as prefixes to other classes or to blocks. In this section we give an example of a class TWLIST, which is intended to be used as a prefix to a block, and to make available within that block the concept of two-way chained cyclic lists. Such a list consists of a *list head*, which contains two pointers, one to the first element of the chain and one to the last. Each *link* in the chain must also contain two pointers, suc which points to the successor in the list (or the list head if there is none), and pred which points to the predecessor in the list (or the list head if there is none). In an empty list, the two pointers from the list head point to the list head itself.

Each pointer in the system must be capable of pointing either to another link in the list or to a list head. Therefore these pointers must be qualified by a class which embraces both links and heads, i.e. a class "linkage" of which they are both subclasses. Since both list heads and links require two reference attributes, suc and pred can be declared as attributes of the prefix class linkage.

The single concept of a two-way list is represented by the triple of classes linkage, link, and list head. In order to indicate that they are to be considered in conjunction as a single concept, the declarations for all three classes are grouped together in a single class declaration TWLIST, which is to be used as a prefix to any block which requires to use the concept. Within such a block the "link" class is intended to be used as a prefix to other classes specifying the nature of the items; for example, if stock items were to be held in a two-way list instead of in a binary search tree, the declaration would be:

   link **class** stock; . . . as before . . . ;

It is now necessary to decide on a basic set of operations on lists and links. A link I should be removable from its list by a procedure statement

$$I.\text{out};$$

and it should be capable of being reinserted in a list just before link J by a procedure statement:

$$I.\text{precede }(J);$$

Since a link can belong to at most one list, this operation should also remove I from any list it happens to belong to before. Finally a link should be insertable as the last item of a list with head H by a procedure statement:

$$I.\text{into }(H);$$

For a list head H, it seems useful to define the following functions

$$H.\text{empty},$$

which tests whether the list is empty,

$$H.\text{first}$$

which yields H's first item, if any; otherwise **none**, and

$$H.\text{last}$$

which yields H's last item, if any; otherwise **none**.

The declaration of the class TWLIST can now be given:

```
1.  class TWLIST;
2.  begin class linkage; begin ref (linkage) suc, pred; end;
3.      linkage class link;
4.      begin procedure out;
5.          if suc =/= none then
6.          begin suc.pred: — pred; pred.suc: — suc;
7.              suc: — pred: — none
8.          end of out;
9.          procedure precede (x); ref (linkage) x;
10.         begin out; suc: — x; pred: — x.pred;
11.             suc.pred: — pred.suc: — this link
12.         end of precede;
13.         procedure into (L); ref (list) L;
14.             precede (L);
            comment suc and pred of a link object should have the
            standard initial value none indicating no list membership;
15.     end of link;
```

16.   linkage **class** list;

17.   **begin ref** (link) **procedure** first;

18.   first: − **if** empty **then none else** suc;

19.   **ref** (link) **procedure** last;

20.   last: − **if** empty **then none else** pred;

21.   **Boolean procedure** empty;

22.   empty: = suc = = **this** list;

23.   suc: − pred: − **this** list

                comment suc and pred of a list head should be initialized to indicate an empty list;

24.   **end** of list;

25. **end** of TWLIST;

Let P be an *arbitrary* block instance prefixed by TWLIST, which, outside its prefix part, contains no explicit reference assignment to any variable suc or pred of any linkage object. Then the assertions (1) and (2) below are valid throughout the lifetime of P (at times when control is textually outside the body of TWLIST).

(1) Any linkage object x in P is either an object with no list membership, in which case $x.\text{suc} = = x.\text{pred} = = $ **none** and $x \notin$ list, or $x.\text{suc}.\text{pred} = = x.\text{pred}.\text{suc} = = x$.

It follows that all lists contained in P are circular. Furthermore:

(2) Each circular list in P contains exactly one list head, which is an object of the class "list".

The assertions are established by observing that each of the operations below preserves their validity, and that P contains no linkage object initially.

new *link* (or **new** C, $C \subseteq$ linkage–list) generates a link object, which is not a list member (its suc and pred are automatically initialised to **none**).

new *list* (or **new** C, $C \subseteq$ list) generates an "empty" circular list containing the generated list head and initially nothing else.

In the following we assume $x \in$ link, y, $z \in$ linkage, and $L \in$ list. $x \leftrightarrow y$ is an abbreviation for $x.\text{suc} = = y$ & $x = = y.\text{pred}$.

$x.out$ If $z \leftrightarrow x \leftrightarrow y$ the result is $z \leftrightarrow y$ and x is not a list member. (Notice that (2) together with $x \in$ link implies $x =/= y, z$.) If x was not a list member, the result is to do nothing.

$x.precede$ (**y**), where $x =/= y \land z \leftrightarrow y$. The result is $x \leftrightarrow y$ (and $z \leftrightarrow x$ if $x =/= z$). If x was a list member, x is first removed from that list.

$x \, . \, into(L)$, where $z \leftrightarrow L$. The result is $z \leftrightarrow x \leftrightarrow L$, which implies $x = = L \, . \, last$. If x was a list member, x is first removed from that list.

Any use of out, precede, or into not satisfying the above assumptions, is either textually illegal or leads immediately to a run time error and program termination caused by an invalid remote identifier. E.g. the operation $x \, . \, precede \, (y)$ sets $x \, . \, pred$ to **none** if $x = = y$ or y is not a list member. Consequently the remote identifier pred. suc in the body of precede is invalid. Notice that $x \, . \, into \, (L)$ is a "safer" operation, since $x \in link$, $L \in list$ implies that $x =/= L$ and $L \, . \, pred =/= $ **none**.

The assertions (1) and (2) provide a guarantee that our lists are well behaved, provided that no explicit assignment to any variable suc or pred occurs. The construction TWLIST is thus a reliable "mental platform," which in a certain sense *cannot break down*, whatever programming errors are made. When programming on top of TWLIST one is entitled to ignore the list processing details involved in manipulating the circular two-way lists. Each list object may be regarded as representing an *ordered set* of link objects, with the proviso that a link object may be member of at most one such set at a time. The last fact is reflected in the design of the procedures into and precede. Explicit use of the attributes suc and pred, e.g. for scanning through a list, may, however, require the user to be conscious of the fact that the "last" member has a successor and the "first" member a predecessor, which are both identical to the list object itself. A design alternative is to suppress this fact by declaring the following procedures as attributes to link.

> **ref** (link) **procedure** successor;
>> **inspect** suc **when** list **do** successor: − **none**
>> **otherwise** successor: − suc;
>
> **ref** (link) **procedure** predecessor;
>> **inspect** pred **when** list **do** predecessor: − **none**
>> **otherwise** predecessor: − pred;

Note the construction

> **inspect** r **when** C **do**. . .

enables the programmer to test whether the object referenced by r belongs to one of its possible subclasses C.

7. CONCEPT HIERARCHIES

At the outset of a programming project there is a *problem*, more or less precisely defined and understood in terms of certain problem oriented concepts, and a *programming language*, perhaps a general purpose one, providing some (machine oriented) basic concepts, hopefully precisely defined and completely understood. There is a *conceptual distance* between the two, which must be bridged by our piece of program. We may picture that distance as a vertical one, the given programming language being the ground level.

Our difficulty in bridging such gaps is the fact that we have to work sequentially on one simple part problem at a time, not always knowing in advance whether they are the *right problems*.

In order to better overcome such difficulties we may build pyramids. Unlike the Egyptian ones ours are either standing on their heads (bottom-up construction) or hanging in the air (top-down construction). The construction principle involved is best called *abstraction*; we concentrate on features common to many phenomena, and we abstract *away* features too far removed from the conceptual level at which we are working. Thereby we have a better chance of formulating concepts which are indeed useful at a later stage.

In the bottom-up case we start at the basic language level and construct abstract concepts capable of capturing a variety of phenomena in some problem area. In the top-down case [8, 9] we formulate the solution to a given problem in terms of concepts, which are capable of being implemented (and interpreted) in many ways, and which are perhaps not yet fully understood. In either case system construction may consist of adding new layers of pyramids (above or below) until the conceptual gap has finally been bridged. Each such layer will correspond to a conceptual level of understanding.

For instance, given some problem which involves queueing phenomena, we could take TWLIST of the preceding section as the first step of a bottom-up construction. Then, for the remainder of the construction we are free to think and express ourselves in terms of dynamic manipulation of ordered sets of objects.

Layers of conceptual levels may be represented as a *prefix sequence* of class declarations. For example, it is possible to construct a series of class declarations, each one using the previous class as prefix

$$\textbf{class } C_1; \ldots;$$
$$C_1 \textbf{ class } C_2; \ldots;$$
$$\cdots$$
$$C_{n-1} \textbf{ class } C_n; \ldots;$$

The list $C_1, C_2, \ldots, C_{n-1}$ is known as the prefix sequence for C_n. The outermost prefix C_1 is built at the ground level. Every other level rests on the one(s) below, in that it may take advantage of all attributes of its entire prefix sequence. Making use of this language mechanism, bottom-up construction of a program is to plan and write the classes of a prefix sequence one by one in the stated order. The program itself is finally written as a prefixed block on top of the whole sequence.

$$C_n \textbf{ begin } \text{———} \textbf{ end}$$

The top–down strategy would correspond to constructing the members of the prefix sequence, including the prefixed block, in the reverse order. (SIMULA 67 contains additional mechanisms, not considered here, for facilitating top–down and mixed mode construction.)

A well-formed conceptual level (bottom-up) is a set of well-defined inter-related concepts, which may be combined to make more elaborate concepts. It may serve for further construction as a mental platform, raised above ground towards some application area, i.e. as an "application language". A preconstructed application language may serve to shorten the conceptual gap that has to be bridged for many problems in the area. The usefulness of such a platform is closely related to its ruggedness, that is with the way in which it tolerates or even forestalls misuse. As we saw in the last section TWLIST supplies an exceptionally rugged mental platform; and in this section we shall build on it a small but useful application language, which may in its turn be used as a platform for the solution of realistic problems.

7.1. DISCRETE EVENT SIMULATION

Simulation is a method for studying the behaviour of large systems of interacting objects, and evaluating the effect of making changes which would be too expensive to make on an experimental basis in real life. The object of a simulation model could be a production line, a traffic system, a computer system (hardware and software), a social system composed of interacting individuals, etc. The following notions are common to most such systems.

(1) Processes taking place in *parallel*, giving rise to discrete events at irregular intervals of time.

(2) *Queueing* phenomena, arising when an object has to wait for service from a currently busy server.

In order to represent processes occurring in parallel, it is not necessary that the corresponding program components should be multiprogrammed in the computer; but it is necessary that the programs should be able to suspend themselves temporarily, and be resumed later from where they left off. Thus the active objects or "processes" in a simulation will be represented by (semi-)coroutines, operating in *pseudo–parallel* under control of a scheduling mechanism.

For example, in a job shop simulation, an incoming order gives rise to a sequence of events on the shop floor, to satisfy the order. Each order may be regarded as a process whose activity is to proceed from one machine to the next, requesting and obtaining service from it. The sequence of requests is determined by the nature of the order. If the requested machine is free, the order is served immediately, and the machine goes busy for a period equal to the length of the service. Otherwise, the order joins a queue of orders waiting for the machine to become free.

In the implementation of the concept of simulated time, the first requirement is that each process have access to a variable "time" which holds the current time, and which is incremented on appropriate occasions by the time-control mechanism. Note that the updating of this variable must be entirely independent of the passage of computing time during the simulation, since actions which take a long time on a computer might take only a short time in the real world, and vice versa. As far as simulated time is concerned, the active phases of the processes must be instantaneous; "time" does not move until all the participating processes are passive.

Thus in order to simulate the passing of time, a process simulating an active system component must relinquish control for a stated interval T of simulated time; and it must be reactivated again when the time variable has been incremented by T. This will be accomplished by the process calling the procedure

hold (T).

For example, an order which has found its required machine ready to serve it needs to indicate how long this service will take, by the statement

hold (service interval);

The order will now become inactive until all other orders which were due to be reactivated *before* time + service interval have been reactivated, and have relinquished control again. At this point, the given order will be reactivated, and will find that its time has been appropriately incremented.

While a process is held, it will be necessary to record its reactivation time as one of its attributes. It is convenient therefore to use the time attribute of the process itself for this purpose.

The method of holding for a specified interval is possible only if the process knows how long it has to wait before the next "event" in its life. But sometimes it may require to wait until the occurrence of some event in the life of some other process. For example, an order, on finding its required machine busy, must join a queue and wait until the machine is free; and an order on releasing a machine must activate the first other order in the queue (if not empty). Thus two additional procedures are required:

wait (Q),

and activate (X),

where Q refers to the queue (two-way list) on which the calling process is to wait while it is passive, and X refers to some passive process, which is to be removed from its queue and allowed to proceed.

Finally, a means must be provided of starting and stopping the simulation. This may be accomplished by a procedure statement

simulate (start, finish),

where start refers to the process with which the simulation starts, and finish gives the time limit for the simulation. Any process requesting to be held beyond this limit may be ignored. Presumably, the start process will activate other processes to participate in the simulation.

We now proceed to implement the mechanism described above. It will be implemented as a class MINISIM, which is intended to be used as a prefix to a simulation main program. In order to take advantage of the two-way list mechanism, the MINISIM class must be prefixed by TWLIST. This ensures that TWLIST is also available in any simulation program which is prefixed by MINISIM.

A class of objects which are to be capable of participating in a simulation should be declared as a subclass of the "process" class. This will make available to it the necessary time control and queueing mechanisms. Each process must have the capability of inserting itself into a two-way list; therefore the process class itself must be declared as a subclass of the class of links.

Processes waiting for the elapse of their holding interval are held on a unique two-way list known as the sequencing set (SQS). The processes are ordered in accordance with decreasing reactivation times. A specially created finish process is always the first link in SQS, and the last link is always the one that is currently active. Its time represents the current time of the system. When it goes inactive, its predecessor in the SQS will (usually) become the last, and its local time has already been updated to the time at which that process was due to be reactivated.

We are now in a position to give the general structure of MINISIM, omitting for the time being the procedure bodies.

```
TWLIST class MINISIM
  begin ref (list) SQS;
      ref (process) procedure current;
          current: − SQS.last;
      link class process;
        begin real time;
            procedure hold (T); real T;
                . . . . . ;
            procedure wait (Q); ref (list) Q;
                . . . . . ;
            procedure activate (X); ref (process) X;
                . . . . . ;
            detach; comment a new process doesn't actually
```

do anything until it is activated

end of process;

procedure simulate (start, finish);

ref (process) start; **real** finish;

. . . . . ;

end of MINISIM.

We shall give the bodies of the procedures in reverse order.

simulate: **begin** SQS: − **new** list;

new process.into (SQS); current.time: = finish;

if start.time < finish **then** start.into (SQS);

while ¬SQS.empty **do**

begin call (current);

current.out;

comment this ensures that a terminated

or detached process leaves the SQS;

end

end of simulate

wait:**begin** into (Q); resume (current) **end**;

The active process inserts itself into the queue, and thereby leaves the SQS. It also resumes the process on the SQS which is next due to be reactivated. Notice that the standard sequencing mechanism of the simulate procedure must be bypassed, since the old active process already is out of the SQS.

activate:**begin** X.into (SQS); **comment** as its last and current member;

X.time: = time; **comment** i.e. now;

resume (current);

end of activate.

The calling process places X ahead of itself in SQS, but with the same time. Since the calling and the activated process X have the same time, it does not matter to the timing mechanism in what order they are placed; our choice implies that an active phase of X is invoked immediately in real time. Control returns to the calling one at the same moment of simulated time, but after the completion of the active phase of X.

hold:

begin ref (process) P;

   $P: -$ pred;

   comment the holding process is necessarily active, and
   therefore also the last member of SQS. Since the
   finish process never holds, there will always be a
   second-to-last process on SQS

   if $T > 0$ **then** time: $=$ time $+ T$;

   comment set local reactivation time,
   time should never decrease;

   if time $\geqslant P$.time **then**

      begin comment this process must be moved in SQS;
         out; **comment** of SQS, now P is current;
         $P: - SQS$.first; **comment** the finish process;
         if time $< P$.time **then**

            begin comment reactivation time is
               within the time limit;
               while time $< P$.time **do** $P: - P$.suc;
               comment terminates since
                        time $\geqslant$ current.time;
               precede (P)
            end; **comment** ignore a process that would
               exceed the limit;
         resume (current)

      end;

   end of hold;

Notice that a process object is allowed to relinquish control simply by
saying detach or by passage through its **end**. In both cases control returns to
the standard sequencing mechanism of the simulate procedure. The basic
activation instructions call and resume, however, should not be explicitly
applied to process objects; that would illegally bypass the timing mechanism.

7.2. THE LEE ALGORITHM

As a simple but unexpected example of the use of simulated time, we take
the Lee algorithm for finding the shortest path between a city A and a city B
connected by a network of one-way roads. The algorithm may be envisaged

as the propagation of a pulse from the destination city B at equal speed along all roads leading into it. Each time a pulse reaches a city not reached by a previous pulse, it records the road it has come along, and then sends pulses outward along all roads leading into the city. When a pulse reaches a city which has already been reached by another pulse, it dies. When a pulse reaches the city A, the task is completed.

Cities and roads may be represented by classes.

> **class** city; **begin ref** (road) roadsin, wayout; .... **end**
>
> **class** road; **begin real** length; **ref** (road) nextin;
>
>   **ref** (city) source, destination; ... **end**

The variable wayout holds the recommended wayout from the city towards B. For an unvisited city, its value is **none**.

The class representing a pulse takes as parameter the road along which it is first to pass.

> process **class** pulse (rd); **ref** (road) rd;
>
> **begin ref** (city) c; c: − rd.source;
>
>   hold $(rd$.length$)$;
>
>   if c.wayout $=/=$ **none then**
>
>   **begin** c.wayout: − rd;
>
>   if $c = = A$ **then go to** done;
>
>   **comment** stops the simulation by
>
>   going to a non-local label;
>
> rd: − c.roadsin;
>
>   **while** $rd =/=$ **none do**
>
>   **begin** activate (**new** pulse (rd));
>
> rd: − rd.nextin
>
>   **end** propagation of pulses
>
>   **end**
>
> **end** of pulse

The algorithm will be invoked by calling a procedure with parameters indicating the starting and final cities, and an upper limit L on the length of the path that is to be printed. It is assumed that the wayout of every city is initially **none**. The time and process concepts are made available by the prefix MINISIM to the procedure body.

procedure Lee (A, B, L); ref (city) A, B; real L;

    MINISIM begin process class pulse (rd); ref (road) rd;

        ...as before...;

    process class starter;

      begin ref (road) rd;

        $rd: - B$.roadsin;

        while $rd =/=$ none do

          begin activate (new pulse (rd));

            $rd: = rd$.nextin

      end

    end of starter;

      simulate (new starter, L);

  done:end of Lee;

After a procedure statement such as

    Lee (Oslo, Belfast, 1000);

where ref (city) Oslo, Belfast; the required route may be printed out, provided that it exists.

if Oslo.wayout $=/=$ none then

begin ref (city) c; procedure print......; .....;

    print (Oslo.wayout); $c: -$ Oslo.wayout.destination;

    while $c =/=$ Belfast do

    begin print (c); print $(c$.wayout);

      $c: - c$.wayout.destination

    end

end else outtext ('no road connection within limit);

It is assumed for the print procedure that cities and roads are objects belonging to a common class, by having the same prefix to the two classes. The prefix part of an object might contain the necessary identifying text, such as 'London' or 'M1' as data.

7.3. A JOB SHOP MODEL

As a second application of MINISIM we shall design a model of a simple job shop system. The model may be used to evaluate the capacity of the shop in relation to a given order load. The line numbers below refer to the program on page 218.

The system consists of *machine groups* (lines 3–10), numbered from 1 to *nmg* (lines 1, 11), and *order* objects (lines 12–22). The machines of a group are identical and therefore need not be represented individually; however, their number is specified initially by the value of the attribute *nm* (line 3). Associated with the group is also a queue of orders waiting to be processed, which is empty initially (lines 4, 9), and procedures to *request* a machine for processing (lines 5–6) and to *release* it when finished (lines 7–8).

The variable *nm* is used to represent the number of available machines, say *m*, as well as the number of orders, say *w*, waiting in the queue, as described by the following assertion.

$$\textbf{if } nm > 0 \textbf{ then } m = nm \land w = 0$$

$$\textbf{else } m = 0 \land w = abs(nm)$$

The assertion is valid for each machine group (outside the procedure bodies request and release).

When a machine is requested and $m = 0$, the caller must enter the queue and wait for its turn (line 6). When a machine is released and $w \neq 0$, one of the waiting processes should proceed. The first member of the queue is activated and thereby leaves the queue. The queueing discipline is thus first come first served.

The orders are process objects, each of which generates its successor, (line 18) and which goes from one machine group to the next (lines 20–21) according to an individually defined schedule. For a given order the schedule has *n* steps, and for each step $s(s = 1, 2, \ldots, n)$ a machine group number ($mg[s]$) and an associated processing time ($pt[s]$) are given. Thus the order should spend the time $pt[s]$ in being processed at machine group number $mg[s]$ (line 21, hold). Notice that the request statement of line 21 will require some additional amount of simulated time for its completion, if the group *m*group [$mg[s]$] currently has no available machine.

The model is driven by input data. In particular, each order object during its first active phase reads in its own schedule, consisting of length of schedule (line 18) arrival time (inreal, line 15), and the values of *mg* and *pt* (lines 16–17). The main program sets up machine groups of specified sizes (lines 24, 25) and generates the first order at time zero. (The procedures inint, inreal, and lastitem are procedures associated with a standard input file, which is part of the program environment).

It is assumed that the input file starts with the following data:

$$nmg, \text{ timelimit}, nm_1, nm_2, \ldots, nm_{nmg},$$

defining the structure of the job shop; and this is followed by an occurrence of

$$n, T, mg_1, pt_1, mg_2, pt_2, \ldots, mg_n, pt_n,$$

for each order to be generated. Each value T defines the arrival time of the order. It is assumed that the T values are in a non-decreasing sequence.

The JOB SHOP goes as follows.

1. **begin integer** *nmg*; *nmg*: = inint;

2. MINISIM **begin**

3. **class** machine group (*nm*); **integer** *nm*;

4. **begin ref** (list) *Q*;

5.   **procedure** request;

6.   **begin** *nm*: = *nm* − 1; **if** *nm* < 0 **then** current.wait (*Q*) **end**;

7.   **procedure** release;

8.   **begin** *nm*: = *nm* + 1; **if** *nm* ⩽ 0 **then** current.activate (*Q*.first) **end**;

9.   *Q*: − **new** list

10. **end** of machine group;

11. **ref** (machine group) **array** *m*group [1:*nmg*];

12. process **class** order (*n*); **integer** *n*;

13. **begin integer array** *mg*[1:*n*]; **array** *pt*[1:*n*]; **integer** *s*;

14.   **ref** (machine group) *M*;

15.   hold (inreal − time); **comment** arrival time is now;

16.   **for** *s*: = 1 **step** 1 **until** *n* **do**

17.   **begin** *mg*[*s*]: = inint; *pt*[*s*]: = inreal **end**;

18.   **if** ¬lastitem **then** activate (**new** order (inint));

19.   **comment** generate next order, if any;

20.   **for** *s*: = 1 **step** 1 **until** *n* **do**

21.   **begin** *M*: − *m*group [*mg*[*s*]]; *M*.request; hold (*pt*[*s*]);

                                                         M.release **end**

22. **end** of order;

23. **integer** *k*; **real** lim; lim: = inreal;

24. **for** *k*: = 1 **step** 1 **until** *nmg* **do** *m*group [*k*]: − **new** machine group (inint);

25. simulate (**new** order (inint), lim);

26. **comment** initial time is zero by default;

27. **end** of program;

The model above should be augmented by mechanisms for observing its performance. We may for instance very easily include a "reporter" process, which will operate in "parallel" with the model components and give output of relevant state information at regular simulated time intervals.

> process **class** reporter (dt); **real** dt;
>
> **while true do**
>
> **begin** hold (dt);
>
> > give output, e.g. of
> >
> > $m$group $[k].nm \lor (k = 1, 2, \ldots, nmg)$
>
> **end** of reporter;

The first order could generate a reporter object and set it going at system time zero.

> activate (**new** reporter (inreal))

Output will then be given at system time t, $2t$, $3t$, $\ldots$, where t is the actual parameter value.

As a further example we may wish to accumulate for each machine group a histogram of waiting times of orders at the group. Then define the following subclass of machine group, redefining the operation "request".

> machine group **class** Machine Group;
>
> **begin ref** (histogram) H;
>
> > **procedure** request;
> >
> > **begin real** T;
> >
> > > T: = time; nm: = $nm - 1$;
> > >
> > > **if** $nm < 0$ **then** wait (Q);
> > >
> > > H.tabulate (time $- T$)
> >
> > **end** of new request;
> >
> > H: $-$ **new** histogram (X, N)
>
> **end** of Machine Group;

It is assumed that "histogram" is the class defined in section 3.1, and that **array** $X[1:N]$ and **integer** N are nonlocal quantities. Now replace the lower case initials by upper case in the class identifier of lines 11, 14, and 24. Then all machine groups will be objects extended as above, and since the qualification of the reference variable M is strengthened, the "request" of line 21 refers to the new procedure. Thus a histogram of waiting times will be accumulated for each group.

Finally it should be mentioned that the "machine group" concept might have considerable utility as a general purpose synchronisation mechanism for pseudo–parallel processes. It might be useful to phrase it in more abstract terminology and possibly include it as part of a "third floor" platform for "resource oriented" simulation. In fact well known special purpose languages [10, 11] have elaborations of this concept ("facility", "store") as fundamental mechanisms. The analogy to the semaphore mechanism [12] for the synchronisation of truly parallel processes should be noted. The procedures request and release correspond to the P and V operations, respectively.

REFERENCES

(1) Naur, P. (ed.) (1962/63). Revised Report on the Algorithmic Language. ALGOL 60. *Comp. J.*, **5**, pp. 349–367.

(2) Dahl, O.-J., Myhrhaug, B., Nygaard, K. (1968). The Simular 67 Common Base Language. Norwegian Computing Centre, Forskningsveien 1B, Oslo 3.

(3) Wang, A., Dahl, O.-J. (1971). Coroutine Sequencing in a Block Structured Environment. *BIT* **11**, 4, pp. 425–449.

(4) Dahl, O.-J., Nygaard (1966). Simula—an Algol-Based Simulation Language. *Comm. A.C.M.* **9**, 9, pp. 671–678.

(5) Dahl, O.-J. (1968). Discrete Event Simulation Languages. "Programming Languages" (ed. Genuys, F.). pp. 349–395. Academic Press, London.

(6) Hoare, C. A. R. (1968). Record Handling. "Programming Languages" (ed. Genuys, F.). pp. 291–347. Academic Press, London.

(7) Conway, M. E. (1963). Design of a Separable Transition—Diagram Compiler. *Comm. A.C.M.* **6**, 7, pp. 396–408.

(8) Naur, P. (1969). Programming by Actions Clusters. *BIT* **9**, 3, pp. 250–258.

(9) Dijkstra, E. W. (1972). Notes on Structured Programming. "Structured Programming". pp. 1–82. Academic Press, London.

(10) Knuth, D. E., McNeley, J. L. (1964). SOL—A Symbolic Language for General-Purpose Systems Simulation. IEEE Trans. E.C.

(11) IBM, General Purpose Systems Simulator.

(12) Dijkstra, E. W. (1968). Co-operating Sequential Processes. "Programming Languages". pp. 43–112. Academic Press, London.